SPINOZA IN ENGLISH

BRILL'S STUDIES
IN
INTELLECTUAL HISTORY

SPINOZA IN ENGLISH

*A Bibliography
from the Seventeenth Century
to the Present*

BY

WAYNE I. BOUCHER

E.J. BRILL

LEIDEN • NEW YORK • KØBENHAVN • KÖLN

1991

The paper in this book meets the guidelines for permanence and durability of the Committee on Production Guidelines for Book Longevity of the Council on Library Resources.

Library of Congress Cataloging-in-Publication Data

Boucher, Wayne I.
   Spinoza in English: a bibliography from the seventeenth century to the present / by Wayne I. Boucher.
     p.   cm. — (Brill's studies in intellectual history, ISSN 0920-8607 ; v. 28)
   ISBN 9004094997 (alk. paper)
   1. Spinoza, Benedictus de, 1632-1677—Bibliography.   I. Title.
II. Series.
Z8831.B68
[B3998]
016.199'492—dc20   91-24542
                                            CIP

ISSN   0920-8607
ISBN   90 04 09499 7

© *Copyright 1991 by E.J. Brill, Leiden, The Netherlands*

PRINTED IN THE NETHERLANDS

To the Memory of

DAVID C. MORGAN

(1934-1982)

Professor of English Literature, Bibliophile, Friend

Ethics, Part IV, Prop. 67

PREFACE

Baruch! Do you know this Baruch?
You must read Baruch!

— *La Fontaine*

My aim in this bibliography has been to bring together, for the first time, citations to all of the books, book chapters or sections, dissertations, and scholarly papers on Spinoza in the English language, as well as citations to all translations of his works into English.

Because every day of searching reveals new titles, I have no doubt that this bibliography falls short of achieving this objective. Nevertheless, it can claim certain strengths. Within its scope, it includes everything of any significance from earlier Spinoza bibliographies, thus spanning the literature in English from the late 17th century to the present. It corrects errors in many of these bibliographies. It organizes the literature alphabetically by author or editor, but not within arbitrary categories, as has often been done, so that works by the same person are finally presented together. Departing from an inexplicable and irksome scholarly convention, it includes the name of the publisher of the books cited, at least to the extent that time permitted gathering this information, thereby easing the burden on those who might actually want to obtain particular titles. Departing from another irksome convention, it also provides full titles of the journals cited, thereby sparing the user the nuisance of having to look up the abbreviations in still another list. Indeed, where time allowed, it restores other useful bibliographic information so diligently suppressed by earlier authors and bibliographers, and, beginning with references in the mid-19th century, it presents these full citations in a uniform style. Finally, in addition to including titles published since the last major bibliography, it cites dozens of books and articles hitherto overlooked, many of considerable interest and value. Conservatively counted, the total number of citations exceeds 2100, of which a substantial percentage appear for the first time.

Preparation of this bibliography involved, in the first instance, a careful review of standard published sources, beginning with Oko (1964), skipping back to Van der Linde's 1871 *Benedictus Spinoza Bibliografie* (Nieuwkoop: B. de Graaf, 1961), and then working forward through the few references in J. te Winkel's *Catalogus van de boekerij der Vereeniging "Het Spinozahuis"* (The Hague: Gebr. Belinfante, 1914) and J. M. M. Aler's *Catalogus van de bibliotheek der Vereniging Het Spinozahuis te Rijnsburg* (Leiden: E. J. Brill, 1965) to a variety of sometimes quite rich sources, such as M. Hertzberger's catalogue of Prof. Wolf's library (1950) and Van der Werf (1984). I also reviewed the citations in most of the major English-language books on Spinoza from Willis (1870) onward and in many of the dissertations on Spinoza in the last 25 years, in order to help ensure that no obviously relevant source used by these Spinoza scholars was left out of account. I then augmented these results by screening twenty or more computer databases and scanning hundreds of individual books in collections at several research universities and elsewhere.

Throughout this process, I relied heavily on the uniquely valuable Oko bibliography. As any user can attest, however, this volume presents special difficulties, not only because it lacks an index and uses an idiosyncratic topical classification (which may help to explain why, among other problems, different editions of the same work sometimes appear under different headings), but also because Oko was apparently pursuing the will-o'-the-wisp of trying to capture everything that anyone had ever written about Spinoza. This led him to create entry cards on many publications that contain only one or two references to Spinoza, by his own reckoning. But including such works is manifestly absurd, since there is no end to it, and all such references (Oko's and hundreds of others that could easily be specified) have been ignored here, unless they concern very early books and essays, in which Spinoza was rarely considered at length. If, however, Oko explicitly indicated the existence of "many" references to Spinoza in a publication, and this publication was not one that I could locate and independently confirm, I have included it. These citations are always accompanied by a reference to the appropriate page in his bibliography.

More generally, I have identified my sources in the following circumstances (which account for perhaps 25 percent of the citations in this bibliography):

- The document was published before 1850 or so. Though I have been able to confirm some of these citations, and thus in a few instances to add or correct bibliographic detail, it seemed appropriate in effect to thank the original bibliographer, without whom the document would almost surely have been missed.

- The publication is cited by only a single author or bibliographer, and I was unable to locate a copy, for one reason or another. There are one or two interesting cases in the literature in which unpublished manuscripts have been cited. These, of course, have not been included here. But this bibliography recognizes that actual publications are often found and cited by just one Spinoza scholar, a somewhat saddening point which is amply and, I think, reliably established in Oko, Van der Werf, and other sources, including this one.

- The title itself does not make it clear why the publication is relevant to the study of Spinoza. In nearly every case of this sort, a note accompanies the citation. If this note simply describes what is included (e.g., a chapter on Spinoza), this typically means that I have examined the work myself. If the note includes a source reference (or consists solely of this reference), then I am relying on the source's judgment as to the relevance of the work to the study of Spinoza. Oko's citations and those in databases like *Philosopher's Index* are frequent examples here.

- The citation (again, from only one source) could not be confirmed, and it appeared worth including, but the citation itself is fragmentary or otherwise problematical. The highly flawed bibliography by Wetlesen (1968) provides innumerable examples, a few of which I have adapted for use here.

Where no source reference is given for a publication, I have usually either confirmed the details directly or been able to construct a satisfactory citation by integrating details from several different authors' citations to the same document.

Excluded here are novels and other works of fiction, newspaper articles, book reviews (unless they are of substantial length), Masters' theses, undergraduate prize essays, and, with rare exceptions, encyclopedia articles, pamphlets or collections of pamphlets, magazine articles, and books of readings that contain selections from Spinoza.

My decision to admit publications with "many" references to Spinoza proved difficult to follow with any rigor; I certainly had no absolute rule. Obviously, historians like Paulsen and Windelband, whose orientation tends to be more thematic than chronological, but whose discussion of Spinoza is insightful, deserve a place. Similarly, the survey edited by Wiener, an unconventional encyclopedia that abounds with references, had to be cited. And a number of specialized studies, like Rome on Malebranche, Wilson on Leibniz, Redwood on the Enlightenment in England, Merz on nineteenth century thought, Sontag on philosophical theology, Collingwood on method, Robinson on definition, and others, all of which mention Spinoza often but seldom discuss him at any length, are reasonable additions. But, again, there is virtually no end to these publications. Arbitrarily, a line had to be drawn — and so it was — so that the primary focus could remain on publications devoted entirely or in some sustained or otherwise important way to Spinoza.

The order of presentation in the "Works" section beginning on p. 1 is chronological within the categories used, by date of the publication or edition actually cited. The order of presentation in the "Commentaries" section beginning on p. 9 is as follows. Works not attributed to an author or editor precede all others and are listed chronologically. Then, by name of individual, books and other self-contained publications precede articles; edited, co-authored or co-edited works are presented last. In each category, earlier publications precede later ones.

As will be noted, this bibliography is rather thoroughly cross-referenced, especially when it comes to anthologies. If the anthology contains only one or two relevant chapters, a full citation is provided for each in the accompanying note and then repeated under the author's name. If the anthology includes many papers, the authors of contributions in English are listed alphabetically in the note and the full citation is given only at the author's name. To avoid separate citations to those papers by a single author which seemingly form a set of Chinese boxes, something of the publication history is given at the point where the paper appeared finally to come to rest. For this reason, among others, entries in this bibliography are not numbered.

Finally, because this bibliography was undertaken as a guide to research rather than to collecting, the last or apparently most complete edition of a publication has almost always been preferred to the first, when there was a choice. But I have not attempted seriously to track down every reprint or edition. In the case of books, Spinoza studies have benefited greatly in recent years from remarkably vigorous reprinting efforts, sometimes by the most obscure publishers. One practical consequence is that a current guide like *Books in Print* or *Philosopher's Index* needs to be consulted to determine the availability of particular titles. In many cases, I have indicated that a dissertation or a book reprint may be obtained from University Microfilms International (UMI) in Ann Arbor, Michigan, which should be helpful to some users. I have also indicated the accession number of abstracts in electronic databases, such as the *Philosopher's Index, Historical Abstracts*, and others. This number identifies the abstract in the underlying data service, and can be used for ordering photocopies; in the case of *Philosopher's Index*, for example, this is DIALOG Information Services in Palo Alto, California.

I plan to compile another edition of this bibliography in a few years. I would be glad, therefore, to hear from users about any errors of omission or commission in the historical record to this point, as well as about any new and forthcoming publications.

For the moment, I would like to thank the several Spinoza scholars who reviewed various drafts of this manuscript and provided encouragement. Special thanks are owed to Manfred Walther, who not only shared his work and offered specific additions and corrections to mine, but also kindly helped to ensure that certain studies by others then on the verge of publication would be included here.

Wayne I. Boucher

Riverside, California
March 1991

The quotation from La Fontaine is in Jacques Boulenger, *The Seventeenth Century in France* (New York: Capricorn Books, 1963), p. 383.

WORKS OF SPINOZA

Collections

The Chief Works of Benedict de Spinoza, Translated with an introduction by R. H. M. Elwes (London: G. Bell and Sons, 1883-1884). 2 vols.

> In Bohn's Philosophical Library. Vol. I includes the *Theologico-Political Treatise* (followed by Spinoza's notes) and *A Political Treatise* (in the translation of H. A. Gosset). Vol. II includes *On the Improvement of the Understanding, The Ethics*, and a selection from Spinoza's correspondence.

The Chief Works of Benedict de Spinoza, Translated with an introduction by R. H. M. Elwes, 2nd Edition, revised (London: G. Bell and Sons, 1887). 2 vols.

> In Bohn's Philosophical Library.

The Chief Works of Benedict de Spinoza, Translated with an introduction by R. H. M. Elwes (New York: Dover Publications, 1951). 2 vols.

> Reprint of the first edition with a bibliographical note by Francesco Cordasco. Reprinted in Gloucester, MA, by Peter Smith, 1962. The Dover edition was also issued in a single hard-cover volume (1951).

Improvement of the Understanding, Ethics and Correspondence, Translated by R. H. M. Elwes, with introduction by Frank Sewall (Washington, DC: M. Walter Dunne, 1901).

> Also issued under the same title in New York by Willey Book Co. (1901) and in New York by Aladdin Book Company (1901). Reprinted as *Philosophy of Benedict de Spinoza* (New York: Tudor Publishing Co., 1934).

Spinoza Selections, Edited with an introduction by John Wild (New York: Charles Scribner's Sons, 1930).

> Includes the *Improvement of the Understanding* (in the Elwes translation)
> and *Ethics* (in the White-Stirling translation), as well as part of the *Short
> Treatise* and "all of the letters of real philosophical importance" (in the Wolf
> translation).

The Philosophy of Spinoza Selected from His Chief Works, With a life of Spinoza
and an introduction by Joseph Ratner (New York: The Modern Library, 1927).

> A radical rearrangement, occasional abridgement, and attempted integra-
> tion of the *Ethics* (based on the White-Stirling translation) with selections
> from the *Improvement of the Understanding, Tractatus Theologico-Politi-
> cus, A Political Treatise*, and the correspondence (in the Elwes translation),
> with some revisions of these translations. An edition published under the
> same title was issued in New York by Carlton House (n.d.); it is not credited
> to Ratner, and it omits his life of Spinoza and his introduction.

The Collected Works of Spinoza, Edited and translated by Edwin Curley
(Princeton: Princeton University Press, 1985), Vol. I.

> Includes *Treatise on the Emendation of the Intellect; Short Treatise on God,
> Man, and His Well-Being; Descartes' "Principles of Philosophy" with the
> Metaphysical Thoughts; Ethics*; and Letters 1-28 (i.e., through June 1665).

Improvement of the Understanding

*Tractatus de Intellectus emendatione, et de via, qua optime in veram rerum
Cognitionem dirigitur*, Translated with preface by W. Hale White, revised by
Amelia Hutchison Stirling (London: T. Fisher Unwin, 1895).

> First published in London by Duckworth, 1889. Reprinted in Freeport, NY,
> by Books for Libraries, 1969.

On the Improvement of the Understanding, Translated with an introduction by
Joseph Katz, Library of the Liberal Arts, No. 67 (New York: The Bobbs-Merrill
Co., 1958).

Treatise on the Improvement of the Understanding, Translated with introduction, commentary, and index by Paul D. Eisenberg, *Philosophy Research
Archives*, Vol. 3 (1977), pp. 553-679.

How To Improve Your Mind, Translated by R. H. M. Elwes, with biographical
notes by Dagobert D. Runes (New York: Philosophical Library, 1956).

> A complete reprint of the Elwes translation of *On the Improvement of
> Human Understanding*.

Short Treatise

Spinoza's Short Treatise on God, Man, and Human Welfare, Translated by Lydia Gillingham Robinson (Chicago: The Open Court Publishing Co., 1909).

> Includes an essay by Albert Schwegler, "Spinoza and His Metaphysics," as well as a glossary of terms (English, Dutch, German), pp. 169-178.

Spinoza's Short Treatise on God, Man, and His Well-Being, Translated and edited, with an introduction and commentary and a life of Spinoza, by A. Wolf (London: Adam and Charles Black, 1910).

The Book of God, Edited with an introduction by Dagobert D. Runes (New York: Philosophical Library, 1958).

> An abridgement of Spinoza's *Short Treatise on God, Man, and His Well-Being*, based on A. Wolf's translation (1910).

Principles of Cartesian Philosophy

The Principles of Descartes' Philosophy, Religion of Science Library, No. 59, Translated, with an introduction, by Halbert Hains Britan (LaSalle, IL: The Open Court Publishing Co., 1943).

Principles of Cartesian Philosophy, Translated by Harry E. Wedeck, with preface by Dagobert D. Runes (London: Peter Owen Ltd.; New York: Philosophical Library, 1961).

Earlier Philosophical Writings: The Cartesian Principles and Thoughts on Metaphysics, Library of the Liberal Arts, No. 163, Translated by Frank A. Hayes, with introduction by David Bidney (Indianapolis: The Bobbs-Merrill Co., 1963).

Ethics

The Ethics. See Willis (1870).

The Ethics of Benedict de Spinoza, Demonstrated after the Method of Geometers, and Divided into Five Parts, in Which Are Treated Separately: I. Of God, II. Of the Soul, III. Of the Affections or Passions, IV. Of Man's Slavery, or the Force of the Passions, V. Of Man's Freedom, or the Power of the Understanding. From the Latin. With an Introductory Sketch of His Life and Writings (New York: D. Van Nostrand, 1876).

Translator's preface signed "D. D. S." — usually identified as Daniel Drake
Smith. The translator observes that "this is the first time that any of
[Spinoza's] works has been published in the United States" (p. iii), a point
he repeats later (p. xxxvii). A reprint was published in New York and
London by G. P. Putnam's Sons, 1888.

The Ethics. See Smith (1886).

*The Philosophy of Spinoza as Contained in the First, Second, and Fifth Parts
of the "Ethics," and in Extracts from the Third and Fourth,* Translated and
edited with introductory material and notes by George Stuart Fullerton, 2nd
Edition (New York: Henry Holt and Co., 1894).

The first edition, which was flawed, was published in 1892.

*Ethic Demonstrated in Geometrical Order and Divided into Five Parts, Which
Treat (1) Of God; (2) Of the Nature and Origin of the Mind; (3) Of the Nature
& Origin of the Affects; (4) Of Human Bondage, or of the Strength of the Affects;
(5) Of the Power of the Intellect, or of Human Liberty,* Translated by W. Hale
White, revised by Amelia Hutchison Stirling, 4th Edition, revised and corrected
(London: Oxford University Press, 1910).

White's translation was published in the English and Foreign Philosophical
Library (London: Trübner & Co., 1883); the second edition, as revised by
Stirling, was published by Oxford in 1894; the third in 1899.

Spinoza's Ethics and De Intellectus Emendatione, Translated by Andrew Boyle,
with introduction by George Santayana, Everyman's Library, No. 481 (London:
J. M. Dent & Sons; New York: E. P. Dutton & Co., 1910).

See Spinoza, *Ethics* (1959 and 1989).

Ethics, Preceded by On the Improvement of the Understanding, Edited, with
introduction, bibliography, and index, by James Gutmann (New York: Hafner
Publishing Co., 1949).

Includes the Elwes translation of *On the Improvement of the Understanding*
and the White-Stirling 1899 edition of the *Ethics,* each with modifications
by the editor. Also includes an essay on Spinoza by Frederick J. E.
Woodbridge, pp. xxiii-xxxiv, originally presented as an address at Columbia University in 1933.

Spinoza's Ethics and De Intellectus Emendatione, Translated by Andrew Boyle,
with introduction by T. C. Gregory, Everyman's Library, No. 481 (London: J.
M. Dent & Sons; New York: E. P. Dutton & Co., 1959).

Revised version of the 1910 translation. *See* Spinoza, *Ethics* (1910 and 1989).

The Ethics of Spinoza: The Road to Inner Freedom, Edited with an introduction by Dagobert D. Runes (Secaucus, NJ: The Citadel Press, 1976).

> A radical rearrangement and paraphrasing of the Elwes translation of the *Ethics*, with changes and revisions by the editor. Originally published in New York in 1957 by the Philosophical Library.

The Ethics, With introduction by SPR Charter (Malibu, CA: Pangloss Press, Joseph Simon Publisher, 1981).

> The translation is based "mainly" on Elwes (1883).

Ethics, Translated by George Eliot, and edited by Thomas Deegan, Salzburg Studies in English Literature (Salzburg: University of Salzburg, 1981).

The Ethics and Selected Letters, Translated by Samuel Shirley, and edited, with introduction and bibliography, by Seymour Feldman (Indianapolis: Hackett Publishing Co., 1982).

Ethics, Translated by Andrew Boyle, revised by G. H. R. Parkinson, with an introduction and notes by G. H. R. Parkinson, Everyman's Library, No. 1481 (London: J. M. Dent & Sons, 1989).

> *See* Spinoza, *Ethics* (1910 and 1959).

Tractatus Theologico-Politicus *and* Tractatus Politicus

A Treatise Partly Theological, and Partly Political, Containing some few Discourses To prove that the Liberty of Philosophizing (that is, Making Use of Natural Reason) may be allow'd without any prejudice to Piety, or to the Peace of any Common-wealth; And that the Loss of Public Peace and Religion it self must necessarily follow, where such a Liberty of Reasoning is taken away ... Translated out of Latin. London, Printed in the Year, 1689.

> Translation of the *Tractatus Theologico-Politicus*. In Van der Linde, No. 13. Also in Oko (1964), p. 31, and in Hertzberger (1950), No. 377. Full citation in Kingma and Offenberg (1985), No. 20. The first of Spinoza's works to be translated into English. The translator is unknown.

Treatise partly Theological and partly Political, containing Discourses to prove the Liberty of philosophizing, that is, making Use of Natural Reason, translated from the Latin. London 1737.

> In Van der Linde, No. 14, and in Oko (1964), p. 32.

Tractatus Theologico-Politicus: A Critical Inquiry into the History, Purpose, and Authenticity of the Hebrew Scriptures; with the Right to Free Thought and Free Discussion Asserted, and Shown To Be Not Only Consistent but Necessarily Bound up with True Piety and Good Government ... From the Latin. With an introduction and notes by the editor ... London: Trübner & Co., 1862.

> In Van der Linde, No. 15, who attributes this anonymous work to Robert Willis. Reprinted in 1868 with the same title but a different subtitle; Van der Linde, No. 16.

Tractatus Theologico-Politicus, Translated with an introduction by R. H. M. Elwes, Revised edition (London: Routledge, 1895).

> In the catalogue, *Baruch de Spinoza (1632-1677): A Major Collection of 330 Items by and about Spinoza and Spinozism* (Bristol: Thoemmes Antiquarian Books, 1989), No. 22.

Theologico-Political Treatise, Translated, with introduction and notes, by Frank M. Vanderhoof, Unpublished doctoral dissertation, Columbia University, 1952.

> Currently available from UMI (Order No. 00-04599).

Treatise on Politics, Edited by George Jacob Holyoake (London, 1853).

> Citation reported by Oko (1964), p. 2, as being in Charles W. F. Goss, *A Descriptive Bibliography of the Writings of George Jacob Holyoake* (London: Crowther & Goodman, 1908). Probably a reference to the following volume.

A Treatise on Politics, Translated by William Maccall, The Cabinet of Reason, A Library of Freethought, Politics and Culture, Vol. V (London: Holyoake and Co., 1854).

> In Oko (1964), p. 30.

Writings on Political Philosophy, Edited with an introduction by Albert G. A. Balz (New York: D. Appleton-Century Co., 1937).

> Includes the *Tractatus Politicus* and selections from the *Tractatus Theologico-Politicus* in the 1883 Elwes translation, with occasional revisions by the editor.

The Political Works: The Tractatus Theologico-Politicus in Part and the Tractatus Politicus in Full, Edited and translated, with an introduction and notes, by A. G. Wernham (Oxford: The Clarendon Press, 1958).

Spinoza on Freedom of Thought: Selections from Tractatus Theologico-Politicus and Tractatus Politicus, Edited and translated by T. E. Jessop (Montreal: Mario Casalini, Ltd., 1962).

Tractatus Theologico-Politicus, Translated by Samuel Shirley, with introduction by Brad S. Gregory (Leiden: E. J. Brill, 1989).

Hebrew Grammar

Hebrew Grammar, Edited and translated, with an introduction, by Maurice J. Bloom (New York: Philosophical Library, 1962).

> Also published in London by Vision, 1963.

Correspondence

A Letter Expostulatory: To a Convert from Protestant Christianity to Roman Catholicism (London: Trübner and Co., 1869).

> 14pp. A letter to Albert Burgh. In Van der Linde, No. 34. Oko (1964), p. 15, also cites (Ramgate, T. Scott, 1869).

Correspondence. See Willis (1870).

Nachbildung der im Jarhe 1902 noch erhaltenen eigenhändigen Briefe des Benedictus Despinoza, Edited by W. Meijer (The Hague: Von Mouton & Co., 1903).

> Includes facsimile copies of 12 letters by Spinoza (and of the title page of a copy of the *Tractatus Theologico-Politicus* with his inscription), along with two separate inserts, one of which contains a transcription of this material and translations into Dutch, German, and English. The English translations are on pp. 67-84.

The Correspondence of Spinoza, Translated and edited, with introduction and annotations, by A. Wolf (London: Frank Cass & Co., 1966).

> Reprint of the original edition published in New York by Dial Press, 1927, and in London by George Allen & Unwin, 1928.

Letters to Friend and Foe, Edited with a preface by Dagobert D. Runes (New York: Philosophical Library, 1966).

> Based upon the translation of R. H. M. Elwes, with minor changes and revisions by the editor.

Excerpts

Spinoza Dictionary, Edited by Dagobert D. Runes, with a foreword by Albert Einstein (New York: Philosophical Library, 1951).

Reflections and Maxims, Edited by Dagobert D. Runes (New York: Philosophical Library, 1965).

> A brief (92 pp.) version of the preceding.

The Living Thoughts of Spinoza, Selected with an introduction by Arnold Zweig, 2nd Edition (London: Cassell and Company, 1943).

> Selections from Spinoza are from the Elwes translation of the *Improvement of the Understanding, Ethics*, and the correspondence. The introductory essay, pp. 1-32, was translated by Eric Katz and Barrows Mussey. A paperback reprint published under the title, *Arnold Zweig Presents the Living Thoughts of Spinoza* (New York: Premier Books, Fawcett Publications, 1959) includes this essay on pp. 15-53.

Works Attributed to Spinoza

Algebraic Calculation of the Rainbow, With introduction by G. ten Doesschate (Nieukoop: B. de Graaf, 1963).

> Facsimile of the original Dutch text (1687), with introduction (pp. 7-26) in English. Published in the series, Dutch Classics on History of Science, Vol. V, under the supervision of the Netherlands Society for the History of Medicine, Mathematics and Exact Sciences.

Spinoza's Algebraic Calculation of the Rainbow and Calculation of Chances, Edited and translated with an introduction, explanatory notes, and an appendix by Michael J. Petry, International Archives of the History of Ideas, No. 108 (Dordrecht: Martinus Nijhoff, 1985).

See also Popkin and Signer (1987).

COMMENTARIES

———, Lives, English and forein ... including the history of England, and other nations of Europe, from the year 1660, to the year 1690. By several hands ... London, Printed for B. Tooke, 1704. 2 vols.

In Oko (1964), p. 69.

———, An account of the life and writings of Spinosa. To which is added, An abstract of his Theological political treatise. Containing I. His discourses of prophecy. II. Of prophets. III. Of the gift of prophecy to other nations as well as the Jewish. IV. Of ceremonies. V. Of miracles. VI. Of the dependency of religion, and all things relating to it, on the civil magistrate. VII. Of the liberty of thinking and speaking ... London, Printed for W. Boreham, 1720.

In Oko (1964), p. 41. Van der Linde (No. 105) cites a shorter version of the title. The complete citation is given in Kingma and Offenberg (1985), No. 21.

———, An historical account of the life and writings of the late eminently famous Mr. John Toland ... By one of his most intimate friends ... London, J. Roberts, 1722.

In Oko (1964), p. 227.

———, The Christian free-thinker; or, An epistolary discourse concerning freedom of thought; in which are contained observations on the lives and writings of Epicurus, Lucretius, Petronius, Cardan, Bruno, Vanini, and Spinosa. 2d ed. London, printed for J. Robert, 1740.

66pp. In Oko (1964), p. 409.

———, Critical remarks upon the late Lord Viscount Bollingbroke's letters on the study and use of history, as far as they regard sacred history. London, J. Woodyer, 1754.

67pp. In Oko (1964), p. 293.

———, Encyclopaedia Britannica; or, A Dictionary of Arts and Sciences ... By a Society of Gentlemen in Scotland. In Three Volumes. Edinburgh: Printed for A. Bell and C. Macfarquhar ... 1771.

> Includes an article on Spinozism, Vol. III, pp. 621-622. Additionally, the article, "Religion, or Theology," Vol. III, p. 542, lists 22 groups that "the theologian will have to combat principally with," the first of which is "The Atheists, with Spinosa at their head."

———, Encyclopaedia; or, A dictionary of arts, sciences, and miscellaneous literature. Philadelphia, T. Dobson, 1798.

> In Oko (1964), p. 127, citing an article on Spinoza, Vol. 17, pp. 695-697.

———, Encyclopaedia Perthensis; or Universal dictionary of knowledge ... Perth, Mitchell, 1816. 23 vols.

> In Oko (1964), p. 124, citing an article on Spinoza, Vol. 21, pp. 291-293.

———, The London Encyclopaedia, or Universal dictionary of science, art, literature, and practical mechanics. By the original editor of the Encyclopaedia metropolitana, T. Curtis, assisted by professional and other gentlemen. London, T. Tegg, 1829. 22 vols.

> In Oko (1964), p. 126, citing an article on Spinoza, Vol. 21, pp. 12-14.

———, [Article on Spinoza's *Tractatus Theologico-Politicus*], *British Quarterly Review*, Vol. 46 (1848).

> This fragmentary reference is based on details in Farrar (1863), p. 106, who notes that the article is concerned with "Spinoza's theology."

———, "Philosophy of Spinoza," *Southern Quarterly Review*, Vol. 16 (1850), pp. 76-81.

> In Oko (1964), p. 113.

———, "The Religion and Ethics of Spinoza," *The National Quarterly Review*, Vol. 23 (1871), pp. 22-41.

> In Oko (1964), p. 458.

———, *Papers Read Before the Jews' College Literary Society During the Session 1886-7* (London: Office of the *Jewish Chronicle*, 1887).

In Oko (1964), p. 370. Includes essays by H. Behrend, "The Influence of Judaism over Ancient, Mediaeval and Modern Philosophy: Philo, Ibn-Gebirol and Spinoza," pp. 13-27, and Michael Friedlander, "Spinoza, His Life and Philosophy," pp. 163-177.

——, *Religious Systems of the World: A Contribution to the Study of Comparative Religion*, A collection of addresses delivered at South Place Institute, now revised and in some cases rewritten by the authors, together with some others specially written for this volume, 10th Edition (London: Swan Sonnenschein, 1911).

Includes a lecture by Frederick Pollock, "Spinoza," pp. 709-723.

——, *Philosophical Essays in Honor of James Edwin Creighton*, by Former Students in the Sage School of Philosophy of Cornell University, in Commemoration of Twenty-Five Years' Service as Teacher and Scholar (New York: Macmillan, 1917).

Includes essays by Ernest Albee, "The Confusion of Categories in Spinoza's Ethics," pp. 1-25, and Katherine E. Gilbert, "Hegel's Criticisms of Spinoza," pp. 26-41.

——, *Chronicon Spinozanum* (The Hague: Curis Societatis Spinozanae, 1921-1927). 5 vols.

Vol I (1921) includes papers in English by L. Roth, F. Pollock, and H. Wolfson; Vol. II (1922), by A. Oko, L. Roth, A. Wolf, and H. Wolfson; Vol. III (1923), by M. Cohen, F. Thilly, and H. Wolfson; Vol. IV (1926), by G. Tawney, A. Wolf, and H. Wolfson; Vol. V (1927), by S. Alexander.

——, *Baruch Spinoza*, Addresses and messages delivered and read at the College of the City of New York on the occasion of the tercentenary of Spinoza, November 23, 1932 (New York: Spinoza Institute of America, 1933).

In Oko (1964), p. 185. Includes essays by W. Bernard, I. Husik, G. Mason, I. Muraskin, J. Shatsky, and H. Waton, as well as messages from A. Einstein, F. Pollock, S. Alexander, C. Brunner, L. Polak, C. Gebhardt, and L. Brunschvicg.

——, *Septimana Spinozana* (The Hague: Curis Societatis Spinozanae, Martinus Nijhoff, 1933).

Includes papers in English by S. Alexander, I. Edman, H. Hallett, F. Pollock, and G. Santayana.

——, *Classics in Philosophy and Ethics* (New York: Philosophical Library, 1960).

In Curley (1975), p. 271. Includes a selection from Spinoza entitled, "The Nature of God"; Curley calls attention to "the introductory reading guide" by C. E. M. Joad in this book.

——, *Akten Des II. Internationalen Leibniz-Kongresses,* Hannover, 17.-22. Juli 1972. Vol. 3: *Metaphysik-Ethik-Ästhetik-Monadenlehre* (Wiesbaden: Steiner, 1975).

In Van der Werf (1984), No. 1045, citing an essay by Jacquelyn A. K. Kegley, "Spinoza's God and Laplace's World Formula," pp. 25-35.

——, *Leibniz à Paris (1672-1676).* Symposium de la G. W. Leibniz-Gesellschaft (Hannover) et du Centre national de la recherche scientifique (Paris) à Chantilly (France) du 14 au 18 novembre 1976. Vol. 2: *La philosophie de Leibniz* (Wiesbaden, 1978).

In Van der Werf (1984), No. 1469, citing an essay by G. H. R. Parkinson, "Leibniz's Paris Writings in Relation to Spinoza," Vol. 2, pp. 73-89.

——, *L'aventure de l'esprit: Mélanges Alexandre Koyré, publies à l'occasion de son 70ée anniversaire* (Paris: Hermann, 1964). 2 vols.

Includes a paper by A. Rupert Hall and Marie Ross Hall, "Philosophy and Natural Philosophy: Boyle and Spinoza," Vol. II, pp. 241-256.

——, *Theoria cum praxi. Zum Verhältnis von Theorie und Praxis im 17. und 18. Jahrhundert.* Akten Des III. Internationalen Leibniz-Kongresses, Hannover. 12. bis 17. November 1977. Vol. 2: *Spinoza* (Wiesbaden: Steiner, 1981).

In Van der Werf (1984), No. 1889. Includes essays by G. H. R. Parkinson, "Spinoza's Concept of the Rational Act," pp. 1-19, and S. Cremaschi, "Concepts of Force in Spinoza's Psychology," pp. 138-144.

——, *Studia Spinozana* (Alling: Walther & Walther Verlag, 1985-1987; Würzburg: Königshausen & Neumann Verlag, 1988-).

This series, "which seeks to continue in the tradition of *Chronicon Spinozanum,*" has produced six volumes to date, each containing a variety of articles, news, and reviews, including most particularly essays focused on a central theme (under the direction of a special editorial team).

The first volumes and the authors of papers in English on the central theme and other topics (excluding book reviews, conference reports, etc.) are as follows:

- Vol. 1, *Spinoza's Philosophy of Society,* Edited by E. Giancotti Boscherini, A. Matheron, and M. Walther (1985), with papers by H. Blom, H. Blom and J. Kerkhoven, D. Den Uyl, M. Petry and G. van Suchtelen, G. van der Wal, and Y. Yovel.

- Vol. 2, *Spinoza's Epistemology*, Edited by E. Curley, W. Klever, and F. Mignini (1986), with papers by F. Biasutti, E. Curley, H. De Dijn, J. De Vet, J. Dienstag, G. Floistad, D. Garret, E. Harris, H. Hubbeling, G. Jongeneelen, W. Klever, and F. Mignini.

- Vol. 3, *Spinoza and Hobbes*, Edited by M. Bertman, H. De Dijn, and M. Walther (1987), with papers by H. De Dijn, D. Den Uyl and S. Warner, G. Jongeneelen, W. Klever, Z. Levy, and W. Sacksteder.

- Vol. 4, *Spinoza's Early Writings*, Edited by F. Mignini, P.-F. Moreau, and G. van Suchtelen (1988), with papers by A. Beavers and L. Rice, W. Klever, A. Klijnsmit, R. Popkin, and W. van Bunge.

- Vol. 5, *Spinoza and Literature*, Edited by M. Bollacher, R. Henrard, and W. Klever (1989), with papers by M. Abadi, J. Cook, R. Elovaara, G. Floistad, A. Hart, W. Klever, A. Negri, W. van Bunge, and M. Walther.

- Vol. 6, *Spinoza and Leibniz*, Edited by E. Curley, A. Heinekamp, and M. Walther (1990), with papers by F. Biasutti, M. Dascal, D. Garrett, W. Klever, Z. Levy, O. Pombo, J. de Salas Ortueta, and E. Yakira.

Planned issues in this series include Vol. 7 (1991), *The Ethics in the "Ethics"*; Vol. 8 (1992), *Spinoza and Socialist Theory*; and Vol. 9 (1993), *Spinoza's Psychology and Social Psychology*.

Abadi, Marcelo, "Spinoza in Borges' Looking Glass," in *Studia Spinozana*, Vol. 5 (1989), pp. 29-42.

Abanuka, B., *The First Part of Spinoza's Ethics: A Reinterpretation*, Unpublished doctoral dissertation, Leuven, 1961.

In Van der Werf (1984), No. 89.

Abbott, George F., *Israel in Europe* (London and New York: Macmillan Co., 1907).

> Includes a section on Spinoza, pp. 251-254.

Abbott, William R., *Sense Experience in Spinoza's Theory of Knowledge*, Unpublished doctoral dissertation, Ohio State University, 1966.

> Currently available from UMI (Order No. 66-09993).

Abraham, Robert D., "Spinoza's Concept of Notions: A Functional Interpretation," *Revue internationale de philosophie*, Vol. 31 (1977), pp. 27-38.

Abrahams, Israel, *Chapters on Jewish Literature* (Philadelphia: The Jewish Publication Society of America, 1899).

> In Oko (1964), p. 76, citing references to Spinoza, especially in pp. 243-252.

[Abu Bakr ibn al-Tufail, Abu Ja'far]　The improvement of human reason, exhibited in the life of Hai ebn Yokdhan: written in Arabick above 500 years ago, by Abu Jaafar ebn Tophail ... newly translated from the original Arabick, by Simon Ockley ... With an appendix, in which the possibility of man's attaining the true knowledge of God, and things necessary to salvation, with instruction, is briefly consider'd. London, Printed and sold by E. Powell, 1708.

> In Oko (1964), p. 413.

Aciman, André, A., "Was Spinoza a Heretic?" *Commentary*, Vol. 90, No. 2 (1990), pp. 39-43.

Adams, Henry Cadwallader, *The History of the Jews from the War with Rome to the Present Time* (London: The Religious Tract Society, 1887).

> Includes a section on Spinoza, pp. 295-298.

Adamson, Robert, *The Development of Modern Philosophy, With Other Lectures and Essays*, Edited by W. R. Sorley (Edinburgh: William Blackwood and Sons, 1903). 2 vols.

> Includes a chapter on Spinoza, Vol. I, pp. 58-66, and other references. This first volume was published separately by Blackwood in 1930.

Adler, Felix, *Creed and Deed: A Series of Discourses* (New York: Published for the Society for Ethical Culture by G. P. Putnam's Sons, 1890).

> Includes a section on Spinoza.

Adler, Jacob, "Spinoza's Theory of Reference and the Origin of the Attributes: A Sketch," *Southwest Philosophy Review*, Vol. 3 (1986), pp. 40-50.

Adler, Jacob, "The Development of Three Concepts in Spinoza," *Southwest Philosophy Review*, Vol. 5 (January 1989), pp. 23-32.

Adler, Jacob, "Divine Attributes in Spinoza: Intrinsic and Relational," *Philosophy and Theology*, Vol. 4 (Fall 1989), pp. 32-52.

Adler, Mortimer J., *The Idea of Freedom: A Dialectical Examination of the Conceptions of Freedom* (Garden City, NY: Doubleday & Co., 1958).

   Includes many references to Spinoza.

Adlerblum, Nima H., *A Study of Gersonides in His Proper Perspective* (New York: Columbia University Press, 1926).

   From the author's doctoral dissertation, Columbia University. Includes a section on Spinoza, pp. 126-130.

Afnan, Ruhi M., *The Revelation of Baha'u'llah and the Bab* (New York: Philosophical Library, 1977). 2 vols.

   Includes a section on Spinoza in Book 2.

Agassi, Joseph, *Towards a Rational Philosophical Anthropology* (The Hague: Martinus Nijhoff, 1977).

   Includes many references to Spinoza.

Agassi, Joseph, "Towards a Canonic Version of Classical Political Theory," in Grene and Nails (1986), pp. 153-170.

Agrawal, Brahma Swarup, "Mechanism in Knowledge," *Indian Philosophy and Culture*, Vol. 6 (June-September 1961), pp. 357-360.

   In *Philosopher's Index*, No. 067185, citing references to Spinoza and Sankara.

Agrawal, Brahma Swarup, "Absolutism and Pantheism," *Darshana International*, Vol. 7 (April 1967), pp. 23-27.

   In *Philosopher's Index*, No. 023781, citing references to Spinoza and Sankara.

Agus, Jacob B., *The Vision and the Way: An Interpretation of Jewish Ethics* (New York: Frederick Ungar, 1965).

> In Dienstag (1986), p. 375, citing a chapter, "Universality of Judaism," pp. 234-252, which discusses differences between Spinoza and Maimonides on the Seven Commandments of Noah.

Akkerman, F., *Studies in the Posthumous Works of Spinoza: On Style, Earliest Translation and Reception, Earliest and Modern Edition of Some Texts* (Groningen: Rijksuniversiteit Groningen, 1980).

Akkerman, F., "J. H. Glazeman, An Early Translator of Spinoza," in De Deugd (1984), pp. 23-29.

Akkerman, F., and H. G. Hubbeling, "The Preface to Spinoza's Posthumous Works, 1677, and Its Author, Jarig Jelles (c. 1619/20-1683)," *Lias*, Vol. 6, No. 1 (1979), pp. 103-173.

Akselrod, L. I., "Spinoza and Materialism," in Kline (1952), pp. 61-89.

> Albee, Ernest, "The Confusion of Categories in Spinoza's Ethics," in *Philosophical Essays in Honor of...Creighton* (1917), pp. 1-25.

Aldrich, Virgil, "Categories and Spinoza's Attributes," *Pacific Philosophical Quarterly*, Vol. 61, Nos. 1-2 (January-April 1980), pp. 156-166.

Alexander, Samuel, *Spinoza and Time*, With an Afterword by Viscount Haldane (London: G. Allen & Unwin, 1921).

> Fourth Arthur Davis Memorial Lecture. An extract is reprinted in Kashap (1972), pp. 68-85. The full essay was reprinted in Alexander (1939), pp. 349-385.

Alexander, Samuel, *Spinoza: An Address*, Delivered in London, March 13, 1927 (London: The Liberal Jewish Union, 1927). 18pp.

Alexander, Samuel, *Spinoza*, An address in commemoration of the tercentenary of Spinoza's birth, given on October 31, 1932 (Manchester: Manchester University Press, 1933). 20pp.

> Manchester University Lectures, No. 29. Currently available from UMI Out-of-Print Books on Demand (Order No. OP42458). Reprinted in Alexander (1939), pp. 332-348.

Alexander, Samuel, *Philosophical and Literary Pieces*, Edited, with a memoir, by his literary executor [John Laird] (London: Macmillan and Co., 1939).

Includes Alexander (1933), pp. 332-348, and Alexander (1921), pp. 349-385.

Alexander, Samuel, "Lessons from Spinoza," in *Chronicon Spinozanum*, Vol. V (1927), pp. 14-29.

Alexander, Samuel, "Spinoza and Philosophy of Religion," in *Septimana Spinozana* (1933), pp. 127-133.

Allen, Harold J., "Spinoza's Naturalism and Our Contemporary Neo-Cartesians," in Wilbur (1976), pp. 133-155.

Allison, Henry E., *Benedict de Spinoza: An Introduction*, Revised edition (New Haven: Yale University Press, 1987).

Allison, Henry E., "Kant's Critique of Spinoza," in Kennington (1980), Chap. 12, pp. 199-228.

Allison, Henry E., "Lessing's Spinozistic Exercises," in *Humanität und Dialog: Lessing und Mendelssohn in neuer Sicht*, Supplement to E. Bahr, E. P. Harris, and L. G. Lyons (eds.), *Lessing Yearbook* (Detroit and Munich, 1982), pp. 223-233.

In Bell (1984), p. 180.

Allison, Henry, E., "Spinoza's Doctrine of the Eternity of the Mind: Comments on Matson," in Curley and Moreau (1990), pp. 96-101.

See Matson (1990).

Alon, I., "Between Fatalism and Causality: Al-Ash'ari and Spinoza," in Scharfstein (1978), pp. 218-234.

Alpern, Henry, *The March of Philosophy* (New York: Dial Press, 1934).

Includes a chapter on Spinoza, pp. 119-151, and many other references.

Altmann, Alexander (ed.), *Biblical and Other Studies* (Cambridge: Harvard University Press, 1963).

Includes an essay by Arthur Hyman, "Spinoza's Dogmas of Universal Faith in the Light of Their Medieval Jewish Background," pp. 183-195.

Altmann, Alexander, *Studies in Religious Philosophy and Mysticism* (Ithaca: Cornell University Press, 1969).

Includes the author's essay, "Moses Mendelssohn on Leibniz and Spinoza,"
pp. 246-274, which was first published in Loewe (1966), pp. 15-45.

Altmann, Alexander, *Moses Mendelssohn: A Biographical Study* (University,
AL: University of Alabama Press, 1973).

Includes a section on the Mendelssohn-Jacobi correspondence, pp. 606-
652, as well as many other references to Spinoza.

Amryc, C., *Pantheism: The Light and Hope of Modern Reason* (Privately
printed, 1898).

In Hertzberger (1950), No. 235, noting that "C. Amryc" is probably an
anagram of "C. Mayo," which is the author's real name.

Amstutz, Jakob, "Philosophers on Death," *Essence*, Vol. 2, pp. 129-138.

In *Philosopher's Index*, No. 070252; no date given.

[Anderson, George] A remonstrance against Lord Viscount Bolingbroke's
philosophical religion, addressed to David Mallet, Esq., the publisher. Edinburgh, 1756.

In Oko (1964), p. 197.

Anderson, Robert Fendel, *Hume's First Principles* (Lincoln: University of
Nebraska, 1966).

Includes a section on Spinoza's doctrine of substance, pp. 79-83.

Anton, John P. (ed.), *Naturalism and Historical Understanding: Essays on the
Philosophy of John Herman Randall, Jr.* (Albany: State University of New York
Press, 1967).

Includes an essay by George L. Kline, "Randall's Reinterpretation of the
Philosophies of Descartes, Spinoza, and Leibniz," pp. 83-93, and other
references.

Aquila, Richard E., "The Identity of Thought and Object in Spinoza," *Journal
of the History of Ideas*, Vol. 16 (July 1978), pp. 271-288.

Aquila, Richard E., "States of Affairs and Identity of Attributes in Spinoza,"
Midwest Studies in Philosophy, Vol. 8 (1983), pp. 161-180.

Arber, Agnes, *The Manifold and The One* (London: John Murray, 1957).

Includes many references to Spinoza.

Arber, Agnes, "Spinoza and Boethius' *De Consolatione Philosophiae*," *Isis*, Vol. 34 (1943), pp. 399-403.

[Argens, Jean Baptiste de Boyer] The Jewish spy: being a philosophical, historical and critical correspondence, by letters which lately pass'd between certain Jews in Turkey, Italy, France, &c. Translated from the originals into French by the Marquis d'Argens; and now done into English. London, Printed for D. Browne and R. Hett, 1739.

> In Oko (1964), p. 197. Oko also cites on p. 77 a 4-volume edition under the same title, published in Dublin, 1753.

Ariew, Roger, "The Infinite in Spinoza's Philosophy," in Curley and Moreau (1990), pp. 16-31.

Armstrong-Buck, Susan, "Whitehead's Metaphysical System as a Foundation for Environmental Ethics," *Environmental Ethics*, Vol. 8 (Fall 1986), pp. 241-259.

> Compares the views of Spinoza and several other philosophers to those of Whitehead.

Arnold, Matthew, *Essays in Criticism*, First Series (London: Macmillan and Co., 1884).

> Includes an essay, "Spinoza and the Bible," pp. 307-344.

Arnold, Matthew, *Essays Literary & Critical*, Everyman's Library, No. 115 (London: J. M. Dent, 1906).

> Includes an essay, "A Word More about Spinoza," pp. 174-185. Also in *Macmillan's Magazine*, Vol. 9 (December 1863), pp. 136-142.

Arnold, Matthew, *Essays, Letters, and Reviews*, Collected and edited by Fraser Neiman (Cambridge: Harvard University Press, 1960).

> Includes an essay, "The Bishop and the Philosopher," pp. 43-68. Originally in *Macmillan's Magazine*, Vol. 7 (1861), pp. 241-256, under the title, "Spinoza and Colenso."

Arnold, Sydney, "Spinoza: A New Orientation" (Excerpt), *Acta Spinozana*, Vol. II (1965), pp. 13-16.

> In Rice (1967), p. 296.

Art, Bradford Lee, *The Mysterious Abyss of Existence: Groundwork for the Life of the Virtuous Sage*, Unpublished doctoral dissertation, Brown University, 1985.

> Offers a view of the "virtuous sage" based on a reading of Spinoza's *Ethics* and Lao Tse's *Tao Te Ching*. Currently available from UMI (Order No. 85-19803).

Ashton, Rosemary, *The German Idea: Four English Writers and the Reception of German Thought, 1800-1860* (Cambridge: Cambridge University Press, 1980).

> Includes sections on Spinoza and Lewes, pp. 126-128, and on Spinoza and George Eliot, pp. 155-159.

Atkins, Dorothy J., *George Eliot and Spinoza* (Salzburg: Institute for English Language and Literature, University of Salzburg, 1978).

> From the author's doctoral dissertation of the same title, University of Nebraska, 1977. The latter is currently available from UMI (Order No. 77-32112).

Atlas, Samuel, *From Critical to Speculative Idealism: The Philosophy of Solomon Maimon* (The Hague: Martinus Nijhoff, 1964).

> Includes references to Spinoza.

Atlas, Samuel, "Moses in the Philosophy of Maimonides, Spinoza, and Solomon Maimon," *Hebrew Union College Annual*, Vol. 25 (1954), pp. 369-400.

> In Dienstag (1986), p. 376.

Atlas, Samuel, "Solomon Maimon and Spinoza," *Hebrew Union College Annual*, Vol. 30 (1959), pp. 233-257.

Augustijn, C., P. N. Holtrop, G. H. M. Posthumus Meyjer, and E. G. E. van der Wall (eds.), *Kerkhistorische opstellen aangeboden aan Prof. dr. J. van den Berg* (Kampen: Kok, 1987).

> In Van Bunge (1989), p. 249, citing an essay by Richard H. Popkin, "Some Seventeenth-Century Interpretations of Spinoza's Ideas," pp. 63-74.

Avineri, Shlomo, "Socialism and Judaism in Moses Hess's *Holy History of Mankind*," *Review of Politics*, Vol. 45, No. 2 (1983), pp. 234-253.

Discusses Hess's socialist utopian vision, the driving force of which is "a new social synthesis of Catholicism and Judaism with Spinozan rationalism." — *Historical Abstracts*, No. 1088702.

Bachem, R. "Rediscovery of Spinoza by Schleiermacher, Arnold and Renan," *Revue de littérature comparée*, Vol. 41, No. 4 (1967), pp. 581-583.

In Curley (1975), p. 292.

Bahm, A. J., *Philosophy: An Introduction* (London: Chapman, 1953).

In *Philosopher's Index*, No. 075559.

Bain, Alexander, and T. Whittaker (eds.), *Philosophical Remains of George Croom Robertson*, With a memoir (London and Edinburgh: Williams and Norgate, 1894).

Includes a chapter, "Leibnitz and Spinoza," pp. 334-342.

Baker, A. E., *How to Understand Philosophy: From Socrates to Bergson* (New York: George H. Doran, 1926).

Includes a chapter, "Spinoza and Leibnitz," pp. 150-166.

Bakker, Jonathan B., *Spinoza's Theory of the Attributes and the Relation of Mind and Body*, Unpublished doctoral dissertation, University of Connecticut, 1978.

Currently available from UMI (Order No. 79-11337).

Bakker, Jonathan B., "Did Spinoza Have a Double Aspect Theory?" *International Studies in Philosophy*, Vol. 14, No. 1 (Spring 1982), pp. 1-16.

Bakker, Jonathan B., "Deborin's Materialist Interpretation of Spinoza," *Studies in Soviet Thought* (Netherlands), Vol. 24, No. 3 (October 1982), pp. 175-183.

Baldwin, James Mark, *Fragments in Philosophy and Science, Being Collected Essays and Addresses* (New York: C. Scribner's Sons, 1902).

Also published under the same title in London by John C. Nimmo, Ltd., 1903. Includes an essay, "The Idealism of Spinoza," pp. 24-41, originally published in *The Presbyterian Review*, Vol. 10 (January 1889), pp. 65-76.

Baldwin, James Mark, *History of Psychology: A Sketch and An Interpretation* (London: Printed for the Rationalist Press Association, Ltd., by Watts & Co., 1913). 2 vols.

Includes a section on Spinoza, Vol. 1, pp. 117-121.

Balet, Leo, *Rembrandt and Spinoza* (New York: Philosophical Library, 1962).

Balz, Albert G. A., *Idea and Essence in the Philosophies of Hobbes and Spinoza* (New York: AMS Press, 1967).

> Originally published by Columbia University Press, 1918, and in the *Archives of Philosophy*, No. 10 (January 1918). Based on the author's doctoral dissertation of the same title, Columbia University, 1916.

Balz, Albert G. A., *Cartesian Studies* (New York: Columbia University Press, 1951).

> Includes an essay, "Cartesian Refutations of Spinoza," pp. 218-241, originally in *The Philosophical Review*, Vol. 46 (1937), pp. 461-484. This book is currently available from UMI Out-of-Print Books on Demand (Order No. OP71624).

Balz, Albert G. A. *See* Spinoza, *Writings on Political Philosophy* (1937).

Bamberger, F., "The Early Editions of Spinoza's *Tractatus Theologico-Politicus*," *Studies in Bibliography and Booklore*, Vol. 5 (1961), pp. 9-33.

> In Kingma and Offenberg (1985), p. 6.

Banerjee, Nikunja Vihari, "Rationalism," in Radhakrishnan (1952), Vol. 2, pp. 201-222.

> Includes a section on Spinoza, pp. 208-215.

Barcan-Marcus, R., "Bar-On on Spinoza's Ontological Proof," in Rotenstreich and Schneider (1983), pp. 110-119.

Barker, H., "Notes on the Second Part of Spinoza's *Ethics*," in Kashap (1972), Part I, pp. 101-122; Part II, pp. 123-144; Part III, pp. 145-167.

> Originally in *Mind*, Vol. 47, No. 186 (1938), pp. 157-179; No. 187, pp. 281-302; and No. 188, pp. 417-439.

Barnard, Frederick M., "Spinozism," in Edwards (1967), Vol. 7, pp. 541-544.

Barnhart, J. E., *Religion and the Challenge of Philosophy* (Totowa, NJ: Littlefield, Adams & Co., 1975).

> Includes a section, "Spinoza's Attempt To Eliminate Anthropomorphic Talk of God," pp. 136-141, and other references.

Barnhart, J. E., "No Glue in the Universe: Hume's Revolution," *Southwest Philosophy Review*, Vol. 5 (January 1989), pp. 39-45.

In *Philosopher's Index*, No. 161708.

Bar-On, A. Z., "The Ontological Proof—Spinoza's Version," in Rotenstreich and Schneider (1983), pp. 101-109.

Bartuschat, W., "The Ontological Basis of Spinoza's Theory of Ethics," in De Deugd (1984), pp. 30-36.

Baruch, S. *See* Oko (1914-1915).

[Basnage, Jacques] The history of the jews, from Jesus Christ to the present time: containing their antiquities, their religion, their rites, the dispersion of the ten tribes in the East and the persecutions this nation has suffer'd in the West. Being a supplement and continuation of the History of Josephus. Written in French by Mr. Basnage. Translated into English by Tho. Taylor, A. M. London, Printed for T. Bever and B. Lintot [etc.]. 1708.

In Oko (1964), p. 363, citing a section on Spinoza, pp. 741-743.

Battisti, Giuseppa S., "Democracy in Spinoza's Unfinished *Tractatus Politicus*," *Journal of the History of Ideas*, Vol. 38, No. 4 (October-December 1977), pp. 623-634.

Bax, E. Belfort, *A Handbook of the History of Philosophy* (London, 1886).

In Hertzberger (1950), No. 42, citing a section on Spinoza, pp. 157-167.

Baxter, Andrew. An enquiry into the nature of the human soul; wherein the immateriality of the soul is evinced from the principles of reason and philosophy ... London, Printed by James Bettenham, for the author [1737?].

In Oko (1964), p. 421. Reprinted in Bristol by Thoemmes, 1991.

[Baxter, Richard] Richard Baxter's Catholick theologie: plain, pure, peaceable: for pacification of the dogmatical word-warriours ... In three books ... London, Printed by Robert White, for Nevill Simons, 1675. 2 vols.

In Oko (1964), p. 346, who notes that the third book was never published, and that the first book is in three parts, with separate title pages and pagination. Spinoza is referred to in Book 1, part 3, pp. 108, 114, 118.

Bayle, Pierre. Miscellaneous reflections, occasion'd by the comet which appear'd in December 1680. Chiefly tending to explode popular superstitions. Written to a doctor of the Sorbon, by Mr. Bayle. Translated from the French. To which is added, the author's life ... London, Printed, 1708.

> In Oko (1964), p. 83, citing a reference to Spinoza, pp. 375-376.

Bayle, Pierre. An Historical and Critical Dictionary. Translated into English. London, C. Harper [etc.], 1710. 4 vols. in folio.

> First English edition of the French original published in Rotterdam in 1697. The article on Spinoza appears in Vol. 3, pp. 2780-2805. In Hertzberger (1950), No. 3; Oko (1964), p. 82; and Walther (1991), p. 15. Walther also cites a second edition, edited by Des Maizeax, published in five volumes in London (1734-1738), with the article on Spinoza in Vol. 5, pp. 199-224, as well as a ten-volume edition edited by G. Strahan (1734-1741) with this article in Vol. 9, pp. 347-372. Hertzberger, No. 4, cites a selected and abridged edition of 1826 in 4 vols., with the Spinoza article in Vol. III, pp. 271-341; Walther identifies the publisher as Hunt & Clarke. (A section from the original French article is translated in Wolf [1927], pp. 160-164.)

Bayle, Pierre, *Selections from Bayle's Dictionary*, Edited by E. A. Beller and M. DuP. Lee, Jr. (Princeton: Princeton University Press, 1952).

> Includes an abridged version of the article on Spinoza, pp. 291-312. The text is based on the second edition of the English translation (1734-1738), which is cited by Oko (1964), p. 82, as having been published in London by J. J. and P. Knapton, and including this article in Vol. 5, pp. 199-224.

Bayle, Pierre, *Historical and Critical Dictionary: Selections*, Edited and translated by Richard H. Popkin and Craig Brush (Indianapolis: Bobbs-Merrill, 1965).

> The article on Spinoza appears on pp. 288-338.

Beavers, Anthony F., and Lee C. Rice, "Doubt and Belief in the *Tractatus De Intellectus Emendatione*," in *Studia Spinozana*, Vol. 4 (1988), pp. 93-119.

Beck, Lewis White, *Six Secular Philosophers: Religious Themes in the Thought of Spinoza, Hume, Kant, Nietzsche, William James, and Santayana* (New York: Harper and Row, 1960).

> Includes a section on Spinoza, pp. 27-41.

Beck, Robert N., "The Attribute of Thought," in Wilbur (1976), pp. 1-12.

Beck, Robert N., "Some Idealistic Themes in the *Ethics*," in Kennington (1980), Chap. 5, pp. 73-88.

Bedford, R. D., *The Defence of Truth: Herbert of Cherbury and the Seventeenth Century* (Manchester: Manchester University Press, 1979).

> In Van der Werf (1984), No. 207.

Behrend, H., "The Influence of Judaism over Ancient, Mediaeval and Modern Philosophy: Philo, Ibn-Gibirol and Spinoza," in Jews' College Literary Society, *Papers*...(1887), pp. 13-27.

> Originally in the *Jewish Chronicle* (London), November 26, 1886, pp. 11-12; December 3, p. 11; and December 10, pp. 14-15. Cited in Oko (1964), p. 423.

Beiser, Frederick C., *The Fate of Reason: German Philosophy from Kant to Fichte* (Cambridge: Harvard University Press, 1987).

> Includes many references to Spinoza, especially in the chapters, "Jacobi and the Pantheism Controversy," and "Mendelssohn and the Pantheism Controversy," and in the section, "Herder and the Pantheism Controversy."

Bekker, B. The world bewitch'd, or an examination of the common opinions concerning spirits. Transl. from a French copy. Vol. I. London, 1695.

> In Hertzberger (1950), No. 761. Only Vol. I was published. It includes some passages on Spinoza.

Belaief, Gail, *Spinoza's Philosophy of Law*, Studies in Philosophy, No. 24 (The Hague: Mouton, 1971).

> From the author's doctoral dissertation at Columbia University, 1963. The latter is currently available from UMI (Order No. 64-09174).

Belaief, Gail, "The Relation Between Civil Law and a Higher Law: A Study of Spinoza's Legal Philosophy," *The Monist*, Vol. 49 (July 1965), pp. 504-518.

Bell, David, *Spinoza in Germany from 1670 to the Age of Goethe*, Bithell Series of Dissertations, Vol. 7 (London: Institute of Germanic Studies, University of London, 1984).

> From the author's doctoral dissertation, Harvard University, 1980.

Benardete, José, "Spinozistic Anomalies," in Kennington (1980), Chap. 4, pp. 53-72.

Benardete, José, "Therapeutics and Hermeneutics," in Curley and Moreau (1990), pp. 209-220.

Benn, Alfred William, *The History of English Rationalism in the Nineteenth Century* (London and New York: Longmans, Green, and Co., 1906). 2 vols.

Includes a section on Spinoza, Vol. I, pp. 94-103. Reprinted in New York by Russell & Russell, 1962.

Benn, Alfred William, *History of Modern Philosophy*, With preface and additional chapter by Robert Arch (London: Printed for the Rationalist Press Association, Ltd., by Watts & Co., 1930).

A new edition of the original 1912 version published by Watts. Includes a section on Spinoza, pp. 38-48, and other references.

Bennett, De Robigne Mortimer, *The World's Sages, Infidels, and Thinkers, Being Biographical Sketches of Leading Philosophers, Teachers, Reformers, Innovators, Founders of New Schools of Thought, Eminent Scientists, etc.* (New York: Liberal and Scientific Publishing House, 1876).

In Oko (1964), p. 42, citing a section on Spinoza, pp. 395-402.

Bennett, Jonathan, *A Study of Spinoza's Ethics* (Indianapolis: Hackett Publishing Co.; Cambridge: Cambridge University Press, 1984).

Bennett, Jonathan, "A Note on Descartes and Spinoza," *The Philosophical Review*, Vol. 74, No. 3 (July 1965), pp. 379-380.

See Donagan (1965).

Bennett, Jonathan, "Accountability," in Van Straaten (1980), pp. 14-47.

Bennett, Jonathan, "Spinoza's Vacuum Argument," *Midwest Studies in Philosophy*, Vol. 5 (1980), pp. 391-399.

Bennett, Jonathan, "Spinoza's Mind-Body Identity Thesis," *The Journal of Philosophy*, Vol. 78, No. 10 (October 1981), pp. 573-584.

Bennett, Jonathan, "Teleology and Spinoza's Conatus," *Midwest Studies in Philosophy*, Vol. 8 (1983), pp. 143-160.

Bennett, Jonathan, "Spinoza on Error," *Philosophical Papers*, Vol. 15 (August 1986), pp. 59-73.

Bennett, Jonathan, "Response to Garber and Ree," in Hare (1988), pp. 62-69.

Bennett, Jonathan, "Spinoza and Teleology: A Reply to Curley," in Curley and Moreau (1990), pp. 53-57.

Ben-Shlomo, J., "Reply to Professor Hampshire," in Rotenstreich and Schneider (1983), pp. 142-146.

Bentley, Richard. The folly and unreasonableness of atheism demonstrated from the advantage and pleasure of a religious life, the faculties of humane souls, the structure of animate bodies, & the origin and frame of the world: in eight sermons preached at the lecture founded by the Honourable Robert Boyle ... in the first year, MDCXCII. By Richard Bentley ... The fourth edition corrected. London, Printed by J. H. for H. Mortlock, 1699.

> In Oko (1964), p. 387; in Hertzberger (1950), No. 763, citing the first edition (1693). Also published as part of Blackall (1700).

[Bentley, Richard] Remarks upon a late discourse of free-thinking in a letter to F. H. By Phileleutherus Lipsiensis [pseud.]. The seventh edition. London, W. Thurlbourn, 1757.

> In Oko (1964), p. 409, who identifies "F. H." as Francis Hare, D.D. The discourse referred to is Collins (1713). Hertzberger (1950), No. 790, cites the fifth edition, which was printed for John Morphew and Cornelius Crownfield in Cambridge, 1716.

Bentley, Richard. Sermons preached at Boyle's lecture; remarks upon a discourse of free-thinking; proposals for an edition of the Greek Testament; etc., etc. By Richard Bentley, D. D. Edited with notes, by the Rev. Alexander Dyce. London, F. Macpherson, 1838.

> In Oko (1964), p. 199. Hertzberger (1950), No. 764, cites the 6th edition (1735).

[Bergier, F.] The life of Lewis of Bourbon, late prince of Condé. Digested into annals. With many curious remarks on the transactions of Europe for these last sixty years. Done out of French. London, T. Goodwin, 1693.

> In Hertzberger (1950), No. 287. 2 vols. in one. Includes references to Spinoza and his visit to the Conde, Part 2, pp. 173-174. Oko attributes this work to Pierre Coste.

Bergmann, Samuel Hugo, *The Philosophy of Solomon Maimon* (Jerusalem, 1967).

> Includes a section on Spinoza and Maimon.

Bergson, Henri, *Creative Evolution*, Translated by Arthur Mitchell (New York: Henry Holt and Co., 1911).

> Includes a section on Spinoza, pp. 347-354.

Berlin, Isaiah, *Vico and Herder: Two Studies in the History of Ideas* (New York: The Viking Press, 1976).

> Includes many references to Spinoza.

Berman, David, "Spinoza's Spiders, Schopenhauer's Dogs," *Philosophical Studies*, Vol. 29 (Winter 1982-1983), pp. 202-209.

Bernard, Walter, *The Philosophy of Spinoza and Brunner* (New York: Spinoza Institute of America, 1934).

> From the author's doctoral dissertation, New York University, 1933. The latter is currently available from UMI (Order No. 73-17723). The book version is currently available from UMI Out-of-Print Books on Demand (Order No. OP55118).

Bernard, Walter, "Free Will or Determinism?" in *Baruch Spinoza* (Spinoza Institute of America, 1933).

Bernard, Walter, "Freud and Spinoza," *Psychiatry*, Vol. 9 (1946), pp. 99-109.

> In Feuer (1958), p. 299.

Bernard, Walter, "Psychotherapeutic Principles in Spinoza's *Ethics*," in Hessing (1977), pp. 63-80.

Bernard, Walter, "Spinoza's Influence on the Rise of Scientific Psychology: A Neglected Chapter in the History of Psychology," *Journal of the History of the Behavioral Sciences*, Vol. 8, No. 2 (1972), pp. 208-215.

Berolzheimer, Fritz, *The World's Legal Philosophies*, Translated by Rachel Szold Jastrow, with an introduction by Sir John Macdonnel and Albert Kocouek (Boston: The Boston Book Co., 1912).

> Includes a section on Spinoza, pp. 127-132.

Bertman, Martin A., "Hobbes' and Spinoza's Politics," in Giancotti Boscherini (1985), pp. 321-331.

Bertman, Martin A. See *Studia Spinozana*, Vol. 3 (1986).

Bertman, Martin A., "Rational Pursuit in Spinoza's *Tractatus de Intellectus Emandatione*," *The New Scholasticism*, Vol. 44 (Spring 1970), pp. 236-248.

Bertman, Martin A., "The Hebrew Encounter with Evil," *Apeiron*, Vol. 9 (1975), pp. 43-47.

> In Van der Werf (1984), No. 247.

Berube, C. (ed.), *Regnum hominis et regnum Dei* (Rome, 1978).

> In Van der Werf (1984), No. 446, citing an essay by D. A. Cress, "Duns Scotus, Spinoza and the Ontological Argument," pp. 389-399.

Bevan, Edwyn Robert (ed.), *The Legacy of Israel* (Oxford: Oxford University Press, 1927).

> Includes an essay by Leon Roth, "Jewish Thought in the Modern World," which contains a section on Spinoza, pp. 449-457.

Biasutti, Franco, "Truth and Certainty in Spinoza's Epistemology," in *Studia Spinozana*, Vol. 2 (1986), pp. 109-127.

Biasutti, Franco, "Reason and Experience in Spinoza and Leibniz," in *Studia Spinozana* (1990), pp. 45-71.

Bickel, Lothar, "On Relationships Between Psychoanalysis and a Dynamic Psychology," in Hessing (1977), pp. 81-89.

Biddle, Stephen Anthony, *Spinoza's Moral Philosophy*, Unpublished doctoral dissertation, Bryn Mawr College, 1980.

> Currently available from UMI (Order No. 81-03595).

Bidney, David, *The Psychology and Ethics of Spinoza: A Study in the History and Logic of Ideas*, 2nd Edition (New York: Russell & Russell, 1962).

> This study is described by the author as a "sequel" to his doctoral dissertation, *The Idea of Value in the Metaphysics of Spinoza*, Yale University, 1932.

Bidney, David. *See* Spinoza, *Earlier Philosophical Writings* (1963).

Bidney, David, "Value and Reality in the Metaphysics of Spinoza," *The Philosophical Review*, Vol. 45, No. 3 (May 1936), pp. 229-244.

The author describes this paper as a 'partial summary' of his dissertation (Bidney, 1962, p. vii).

Bidney, David, "The Problem of Substance in Spinoza and Whitehead," *The Philosophical Review*, Vol. 45 (November 1936), pp. 574-592.

Bidney, David, "Joachim on Spinoza's *Tractatus de Intellectus Emendatione*," *The Philosophical Review*, Vol. 51 (January 1942), pp. 47-64.

Birnbaum, Ruth, "Baruch Spinoza — Martin Buber, Dialectic and Dialogue," *The Personalist*, Vol. 48 (January 1967), pp. 119-128.

[Blackall, Offspring] The sufficiency of a standing revelation in general, and of the Scripture revelation in particular ... and that new revelations cannot reasonably be desir'd ... In eight sermons, preach'd ... at the lecture founded by the Honorable Robert Boyle Esq; in the year MDCC. By Ofspring Blackall ... London, Printed by J. Leake, for Walter Kettilby, 1700.

> In Oko (1964), p. 199, who notes that it is bound with Richard Bentley's *The folly and unreasonableness of atheism demonstrated* (1699).

Blackmore, R. Creation. A philosophical poem. London, 1712.

> In Hertzberger (1950), No. 766. Includes critical references to Spinoza.

Blackwell, Albert L., *Schleiermacher's Early Philosophy of Life: Determinism, Freedom, and Phantasy*, Harvard Theological Studies XXXIII (Chico, CA: Scholars Press, 1982).

> Includes a chapter, "Schleiermacher's Debt to Spinoza and Plato," pp. 123-136, and many other references.

Blackwell, Kenneth M., *The Spinozistic Ethics of Bertrand Russell* (London: Allen & Unwin, 1985).

> From the author's doctoral dissertation, *Bertrand Russell's Spinozistic Ethic of Impersonal Self-Enlargement*, University of Guelph (Canada), 1981.

Blair, R. G., "Imagination and Freedom in Spinoza and Sartre," *Journal of the British Society for Phenomenology*, Vol. 1 (May 1970), pp. 13-16.

Blair, R. G., "Spinoza's Account of Imagination," in Grene (1979), pp. 318-328.

Blakey, Robert, *History of the Philosophy of Mind: Embracing the Opinions of All Writers on Mental Science from the Earliest Period to the Present Time* (London: Longman, Brown, Green and Longmans, 1850). 4 vols.

> In Oko (1964), p. 131, citing two chapters on Spinoza, Vol. 2, pp. 355-384 and pp. 455-460.

Blakey, Robert, *The History of Political Literature from the Earliest Times* (London: R. Bentley, 1855). 2 vols.

> In Oko (1964), p. 289.

[Blakey, Robert] *Memoirs of Dr. Robert Blakey*, Professor of Logic and Metaphysics, Queen's College, Belfast ... Edited by the Rev. Henry Miller ... London, Trübner & Co., 1879.

> In Oko (1964), p. 230.

Blanshard, Brand, *Reason and Goodness* (New York: Macmillan, 1961).

> In *Philosopher's Index*, No. 015485.

Blanshard, Brand, *Reason and Analysis* (LaSalle, IL: Open Court Publishing Co., 1964).

> Includes a section on Spinoza, pp. 73-78, and other references.

Blau, Joseph L., *The Story of Jewish Philosophy* (New York: Random House, 1962).

> Includes a discussion of Spinoza.

Blewett, George John, *The Study of Nature and the Vision of God: With Other Essays in Philosophy* (Toronto: William Briggs, 1907).

> Includes a chapter, "The Metaphysic of Spinoza," pp. 111-199.

Blom, Hans, "Political Science in the Golden Age: Criticism, History and Theory in Dutch Seventeenth Century Political Thought," *The Netherlands Journal of Sociology*, Vol. 15 (1979), pp. 47-71.

> In Van der Werf (1984), No. 278, citing a section on Spinoza's "scientific politics," pp. 60-65.

Blom, Hans W., "Virtue and Political Science: An Interpretation of Spinoza's Political Philosophy," in *Studia Spinozana*, Vol. 1 (1985), pp. 209-230.

Blom, Hans W., "Virtue and Republicanism: Spinoza's Political Philosophy in the Context of the Dutch Republic," in Koenigsberger (1988), pp. 195-212.

Blom, Hans W., and J. M Kerkhoven, "A Letter Concerning an Early Draft of Spinoza's Treatise on Religion and Politics?" in *Studia Spinozana*, Vol. 1 (1985), pp. 371-378.

Blomgren, Carl A., *The Doctrine of Substance, as Held by Descartes, Spinoza, and Leibniz*, Unpublished doctoral dissertation, Yale University, 1893.

Bloom, M. J. *See* Spinoza, *Hebrew Grammar* (1962).

Blount, Charles. Anima mundi: or, An historical narration of the opinions of the ancients concerning man's soul after this life: according to unenlightened nature. By Charles Blount, gent. ... London, Printed in the year 1679.

>   In Oko (1964), p. 421, who notes that this document also appears in *The miscellaneous works of Charles Blount* (1695).

Blount, Charles. Miracles, no violations of the laws of nature ... London: Printed for Robert Sollers, 1683.

>   In Oko (1964), p. 435, who notes that this is mainly a translation of the sixth chapter of Spinoza's *Tractatus Theologico-Politicus*, along with a translation of part of a chapter in Hobbe's *Leviathan* on miracles.

Blount, Charles. Religio laici, written in a letter to John Dryden, Esq. London, printed for R. Bentley and S. Magnus, 1683. 95 pp.

>   In Oko (1964), p. 200.

Blount, Charles. The oracles of reason: consisting of [16 sections]. In several letters to Mr. Hobbs and other persons of eminent quality and learning. By Char. Blount esq; Mr. Gildon and others. London, Printed 1693.

>   In Oko (1964), p. 199, who gives the titles of the 16 sections.

Bluh, Otto, "Newton and Spinoza," *Nature*, Vol. 135 (April 27, 1935), pp. 658-659.

>   Curley (1975), p. 293, cites what is apparently a reprint of this article in *Proceedings of the Tenth International Congress on the History of Sciences,* 1962 (Paris: Hermann, 1964), pp. 701-703.

Blunt, John Henry, *Dictionary of Doctrinal and Historical Theology*, 2nd Edition (London: Rivingtons, 1872).

> Includes an article, "Spinozism," pp. 707-710.

Blunt, John Henry, *Dictionary of Sects, Heresies, Ecclesiastical Parties, and Schools of Religious Thought* (London: Rivingtons, 1874).

> Includes a section on Spinoza, pp. 570-577.

Boedder, Bernard, *Natural Theology* (London: Longmans, Green, 1891).

> Includes an appendix, "Examination of Propositions I-VI in Spinoza's Ethics," pp. 449-460.

Bollacher, M. See *Studia Spinozana*, Vol. 5 (1989).

Bontempo, Charles J., and S. Jack Odell (eds.), *The Owl of Minerva: Philosophers on Philosophy* (New York: McGraw-Hill, 1975).

> In Van der Werf (1984), No. 1517, citing an essay by Karl R. Popper, "How I See Philosophy," pp. 41-55.

Boole, George, *An Investigation of the Laws of Thought, on Which Are Founded the Mathematical Theories of Logic and Probabilities* (New York: Dover Publications, 1958).

> First American printing of the original Macmillan edition, published in 1854. Includes a chapter, "Clarke and Spinoza," pp. 185-218.

Bolton, Martha B., "Spinoza on Cartesian Doubt," *Nous*, Vol. 19, No. 3 (September 1985), pp. 379-395.

Boodin, John Elof, *A Realistic Universe: An Introduction to Metaphysics* (New York: The Macmillan Company, 1916).

> Includes a section on Spinoza's concept of the attributes, pp. 386-389, and other references.

Bosanquet, R. G., "Remarks on Spinoza's *Ethics*," *Mind*, Vol. 54, No. 215 (July 1945), pp. 264-271.

Boscherini, E. *See* Giancotti Boscherini, Emilia.

Bossart, William H., "Metaphysical Experience," *The Review of Metaphysics*, Vol. 15 (September 1961), pp. 34-50.

In *Philosopher's Index*, No. 006920, citing a discussion of Spinoza's formulation of the ontological argument.

Bossart, William H., "Is Philosophy Transcendental?" *The Monist*, Vol. 55 (April 1971), pp. 293-311.

In *Philosopher's Index*, No. 032358, citing references to Spinoza and Kant.

Bourke, Vernon Joseph, *History of Ethics* (Garden City, NY: Doubleday, 1968).

In *Philosopher's Index*, No. 017189, citing references to Aristotle, Spinoza, Leibniz, and Kant.

Bourget, Paul, *Spinoza* (Chicago, 1912).

In Kashap (1972), p. 352.

Bowen, Francis, *Critical Essays on a Few Subjects Connected with the History and Present Condition of Speculative Philosophy* (Boston: H. B. Williams, 1842).

In Oko (1964), p. 230.

Bowen, Francis, *On the Application of Metaphysical and Ethical Science to the Evidences of Religion*, Lectures delivered before the Lowell Institution in Boston, in the Winters of 1848-49 (Boston: C. C. Little and J. Brown, 1849).

In Oko (1964), p. 347.

Bowen, Francis, *Modern Philosophy, from Descartes to Schopenhauer and Hartmann* (New York: Scribner, Armstrong and Co., 1877).

Includes a chapter on Spinoza.

Bowen, Francis, *The Theory of the Innate Ideas in the Writings by Descartes, Spinoza, Pascal and Others* (Albuquerque, NM: American Classical College Press, 1987).

Bowen, Maj., *The Netherlands Display'd, or the Delights of the Low Countries* (London, 1926).

In Hertzberger (1950), No. 9, citing many references to Spinoza.

Bowman, Carroll R., *Systematic Morality: A Study in the Philosophy of Benedict Spinoza*, Unpublished doctoral dissertation, Tulane University, 1966.

Currently available from UMI (Order No. 66-10753).

Bowman, Carroll R., "Spinoza's Doctrine of Attributes," *The Southern Journal of Philosophy*, Vol. 5 (Spring 1967), pp. 59-71.

Bowman, Carroll R., "The Spinozism of Adolph S. Oko," *The Southern Journal of Philosophy*, Vol. 6 (Fall 1968), pp. 172-180.

> "Oko's thought and work are dealt with to the extent that they bear upon the compilation of [his] bibliography" — *Philosopher's Index*, No. 025049.

Bowman, Carroll R., "Spinoza's Idea of the Body," *Idealistic Studies*, Vol. 1 (September 1971), pp. 258-268.

Bowrey, Thomas, *The Papers of Thomas Bowrey, 1669-1713, Discovered in 1913 by John Humphreys...and Now in the Possession of Lieut-Colonel Henry Howard*, Edited by Lieut-Colonel Sir Richard Carnac Temple (London: Printed for the Hakluyt Society, 1927).

> In Oko (1964), p. 60.

[Boyer] d'Argens, [J. B. de]. Jewish letters, or a correspondence philosophical, historical and critical betwixt a Jew and his correspondents, in different parts. Newcastle, J. Fleming, 1746. 4 vols.

> In Hertzberger (1950), No. 771, citing references to Spinoza in Vol. 1. Hertzberger also notes (No. 772) that *The Jewish Spy* (1766) is merely the title of the third edition of *Jewish Letters*.

Boyle, Andrew. *See* Spinoza, *Ethics* (1910, 1959, and 1989).

[Boyle, Robert] Reasons why a Protestant should not turn papist: or, Protestant prejudices against the Roman Catholic religion; propos'd, in a letter to a Romish priest. By a person of quality. London, Printed by H. Clark for John Taylor, 1687.

> In Oko (1964), p. 200.

[Bradlaugh, Charles] *Half-Hours with the Freethinkers*, Edited by Iconoclast, A. Collins [pseud.], & J. Watts, 3rd Edition (London: F. Farrah, 1868).

> In Oko (1964), p. 43, citing a section on Spinoza. Hertzberger (1950), No. 244, cites a London edition of 1856-1857, attributing it not to Bradlaugh, but to Collins and Watts, and identifying Part 7, pp. 49-56, as being on Spinoza. Oko (1964), p. 43, also identifies a reprint under the title, *Biographies of Ancient and Modern Freethinkers* (New York: P. Eckler, 1913), with the Spinoza biography on pp. 60-76.

[Bradlaugh, Charles] *The Bible: What It Is; Its Authorship & Authenticity.* Book I. By Iconoclast. (London: Austin, 1870).

> In Oko (1964), p. 395.

Bradshaw, Marion John, *Philosophical Translations of Faith: A Contribution Towards the Philosophy of Religion* (Oxford: Oxford University Press; New York: Columbia University Press, 1941).

> In *Philosopher's Index*, No. 076571 (repeated as No. 018035), citing discussion of Descartes, Pascal, Spinoza, Leibniz, Hobbes, and Locke.

Braham, E. G., "Spinoza and Immortality," *The Open Court*, Vol. 41 (October 1927), pp. 577-582.

Brandom, Robert, "Adequacy and the Individuation of Ideas in Spinoza's *Ethics,*" *Journal of the History of Philosophy*, Vol. 14 (April 1976), pp. 147-162.

Brandt, Richard B., *The Philosophy of Schleiermacher: The Development of His Theory of Scientific and Religious Knowledge* (New York: Greenwood Press, 1968).

> Includes a section, "The Influence of Spinoza," pp. 35-41, and many other references.

Brann, Henry Walter, "Spinoza and the Kabbalah," *Hartwick Review*, Vol. 3 (1967), pp. 61-66.

Brann, Henry Walter, "Freud as Philosopher," *Imago*, Vol. 27, No. 2 (1970), pp. 122-139.

> In *Mental Health Abstracts*, No. 0004955, citing a discussion of why Freud's views fell short of becoming a "monistic system equalling those of Spinoza and Hegel."

Brann, Henry Walter, "Schopenhauer and Spinoza," *Journal of the History of Philosophy*, Vol. 10 (April 1972), pp. 181-196.

Brann, Henry Walter, "Spinoza and Karl Marx," *Judaica*, Vol. 31, No. 1 (1975), pp. 27-40.

Brann, Henry Walter, "Spinoza and the Kabbalah," in Hessing (1977), pp. 108-118.

Bratton, F. G., *Maimonides: Medieval Modernist* (Boston: Beacon Press, 1967).

In *Philosopher's Index*, No. 015651.

Bratton, F. G., "Precursors of Biblical Criticism," *Journal of Biblical Literature*, Vol. 50, No. 3 (1931), pp. 182-185.

Includes many references to Spinoza.

Braune, Ronald A. (ed.), *Jewish Civilization* (Philadelphia: Reconstructionist Rabbinical College, 1979).

In Dienstag (1986), p. 395, citing an essay by Henry D. Morris, "Interpretation and Reinterpretation in Maimonides and Spinoza," Vol. 1, pp. 75-88.

Brecher, E. M., "*Conatus* in Spinoza's Ethics," *Psychological Review*, Vol. 40 (July 1933), pp. 388-390.

Brehier, Emile, *The History of Philosophy: The Seventeenth Century*, Translated by Wade Baskin (Chicago: University of Chicago Press, 1966).

Includes a chapter on Spinoza, pp. 155-196.

Brennan, Joseph Gerard, *The Meaning of Philosophy: A Survey of the Problems of Philosophy and of the Opinions of the Philosophers* (New York: Harper & Brothers, 1953).

Includes a section, "Spinoza's Concept of God," pp. 281-284, and other references.

Breslauer, S. Daniel, "Spinoza's Theological-Political Treatise and A. J. Heschel's Theology of Biblical Language," *Yearbook of the Central Conference of American Rabbis*, Vol. 24 (1977), pp. 19-27.

Breslauer, S. Daniel, "Baruch Spinoza: What Manner of Zionist?" *Hebrew Studies*, Vol. 18 (1977), pp. 127-131.

Brett, George Sidney, *A History of Psychology* (London, 1921).

In Hertzberger (1950), No. 52, citing Vol. II, *Medieval and Early Modern Period*.

[Briggs, Samuel, ed.] De tribus impostoribus, A. D. 1230. The three impostors, translated (with notes and comments) from a French manuscript of the work written in the year 1716, with a dissertation on the original treatise and a bibliography of the various editions. By Alcofribas Nasier, the later [pseud.]. Privately printed for the subscribers, 1904.

> In Oko (1964), p. 536. Oko's note: "Contains English translations of two works. The first (pp. 26-109) is a translation of the work in French which appeared in 1719 as 2d part of *La vie et l'esprit de m. Benoit de Spinoza*, and later under the title *Traite des trois imposteurs*....The second (pp. 111-144) is a translation of the Latin work with which the former was long confused, *De tribus impostoribus* (translated from 1876 ed. of Emil Weller)." Includes references to Spinoza, pp. 10-11.

Britan, H. H. *See* Spinoza, *Principles of Descartes' Philosophy* (1943).

Broad, C. D., *Five Types of Ethical Theory* (Paterson, NJ: Littlefield, Adams & Co., 1959).

> Includes a chapter on Spinoza, pp. 15-52.

Broad, C. D., *Leibniz: An Introduction*, Edited by C. Lewy (London: Cambridge University Press, 1975).

> Includes a section on Spinoza's solution of the mind-body problem, pp. 119-122, and many other references.

Broad, C. D., "Prof. Hallett's *Aeternitas*," *Mind*, Vol. 42 (April 1933), pp. 150-169; (July 1933), pp. 299-318.

> A review of Hallett (1930). Hallett's reply appeared in *Mind*, Vol. 43 (April 1934), pp. 275-278.

Broad, C. D., "Spinoza's Doctrine of Human Immortality," *Mélanges Anders Karitz* (1946), pp. 139-148.

> This citation is based on Wetlesen (1968), p. 52.

Brophy, John M., *Benedict Spinoza: The Enigma*, Unpublished doctoral dissertation, Fordham University, 1934.

Brown, Gregory, *Mathematical Reasoning, Architectonics, and the Pre-Established Harmony in Leibniz*, Unpublished doctoral dissertation, University of Maryland, 1980.

> Includes material on Spinoza. Currently available from UMI (Order No. 81-16457).

Brown, Robert F., *The Later Philosophy of Schelling: The Influence of Boehme on the Works of 1809-1815* (Lewisburg: Bucknell University Press: Cranbury, NJ: Associated University Presses, 1977).

> Includes a section that focuses on Spinoza, "The Problem of Pantheism," pp. 119-124, and many other references.

Brown, Hugh, "A Philosopher's Tragedy: Shakespeare and Spinoza," *Hibbert Journal*, Vol. 27, No. 2 (January 1929), pp. 299-313.

Brown, Norman O., "Philosophy and Prophecy: Spinoza's Hermeneutics," *Political Theory*, Vol. 14, No. 2 (May 1986), pp. 195-213.

[Brown, Thomas] Miracles work's above and contrary to nature: or, An answer to a late translation out of Spinoza's Tractatus theologico-politicus, Mr. Hobb's Leviathan, &c. Published to undermine the truth and authority of miracles, Scriptures, and religion, in a treatise entituled Miracles no violation of the laws of nature ... London, S. Smith, 1683.

> In Oko (1964), p. 435, and in Hertzberger (1950), No. 622. *See* Blount (1683).

Brown, Thomas, *Inquiry into the Relation of Cause and Effect*, 4th Edition (London: H. G. Bohn, 1835).

> In Oko (1964), p. 399.

Browne, J. H., "Spinoza," *Overland Monthly*, Vol. 13, pp. 314 ff.

> This citation is based on information in *Poole's Index*, Vol. 1 (1802-1881).

Browne, Lewis, *Blessed Spinoza: A Biography of the Philosopher* (New York: The Macmillan Company, 1932).

> Currently available from UMI Out-of-Print Books on Demand (Order No. OP52420).

Bruder, Kenneth John, *Baruch Spinoza's Logic of the One, or One Act of Love* (1970).

> Apparently a book based on the author's doctoral dissertation of the same title at the Albert-Ludwigs-Universität at Freiburg.

Brunner, Constantin, *Science, Spirit, Superstition: A New Enquiry into Human Thought*, Abridged and translated by Abraham Suhl, revised and edited, with a preface, by Walter Bernard (London: George Allen & Unwin; Toronto: University of Toronto Press, 1968).

Includes a section, "Spinoza's Attributes," pp. 442-461, and many other references.

Brush, Craig B., *Montaigne and Bayle: Variations on the Theme of Skepticism* (The Hague: Martinus Nijhoff, 1966).

Includes a section on Bayle's treatment of Spinoza in the *Dictionary*, pp. 274-277, and other references.

Brushlinski, V. K., "Spinoza's Substance and Finite Things," in Kline (1952), pp. 120-130.

Bryant, Jacob. An address to Dr. Priestly upon his Doctrine of philosophical necessity illustrated. London, Printed for T. Cadell, 1780.

In Oko (1964), p. 230.

[Bryant, Jacob] A treatise upon the authenticity of the Scriptures, and the truth of the Christian religion. 2d ed. Cambridge, Printed by J. Archdeacon for T. Cadell, and P. Elmsly, London, 1793.

In Oko (1964), p. 347.

Brykman, Genevieve, "Bayle's Case for Spinoza," *Proceedings of the Aristotelian Society*, Vol. 88 (1987-1988), pp. 259-270.

Buchanan, James, *Modern Atheism: Under Its Forms of Pantheism, Materialism, Secularism, Development, and Natural Laws* (Boston: Gould & Lincoln, 1867).

Includes a chapter, "The System of Spinoza," pp. 142-161.

Buchwalter, Andrew James, *Philosophy and Politics in the Thought of G. W. F. Hegel*, Unpublished doctoral dissertation, Boston University, 1989. 2 vols.

Includes material on Spinoza. Currently available from UMI (Order No. 88-20457).

Bucke, Richard Maurice, *Cosmic Consciousness: A Study in the Evolution of the Human Mind*, 4th Edition, corrected and entirely re-set (New York: E. P. Dutton & Co., 1923).

Includes a section on Spinoza, pp. 276-282. The first edition (Philadelphia: Innes & Sons, 1901) includes the Spinoza section on pp. 228-233.

Burgess, Joseph B., *Introduction to the History of Philosophy* (New York: McGraw-Hill Book Co., 1939).

Includes a chapter, "Rationalist Approach to Philosophy: Baruch Spinoza," pp. 256-273, and other references.

Burkhill, T. Alec, *God and Reality in Modern Thought* (Englewood Cliffs, NJ: Prentice Hall, 1963).

Includes a discussion of Spinoza, pp. 145-149, and other references.

Burkhill, T. Alec, "Theism and Absolutism," *Philosophy*, Vol. 19 (July 1944), pp. 117-129.

In *Philosopher's Index*, No. 063144, citing references to Spinoza and Royce.

Burns, C. Delisle, *The Growth of Modern Philosophy* (London: S. Low, Marston & Co., 1909).

Includes a chapter, "Spinoza and Leibnitz," pp. 38-55. This volume was published in New York by the University Lecturer's Association, n.d.

Burstein, N., *Ideas and Ideals*, Foreword by Rabbi Professor Sir Hermann Gollancz (London: K. S. Bhat, 1932).

Includes a chapter on Spinoza.

Burtt, Edwin A., *Types of Religious Philosophy*, Revised edition (New York: Harper & Brothers, 1951).

Includes a section, "Spinoza's Philosophy of Religion," pp. 181-192, and many other references.

Bush, N. R., *The Marquis D'Argens and His Philosophical Correspondence* (Ann Arbor, MI: Brothers, 1953).

In *Philosopher's Index*, No. 018570, citing references to Descartes, Spinoza, Bayle, and Locke.

Butler, Benjamin, *The Philosophy of Spinoza* (Boston: Student Outlines Company, 1939).

Byrne, Laura M., *Hegel's Critique of Spinoza's Concept of Substance*, Unpublished doctoral dissertation, University of Toronto, 1988.

Byrne, Laura M., "Reason and Emotion in Spinoza's *Ethics*: The Two Infinities," in Hunter (1991).

Cadbury, H. J., "Spinoza and a Quaker Document of 1657," *Medieval and Renaissance Studies*, Vol. F, The Warburg Institute (1943), pp. 130-132.

In Walther (1991), p. 91.

Cahn, Zvi, *The Philosophy of Judaism* (New York: Macmillan, 1962).

In *Philosopher's Index*, No. 018962.

Caird, Edward, *Essays on Literature and Philosophy* (Glasgow: J. Maclehose; New York: Macmillan and Co., 1892). 2 vols.

Includes a section on Spinoza, Vol. 2, pp. 332-383, in the essay, "Cartesianism," and other references.

Caird, John, *Spinoza* (Edinburgh: William Blackwood and Sons, 1888).

Currently available from UMI Out-of-Print Books on Demand (Order No. OP52553); the 1888 edition published in Philadelphia by Lippincott is also available (Order No. BH05541).

Cairns, Huntington, *Legal Philosophy from Plato to Hegel* (Baltimore: Johns Hopkins University Press, 1949).

In *Philosopher's Index*, No. 017290. Currently available from UMI Out-of-Print Books on Demand (Order No. 2004957).

Cairns, Huntington, "Spinoza's Theory of Law," *Columbia Law Review*, Vol. 48 (1948), pp. 1032-1048.

Cairns, John, *Unbelief in the Eighteenth Century as Contrasted with Its Earlier and Later History*, Being the Cunningham lectures for 1880 (Edinburgh: Adam and Charles Black, 1881).

Includes a section on Spinoza, pp. 50-59, and other references.

Calamy, Edmund. The inspiration of the Holy Writings of the Old and New Testament consider'd and improv'd. In fourteen sermons preach'd at the merchants lecture at Salters Hall. By Edmund Calamy ... To which is added a single sermon in vindication of the divine institution of the office of the ministry, preach'd at the same lecture. London: Printed for T. Parkhurst [etc.], 1710.

In Oko (1964), p. 347, with note: An answer to Leclerc's *Five letters concerning ... the Holy Scriptures.*

Calkins, Mary Whiton, *The Persistent Problems of Philosophy: An Introduction to Metaphysics Through the Study of Modern Systems*, 5th Edition (New York: The Macmillan Co., 1939).

> Includes a chapter, "Monistic Pluralism: The System of Spinoza," pp. 277-306, and a section in the Appendix, "Baruch de Spinoza: The Monistic Pluralist," pp. 490-509.

[Campbell, Archibald] ΑΡΕΤΗ-ΛΟΓΙΑ; or, An enquiry into the original of moral virtue; wherein the false notions of Machiavel, Hobbes, Spinoza, and Mr. Bayle, as they are collected and digested by the author of The fable of the bees, are examin'd and confuted ... To which is prefix'd, a preparatory introduction, in a letter to that author. By Alexander Innes ... Westminster, Printed by J. Cluer and A. Campbell for B. Creake, 1728.

> Oko (1964), p. 201, quotes the *Dictionary of National Biography* as saying that Innes, "employed to make arrangements for its publication, appropriated it to himself." Hertzberger (1950), No. 857, attributes the authorship to Innes. The work was published in 1733 in Campbell's name; see the following citation.

Campbell, Archibald. An enquiry into the original of moral virtue; wherein it is shown (against the author of the "Fable of the Bees" &c.,) that virtue is founded in the nature of things, is unalterable, and eternal ... With some reflections on a late book, entitled An enquiry into the original of our ideas of beauty and virtue. By Archibald Campbell ... Edinburgh, Printed for G. Hamilton, by R. Fleming and company, 1733.

> In Oko (1964), p. 201.

Campbell, John, "Spinoza's Theory of Perfection and Goodness," *The Southern Journal of Philosophy*, Vol. 18, No. 3 (Fall 1980), pp. 259-274.

Campbell, K., *Metaphysics: An Introduction* (Encino, CA, 1976).

> In Van der Werf (1984), No. 365, citing a section on Spinoza, pp. 75-79.

Capek, Milic, "The Doctrine of Necessity Re-Examined," *The Review of Metaphysics*, Vol. 5 (September 1951), pp. 11-54.

> In *Philosopher's Index*, No. 020553, citing discussion of "the logical incompatibility of the classical (Spinoza-LaPlacean) determinism and succession."

Caponigri, Aloysius Robert, *Philosophy from the Renaissance to the Romantic Age* (Notre Dame: Notre Dame University Press, 1963).

In *Philosopher's Index*, No. 019511, citing references to Descartes, Spinoza, Leibniz, Kant, and Hegel.

Carlile, William Warrand, "Natura Naturans," *The Philosophical Review*, Vol. 4 (1895), pp. 624-640.

In Oko (1964), p. 439.

Carr, Spencer, "Spinoza's Distinction Between Rational and Intuitive Knowledge," *The Philosophical Review*, Vol. 87, No. 2 (April 1978), pp. 241-252.

Carriero, John Peter, *Descartes and the Autonomy of the Human Understanding*, Unpublished doctoral dissertation, Harvard University, 1984.

Includes material on Spinoza. Currently available from UMI (Order No. 85-03515).

Carritt, Edgar Frederick, *Morals and Politics: Theories of Their Relation from Hobbes and Spinoza to Marx and Bosanquet* (Oxford: The Clarendon Press, 1935).

Includes a chapter on Spinoza, pp. 40-46, and other references.

[Carroll, William] Remarks upon Mr. Clarke's sermons, preached at St. Paul's against Hobbs, Spinoza, and other atheists. London, Printed for Jonathan Robinson, 1705.

42pp. In Oko (1964), p. 201.

Carroll, William. A Dissertation upon the Tenth Chapter of the Fourth Book of Mr. Locke's Essay, concerning Humane Understanding. Wherein That Author's Endeavours to Establish Spinoza's Atheistical Hypothesis, more especially in that Tenth Chapter, are Discover'd and Confuted ... London: Printed by J. Matthews ... 1706.

In Oko (1964), p. 387. Van der Linde, No. 315, cites this work as follows: A dissertation upon the tenth chapter of the fourth book of Mr. Locke's essay concerning humane understanding; wherein that author's endeavours to establish Spinoza's atheistical hypothesis are confuted. To which is subjoined: A short account of the sense wherein the reasonings of the following pernicious books are to be understood, viz: The reasonableness of Christianity (by J. Locke); Christianity not mysterious (by J. Toland); the rights of the Christian Church (by M. Tindal). London 1706. A facsimile reprint, with a new introduction by John Yolton, was published in Bristol by Thoemmes, 1990.

[Carroll, William] A letter to the Reverend Dr. Benjamin Prat ... wherein the dangerous errors in a late book, intituled, An essay concerning the use of reason in propositions, the evidence whereof depends upon human testimony: are detected, confuted, etc. London, Richard Sare, 1707.

> 24pp. In Oko (1964), p. 201. *See* Collins (1709).

[Carroll, William] Spinoza reviv'd: or, a Treatise proving the book Entitled The rights of the Christian Church &c. (in the most notorious parts of it) to be the same with Spinoza's Rights of the Christian clergy &c. And that both of them are grounded upon downright Atheisme. To which is added A preliminary discourse relating to the said books, by the Reverend Dr. George Hicks ... London. Printed and to be sold by J. Morphew, near Stationers Hall 1709.

> In Van der Linde, No. 55; also in Oko (1964), p. 201, and Hertzberger (1950), No. 429. Hertzberger (1950) notes that Carroll "and his contemporaries" mistakenly attributed *The Rights of the Christian Clergy* to Spinoza. Hertzberger says that it was actually written by Lucius Antistius Constans (pseudonym for Pieter de la Court), adding that the author of *The Rights of the Christian Church* was Matthew Tindal.

Casey, Edward S. (ed.), *The Life of the Transcendental Ego: Essays in Honor of William Earle* (Albany, NY: State University of New York Press, 1986).

> Includes essays by Asher Moore, "Reason and Existence: Or, What Spinoza Was Doing Up In His Room," pp. 3-18, and Forrest Williams, "Some Reflections on Spinoza's *Ethics* as Edifying Ontology," pp. 95-100.

Cassidy, John, "Some Similarities Between Hume's and Spinoza's Ethical Theories," *The Journal of Value Inquiry*, Vol. 13 (Fall 1979), pp. 187-194.

Cassirer, Ernst, *The Philosophy of the Enlightenment*, Translated by Fritz C. A. Koelln and James P. Pettegrove (Boston: Beacon Press, 1955).

> Includes a section on Spinoza, pp. 183-191.

Catlin, George, *The Story of the Political Philosophers* (New York: Whittlesey House, McGraw-Hill Book Co., 1939).

> Includes a section on Spinoza, pp. 248-254, and many other references.

Caverzasi, Peter L., *Belief and Justification in Emotion*, Unpublished doctoral dissertation, New York University, 1985.

> Includes material on Spinoza. Currently available from UMI (Order No. 86-04042).

[Chambers, Ephrain]   Cyclopedia; or, An universal dictionary of arts and sciences; containing an explication of the terms ... in the several arts ... and the several sciences, human and divine. The second edition, corrected and amended with some additions. London, Midwinter, 1733. 2 vols.

> In Oko (1964), p. 122, citing an article, "Spinozism," in Vol. 2. Oko, p. 122, also cites a revised edition published in New York by P. F. Collier in 1876, with an article on Spinoza in Vol. VII [sic], pp. 362-363.

Chambers, L. P., "Spinoza and Modern Thought," in Cory (1931), pp. 7-42.

Charlton, William, "Spinoza's Monism," *The Philosophical Review*, Vol. 90, No. 4 (October 1981), pp. 503-530.

Charter, SPR. *See* Spinoza, *Ethics* (1981).

Chase, H. W., "Address of the Chairman," in Schaub (1933).

Cheyne, T. K., *Founders of Old Testament Criticism: Biographical, Descriptive, and Critical Studies* (London, 1893).

> In Hertzberger (1950), No. 66.

Christian, William A., "Spinoza on Theology and Truth," in Cushman and Grislis (1965), pp. 89-107.

Chubb, J. N., "Spinoza's Arguments for the Existence of God," *Indian Journal of Theology*, Vol. 17, No. 8 (1968), pp. 116-125.

> In Curley (1975), p. 295.

Chuska, Jeffrey Don, *Descartes' "Passions of the Soul": The Psychological Foundation of Modern Political Philosophy*, Unpublished doctoral dissertation, Fordham University, 1984.

> Theorizes that Spinoza's construction of his political philosophy from the *Ethics* provides a "model" for constructing Descartes' political philosophy from his *Passions of the Soul*. Currently available from UMI (Order No. 85-15893).

Clarendon, Edward Hyde. A brief view and survey of the dangerous and pernicious errors to church and state, in Mr. Hobbe's book, entitled Leviathan. [Oxford] Printed at the Theater, 1676.

> In Oko (1964), p. 213.

Clark, Barrett Harper, *Great Short Biographies of the World: A Collection of Short Biographies, Literary Portraits, and Memoirs Chosen from the Literature of the Ancient and Modern World* (New York: R. M. McBride and Co., 1928).

> In Oko (1964), p. 44. Includes a biography of Spinoza, pp. 716-730, based on Lucas; *see* Wolf (1927).

Clark, Mary T., "How Plotinian Is Spinoza's Doctrine of Freedom?" *The New Scholasticism*, Vol. 33 (1959), pp. 273-290.

Clarke, Samuel. A letter to Mr. Dodwell; wherein all the arguments in his Epistolary Discourse against the immortality of the soul are answered ... London, 1706.

> In Hertzberger (1950), No. 785. *See* Dodwell (1708).

Clarke, Samuel. A discourse concerning the being and attributes of God, the obligations of the natural religion, and the truth and certainty of the Christian religion. In answer to Mr. Hobbs, Spinoza, the author of the Oracles of reason, and other deniers of natural and revealed religion. Being sixteen sermons, preach'd ... in the years 1704, and 1705, at the lecture founded by the Honourable Robert Boyle, esq. ... The tenth edition, corrected. London, Printed for John and Paul Knapton, 1749.

> This citation follows Oko. Van der Linde, No. 291, cites two versions of the title page of the fourth edition. McKeon (1928), p. 330, cites the fifth edition. The sixth edition (London, Printed by W. Bothan for J. Knapton, 1725) is cited in Hertzberger (1950), No. 782, with the note that this edition also includes, under separate titles, the sixth edition of the author's *A demonstration of the being and attributes of God, more particularly in answer to Hobbs, Spinoza, and their followers* [first published in 1705] and the sixth edition of *A discourse concerning the unchangeable obligations of natural religion*, along with the third edition of *Several letters to Dr. Clarke from a gentleman in Glocestershire* [J. Butler], *with the answers thereunto*. The tenth edition (above) includes this material, as well as several additions.

Clarke, W. Norris, "A Curious Blindspot in the Anglo-American Tradition of Anti-Theistic Argument," *The Monist*, Vol. 54 (April 1970), pp. 181-200.

> In *Philosopher's Index*, No. 030172, citing references to Descartes, Spinoza, Hume, Mill, and Russell.

Clifford, Martin. A treatise of human reason. London, for Hen. Brome, 1674.

> 91pp. In Oko (1964), p. 203.

Cockayne, Charles A., *The Relation of Spinoza to Hobbes*, Unpublished doctoral dissertation, Yale University, 1908.

[Cockman, Thomas] Free-thinking rightly stated; wherein a discourse (falsely so call'd) is fully consider'd ... London: Printed for George Strahan, 1713.

> In Oko (1964), p. 409, citing a reference to Spinoza on p. 38. *See* Collins (1713).

Coers, Kathy F., *Understanding and the Moral: A Contemporary Adaptation of the Ethics of Spinoza*, Unpublished doctoral dissertation, Emory University, 1988.

> Currently available from UMI (Order No. 88-27424).

[Cohen, Louisa Emily] *Pantheism, and Other Essays*, by L. E. C. (London: K. Paul, Trench, Trübner & Co., 1926).

> In Oko (1964), p. 441.

Cohen, Morris R., *The Faith of a Liberal* (New York: Henry Holt and Co., 1946).

> Includes two essays: "Spinoza: Prophet of Liberalism," pp. 13-19, origi-
> nally in *The New Republic*, Vol. 50 (March 30, 1927), pp. 164-166, and
> "The Intellectual Love of God," pp. 307-319, originally in *The Menorah
> Journal*, Vol. 11, No. 4 (August 1925), pp. 332-341. Van den Wal (1985),
> p. 300, cites a 1946 edition of this book published in Toronto by Oxford
> University Press, with the first essay on pp. 13-46 [sic].

Cohen, Morris R., "*Amor Dei Intellectualis*," in *Chronicon Spinozanum*, Vol. III (1923), pp. 3-19.

> Read before The American Philosophical Association, December 1922.

Cohn, H. H., "Spinoza's Concept of Jewish Law," *Tel Aviv University Studies in Law*, Vol. 3 (1977), pp. 11-44.

> In Van der Werf (1984), No. 404.

[Colerus, Johannes] The life of Benedict de Spinosa. Written by John Colerus, Minister of the Lutheran Church at the Hague ... Done out of French. London. Printed by D. L. And Sold by Benj. Bragg, at the Raven in Pater-Noster-Row, 1706.

> 92 pp. A facsimile reprint of this volume was published in The Hague by
> Martinus Nijhoff, 1906. Also reprinted, with textual notes and corrections,
> as the appendix to Pollock (1899), pp. 383-418.

[Coleridge, S. T.] *The Philosophical Lectures: Hitherto Unpublished*, Edited by Kathleen Coburn (London: Routledge & Kegan Paul, 1949).

> Includes several references to Spinoza.

Colie, Rosalie L., *Light and Enlightenment: A Study of the Cambridge Platonists and the Dutch Arminians* (Cambridge: Cambridge University Press, 1957).

> Discusses Spinoza in Chaps. V and VI. Currently available from UMI Out-of-Print Books on Demand (Order No. 2050767).

Colie, Rosalie L., "Spinoza and the Early English Deists," *Journal of the History of Ideas*, Vol. 20 (January 1959), pp. 23-46.

Colletti, Lucio, *Marxism and Hegel*, Translated by Lawrence Garner (London: New Left Books, 1973).

> Includes a section on Spinoza and Hegel, pp. 28-39.

[Colliber, Samuel] Free Thoughts concerning Souls: In Four Essays: I. Of the Humane Soul consider'd in its own Nature. II. Of the Humane Soul compared with the Souls of Brutes. III. Of the supposed Prae-existent State of Souls. IV. Of the Future States of Souls. To which is added: An Essay on Creation ... London: Printed for R. Robinson ... 1734.

> In Oko (1964), p. 401. Spinoza is explicitly mentioned in "An Essay on Creation," pp. 150, 153, 160, 165, and 167-168. A facsimile reprint, with a new introduction by John Yolton, was published in Bristol by Thoemmes, 1990.

[Colliber, Samuel] An impartial enquiry into the existence and nature of God; being a modest essay towards a more intelligible account of the divine perfections. With remarks on several authors both ancient and modern; and particularly on some passages in Dr. Clarke's Demonstration of the being and attributes of God. In two books. With an appendix concerning the nature of space and duration. The third edition. With considerable additions and improvements, made partly with regard to some objections of the Reverend Mr. Jackson. London, Printed for R. Robinson, 1735.

> In Oko (1964), pp. 413-414. *See* Clarke (1749).

Collingwood, R. G., *An Essay on Philosophical Method* (Oxford: Clarendon Press, 1933).

> Includes many references to Spinoza.

[Collins, Anthony] An essay concerning the use of reason in propositions, the evidence whereof depends upon human testimony. 2nd ed. corr. London, 1709.

> In Hertzberger (1950), No. 789. This volume and the next were issued in a single volume in facsimile reprint by Garland Publishing in New York in 1984 as Vol. 2 in the Garland Series on the Philosophy of John Locke. The first edition (1707) of the essay is currently available from UMI Out-of-Print Books on Demand (Order No. OP35131).

[Collins, Anthony] A discourse of free-thinking, occasion'd by the rise and growth of a sect call'd free-thinkers ... London, 1713.

> In Oko (1964), p. 409; in Hertzberger (1950), No. 790.

[Collins, Anthony] A philosophical inquiry concerning human liberty. Republished with preface by Joseph Priestley. Birmingham, Printed by Thomas Pearson ... 1790.

> In Hertzberger (1950), No. 791. The first edition was printed in London for R. Robinson, 1717. A facsimile reprint of the 1790 edition, with a new introduction by John Stephens, was published in Bristol by Thoemmes, 1990.

Collins, Arthur W., *Thought and Nature: Studies in Rationalist Philosophy* (Notre Dame: Notre Dame University Press, 1985).

> In *Philosopher's Index*, No. 137068, citing references to Descartes, Spinoza, Leibniz, and Kant.

Collins, James, *A History of Modern European Philosophy* (Milwaukee: The Bruce Publishing Co., 1954).

> Includes a chapter on Spinoza, pp. 199-251.

Collins, James, *God in Modern Philosophy* (Chicago: Henry Regnery Co., 1959).

> Includes a chapter, "Spinoza's God as the Totality of Nature," pp. 69-79.

Collins, James, *The Continental Rationalists: Descartes, Spinoza, Leibniz* (Milwaukee: The Bruce Publishing Co., 1967).

Collins, James, *Interpreting Modern Philosophy* (Princeton: Princeton University Press, 1972).

> Includes many references to Spinoza.

Collins, James, *Spinoza on Nature*, With foreword by George Kimball Plochmann (Carbondale: Southern Illinois University Press, 1984).

Collins, James, "God as a Function in Modern Systems of Philosophy," *Proceedings of the American Catholic Philosophical Association*, Vol. 28 (1954), pp. 1-16.

> In *Philosopher's Index*, No. 014307, citing references to Spinoza, Kant, and Hegel.

Collins, James, "Inquiry-Model of Philosophical Advancement," *The Modern Schoolman*, Vol. 52 (November 1974), pp. 3-25.

> Offers a model of how innovation in philosophy occurs, illustrating the process by examples, including the transition from Descartes "to Spinoza and Locke taken together" — *Philosopher's Index*, No. 044746.

Collins, James, "Interpreting Spinoza: A Paradigm for Historical Work," in Hessing (1977), pp. 119-132.

Collins, William Job, *Spinoza, The God-Intoxicated Man: A Short Recount of His Life and Philosophy* (Enfield, UK: Meyers, Brooks, and Co., 1889).

> Oko indicates 21 pp.; paper covers. *Catalogus... "Het Spinozahuis,"* No. 247 (p. vi, above), indicates 55 pp.

Commers, Ronald, "Marx's Concept of Justice and the Two Traditions in European Political Thought," *Philosophica*, Vol. 33 (1984), pp. 107-130.

> In *Philosopher's Index*, No. 130460, citing references to Hobbes, Spinoza, and Marx.

[Condillac, Abbé de] *Philosophical Writings of Étienne Bonnot, Abbé de Condillac*, Translated by Franklin Philip, with the collaboration of Harlan Lane (Hillsdale, NJ: Lawrence Erlbaum Associates, Publishers, 1982). 2 vols.

> Includes the author's *Treatise on Systems* (1746), Chap. 10 of which is entitled, "Eighth and Last Example: Spinozism Refuted," Vol. 1, pp. 81-121.

Conger, G. P., *Theories of Macrocosm and Microcosm in the History of Philosophy*, Unpublished doctoral dissertation, Columbia University, 1922.

> In Wetlesen (1968), p. 47.

Congleton, Ann, *Spinoza, Kierkegaard, and the Eternal Particular*, Unpublished doctoral dissertation, Yale University, 1962.

Cook, J. Thomas, *Understanding Human Freedom in a Naturalistic Context: A Spinozistic Study*, Unpublished doctoral dissertation, Vanderbilt University, 1981.

> Currently available from UMI (Order No. 82-06105).

Cook, J. Thomas, "Self-Knowledge as Self-Preservation?" in Grene and Nails (1986), pp. 191-210.

Cook, J. Thomas, " 'A Whirlwind at My Back ... ': Spinozistic Themes in Malamud's *The Fixer*," in *Studia Spinozana*, Vol. 5 (1989), pp. 15-28.

Cooley, William Forbes, "Spinoza's Pantheistic Argument," *Studies in the History of Ideas*, Vol. 1 (1918), pp. 171-187.

> In Oko (1964), p. 442.

Cooney, Brian, "Arnold Geulincx: A Cartesian Idealist," *Journal of the History of Philosophy*, Vol. 16, No. 2 (April 1978), pp. 167-180.

> In *Philosopher's Index*, No. 058827, citing discussion of Geulincx's metaphysical differences with Descartes, Spinoza, Malebranche, and others.

Cooper, E., "Spinoza: A Tercentenary Appreciation," *The American Zionist*, Vol. 67, No. 8 (1977), pp. 21-25.

Copleston, Frederick C., *A History of Philosophy* (London: Burns and Oates, 1960). 7 vols.

> Includes a chapter on Spinoza, Vol. 4, pp. 205-263.

Copleston, Frederick C., "Pantheism in Spinoza and the German Idealists," *Philosophy*, Vol. 21, No. 78 (April 1946), pp. 42-56.

Copleston, Frederick C., "Spinoza as Metaphysician," in Mandelbaum and Freeman (1975), pp. 215-234.

Cory, Charles Edward (ed.), *Three Philosophical Studies*, Washington University Studies, New Series, Social and Philosophical Sciences, No. 3 (St. Louis: Washington University, 1931).

> Includes an essay by L. P. Chambers, "Spinoza and Modern Thought," pp. 7-42.

Costa, Isaac da, *Israel and the Gentiles: Contributions to the History of the Jews from the Earliest Times to the Present Day* (London: Nisbet, 1850).

> Includes a section on Spinoza, pp. 425-430.

Cottingham, John G., *The Rationalists* (Oxford: Oxford University Press, 1988).

> Vol. 4 in Oxford's *A History of Western Philosophy*.

Cottingham, John G., "The Intellect, the Will, and the Passions: Spinoza's Critique of Descartes," *Journal of the History of Philosophy*, Vol. 26, No. 2 (April 1988), pp. 239-257.

Coupland, W. C. (ed.), *Thoughts and Aspirations of the Ages: Selections in Prose and Verse from the Religious Writings of the World* (London, 1895).

> In Hertzberger (1950), No. 178, citing selections from Spinoza "and his circle."

Craig, Edward, *The Mind of God and the Works of Man* (Oxford: Clarendon Press, 1987).

> Includes a section, "Spinoza: A Part of the Infinite Intellect," pp. 44-51, and many other references.

Craig, William Lane, *The Cosmological Argument from Plato to Leibniz* (New York: Barnes & Noble Books, 1980).

> In Van der Werf (1984), No. 434, citing a section on Spinoza, pp. 236-256, in the London edition (no publisher given).

Craigie, P. C., "The Influence of Spinoza in the Higher Criticism of the Old Testament," *The Evangelical Quarterly*, Vol. 50 (1978), pp. 23-32.

> In Van der Werf (1984), No. 435.

Crain, W. A., "Spinoza," *The Radical* (Boston), Vol. 2 (1867), pp. 170-177.

> Oko (1964), p. 107, identifies the author as W. A. Cram.

Crain, W. A., "Spinoza's Doctrine," *The Radical* (Boston), Vol. 2 (1867), pp. 543-549.

> Oko (1964), p. 292, identifies the author as W. A. Cram.

Cramer, K., W. G. Jacobs, and W. Schmidt-Biggemann (eds.), *Spinozas Ethik und ihre frühe Wirkung* (Wolfenbüttel: Herzog-August Bibliothek, 1981).

> Includes an essay by Michael J. Petry, "Kuyper's Analysis of Spinoza's Axiomatic Method," pp. 1-18.

Cremaschi, S., "Concepts of Force in Spinoza's Psychology," in *Theoria cum praxi* (1981), pp. 138-144.

Cress, D. A., "Duns Scotus, Spinoza and the Ontological Argument," in Berube (1978), pp. 389-399.

Cropsey, Joseph, *Political Philosophy and the Issues of Politics* (Chicago: University of Chicago Press, 1977).

> In Van der Werf (1984), No. 454, citing a chapter, "Political Life and a Natural Order," pp. 221-230.

Cudworth, Ralph. The true intellectual system of the universe: wherein all the reason and philosophy of atheism is confuted, and its impossibility demonstrated, with a treatise concerning eternal and immutable morality. To which are added the notes and dissertations of Dr. J. L. Mosheim, tr. by John Harrison. London, Printed for Thomas Tegg, 1845.

> In Oko (1964), p. 388. Originally published in 1678.

Cunningham, William, *The Influence of Descartes on Metaphysical Speculation in England*, Being a Degree Thesis (London & Cambridge: Macmillan, 1876).

> In Oko (1964), p. 215.

Cunynghame, Sir Henry Hardinge Samuel, *Short Talks Upon Philosophy* (London: Constable & Co., 1923).

> Includes a chapter on Spinoza, pp. 103 ff.

Curley, E. M., *Spinoza's Metaphysics: An Essay in Interpretation* (Cambridge: Harvard University Press, 1969).

> From the author's doctoral dissertation of the same title, Duke University, 1963. The latter is currently available from UMI (Order No. 64-04732).

Curley, E. M., *Behind the Geometrical Method: A Reading of Spinoza's Ethics* (Princeton: Princeton University Press, 1988).

Curley, E. M. *See* Spinoza, *Collected Works* (1985).

Curley, E. M. See *Studia Spinozana*, Vol. 2 (1986) and Vol. 6 (1990).

Curley, E. M., "A Reply to Williamson," *Australasian Journal of Philosophy*, Vol. 51 (August 1973), pp. 162-164.

See Williamson (1973).

Curley, E. M., "Descartes, Spinoza and the Ethics of Belief," in Mandelbaum and Freeman (1975), pp. 159-190.

Curley, E. M., "Bibliography," in Mandelbaum and Freeman (1975), pp. 263-316.

Curley, E. M., "Spinoza as an Expositor of Descartes," in Hessing (1977), pp. 133-142.

Curley, E. M., "Notes on the Immortality of the Soul in Spinoza's Short Treatise," *Giornale critico della filosofia italiana*, Vol. 8 (October-December 1977), pp. 327-336.

Curley, E. M., "Man and Nature in Spinoza," in Wetlesen (1978), pp. 19-26.

Curley, E. M., "Spinoza and Recent Philosophy of Religion," in Shahan and Biro (1978), Chap. 8, pp. 161-175.

Originally in the *Southwestern Journal of Philosophy*, Vol. 8, No. 3 (Fall 1977), pp. 161-175.

Curley, E. M., "Experience in Spinoza's Theory of Knowledge," in Grene (1979), pp. 25-59.

Revised version of a paper read to the Australian Association of Philosophy, Melbourne, August 1968.

Curley, E. M., "Spinoza's Moral Philosophy," in Grene (1979), pp. 354-376.

Revised version of a paper read to the New Zealand Philosophy Association, Hamilton, May 1968.

Curley, E. M., "Spinoza on Miracles," in Giancotti Boscherini (1985), pp. 421-438.

Curley, E. M., "Spinoza's Geometric Method," in *Studia Spinozana*, Vol. 2 (1986), pp. 151-169.

Curley, E. M., "Notes on a Neglected Masterpiece: Spinoza and the Science of Hermeneutics," in Hunter (1991).

Curley, E. M., and Pierre-François Moreau (eds.), *Spinoza: Issues and Directions*, The Proceedings of the Chicago Spinoza Conference (Leiden: E. J. Brill, 1990.)

> In addition to a paper by Curley — "On Bennett's Spinoza: The Issue of Teleology," pp. 39-52 — includes essays in English by H. Allison, R. Ariew, J. Benardete, J. Bennett, H. De Dijn, A. Donagan, W. Doney, P. Eisenberg, D. Garber, D. Garrett, E. Harris, H. Hubbeling, W. Kleves, G. Kline, G. Lloyd, W. Matson, F. Mignini, R. Popkin, L. Rice, A. Rorty, M. Walther, M. Wilson, and Y. Yovel.

Cushman, Henry Ernest, *A Beginner's History of Philosophy* (Boston: Houghton Mifflin Co., 1910-1911). 2 vols.

> Includes a section on Spinoza, Vol. II, pp. 81-106, and other references.

Cushman, R. E., and E. Grislis (eds.), *The Heritage of Christian Thought: Essays in Honor of Robert Lowry Calhoun* (New York: Harper and Row, 1965).

> Includes a chapter by William A. Christian, "Spinoza on Theology and Truth," pp. 89-107.

Cyres, S., *François de Fénélon* (London, 1901).

> In Hertzberger (1950), No. 805, citing a section on Spinoza, pp. 258-262, and other references.

Damle, P. R., "Jottings on the Characteristic and Much Criticized Ethical Positions of Kant and Spinoza," *Indian Philosophical Quarterly*, Vol. 7 (October 1979), pp. 165-170.

Dan, Joseph (ed.), *Binah* (New York: Praeger, 1989). 2 vols.

> Vol. I, entitled *Studies in Jewish History*, includes several articles on the Spanish exiles and the Portuguese Jews in Amsterdam. Vol. II, entitled *Studies in Jewish Thought*, includes an essay by Warren Zev Harvey, "Maimonides and Spinoza on the Knowledge of Good and Evil."

Daniels, C. B., "Spinoza on the Mind-Body Problem: Two Questions," *Mind*, Vol. 85, No. 340 (October 1976), pp. 542-558.

Daniels, C. B., "A Spinozistic Axiomatics in Story Semantics," *Philosophia* (Israel), Vol. 18, No. 4 (1988), pp. 347-356.

Darcus, Roy Lionel, *The Persistence of Kant and Hegel as Theological Models: The Realm of Faith Versus the Realm of Philosophy as the Grounding for the Autonomy of the Human Subject*, Unpublished doctoral dissertation, Concordia University (Canada), 1981.

> Includes material on Spinoza.

Das, S. K., "Spinoza and the Modern World," *Calcutta Review*, Vol. 85 (1942).

> In Wetlesen (1968), p. 58.

Dascal, Marcelo, "Spinoza and Leibniz: Language and Cognition," in *Studia Spinozana* (1990), pp. 103-145.

Davis, Elmer, "The God of Hitler and Spinoza," *Harper's* (July 1940), pp. 186-195.

> In Oko (1964), p. 292.

Davis, Mac, *From Moses to Einstein: They Are All Jews* (New York: Jordan Publishing Co., 1937).

> In Oko (1964), p. 45, citing a biographical sketch of Spinoza.

Davis, P. E., *The Cartesian and Spinozistic Theories of Time*, Unpublished doctoral dissertation, Yale University, 1955.

> In Van der Werf (1984), No. 2196.

Deborin, A. M., "Spinoza's World-View," in Kline (1952), pp. 90-119.

De Burgh, W. G., "Great Thinkers (VIII): Spinoza," *Philosophy*, Vol. 11, No. 43 (1936), pp. 271-287.

De Casseres, Benjamin, *Forty Immortals* (New York: J. Lawren, 1929).

> Includes an essay on Spinoza, pp. 51-56.

De Casseres, Benjamin, *Spinoza: Liberator of God and Man* (New York: E. Wickham Sweetland, 1932).

> According to Oko (1964), p. 107, the author's essay, "The Liberator of God," *The Thinker*, Vol 2, No. 3 (July 1930), pp. 29-56, was reprinted as Chap. 5 of this book.

[De Casseres, Benjamin] *The Works of Benjamin de Casseres* (New York: Gordon Press, 1976).

Reissue of the original 1936 edition.

De Casseres, Benjamin, *Spinoza Against the Rabbis* (New York: B. De Casseres at the Blackstone Publishers, 1937).

58 pp. On cover: "Book No. 14."

De Deugd, Cornelius, *The Significance of Spinoza's First Kind of Knowledge* (Assen, The Netherlands: Van Gorcum, 1966).

De Deugd, Cornelius (ed.), *Spinoza's Political and Theological Thought*, International Symposium Under the Auspices of the Royal Netherlands Academy of Arts and Sciences Commemorating the 350th Anniversary of the Birth of Spinoza (Amsterdam: North-Holland Publishing Co., 1984).

Includes papers by F. Akkerman, W. Bartuschat, K. Hammacher, E. Harris, H. Hubbeling, S. Hutton, Y. Kaplan, W. Klever, Z. Levy, F. Mignini, M. Petry, R. Popkin, L. Rice, W. Sacksteder, and H. Siebrand.

De Deugd, Cornelius, "Old Wine in New Bottles? Tillich and Spinoza," *Talk of God*, Royal Institute of Philosophy Lectures (New York: St. Martin's Press, 1969), Vol. 2, pp. 133-151.

This citation is based on Curley (1975), p. 296.

De Dijn, Herman, "Historical Remarks on Spinoza's Theory of Definition," in Van der Bend (1974), pp. 41-50.

De Dijn, Herman, "The Significance of Spinoza's *Treatise on the Improvement of the Understanding*," *Algemeen Nederlands tijdschrift voor wijsbegeerte*, Vol. 69 (1974), pp. 1-16.

In De Dijn (1986), p. 23.

De Dijn, Herman, "The Articulation of Nature, or the Relation of God-Modes in Spinoza," *Giornale critico della filosofia italiana*, Vol. 8 (October-December 1977), pp. 337-344.

De Dijn, Herman, "The Possibility of an Ethic in a Deterministic System Like Spinoza's," in Wetlesen (1978), pp. 27-35.

De Dijn, Herman, "The Compatibility of Determinism and Moral Attitudes," in Giancotti Boscherini (1985), pp. 205-219.

De Dijn, Herman, "Spinoza's Logic or Art of Perfect Thinking," in *Studia Spinozana*, Vol. 2 (1986), pp. 15-25.

De Dijn, Herman, "Conceptions of Philosophical Method in Spinoza: Logica and Mos Geometricus," *The Review of Metaphysics*, Vol. 40, No. 1 (September 1986).

In Abadi (1989), p. 42.

De Dijn, Herman, "How To Understand Spinoza's Logic or Methodology: A Critical Evaluation of W. N. A. Klever's Commentary on Spinoza's *TIE*," in *Studia Spinozana*, Vol. 3 (1987), pp. 419-429.

See Klever (1987) for a reply.

De Dijn, Herman, "Wisdom and Theoretical Knowledge in Spinoza," in Curley and Moreau (1990), pp. 147-156.

Deegan, Thomas. *See* Spinoza, *Ethics* (1981).

Degen, Peter Anton, *Interpretations of Quantum Physics, the Mystical and the Paranormal: Einstein, Schroedinger, Bohr, Pauli and Jordan*, Unpublished doctoral dissertation, Drew University, 1989.

Includes material on Spinoza. Currently available from UMI (Order number 89-21805).

[De la Court, Pieter] The true interest and political maxims of the republick of Holland and West-Friedland ... Written by John de Witt and other great men in Holland. Pub. by the authority of the States. London, Printed in the year 1702.

Oko (1964), p. 63, cites a 1665 Latin edition with a manuscript note attributing this work to Spinoza. He quotes the *British Museum Catalogue*: "By B. de Spinoza? or, more probably by P. de las Court?"

Delahunty, R. J., *Spinoza* (London: Routledge & Kegan Paul, 1985).

Deleuze, Gilles, *Spinoza: Practical Philosophy*, Translated with a preface by Robert Hurley (San Francisco: City Lights Books, 1988).

Translation of the 1970 French original, a revised and expanded version of which was published in French in 1981.

Deleuze, Gilles, *Expressionism in Philosophy: Spinoza*, Translated by Martin Joughin (New York: Zone Books, 1990).

> Currently available through MIT Press.

De Lucca, John, "Wolfson on Spinoza's Use of the *More Geometrico*," *Dialogue* (Ottawa), Vol. 6 (June 1967), pp. 89-102.

De Mendelssohn, Peter, "Did Spinoza Ever Sit for Rembrandt? Speculations in Amsterdam," *Encounter*, Vol. 49, No. 3 (1977), pp. 57-62.

Demos, Raphael, "Spinoza's Doctrine of Privation," in Kashap (1972), pp. 276-288.

> Originally in *Philosophy*, Vol. 8 (1933), pp. 155-166.

Den Ouden, Bernard, *The Fusion of Naturalism and Humanism* (Lanham, MD: University Press of America, 1979).

> In *Philosopher's Index*, No. 089163.

Den Uyl, Douglas J., *Power, State, and Freedom: An Interpretation of Spinoza's Political Philosophy* (Assen, The Netherlands: Van Gorcum, 1983).

> From the author's doctoral dissertation, *Spinoza's Concept of the State and Political Authority*, Marquette University, 1978. The latter is currently available from UMI (Order No. 80-06524).

Den Uyl, Douglas J., "Passion, State, and Progress: Spinoza and Mandeville on the Nature of Human Association," *Journal of the History of Philosophy*, Vol. 25, No. 3 (July 1987), pp. 369-395.

Den Uyl, Douglas J., "Sociality and Social Contract: A Spinozistic Perspective," in *Studia Spinozana*, Vol. 1 (1985), pp. 19-51.

Den Uyl, Douglas J., and Stuart D. Warner, "Liberalism and Hobbes and Spinoza," in *Studia Spinozana*, Vol. 3 (1987), pp. 261-318.

Derham, W. Physico-theology, or a demonstration of the Being and Attributes of God, from His works of Creation. 2nd ed. London, 1714.

> In Hertzberger (1950), No. 795.

[Descartes, Rene] *The Method, Meditations and Philosophy of Descartes*, Translated with a new introductory essay, historical and critical, by John Veitch, with a special introduction by Frank Sewall (New York: Tudor Publishing Co., n.d.).

> Veitch's introduction includes a section, "Spinoza — Relative to Descartes," pp. 68-88, and other references.

Desmond, Patrick, *Time and Eternity in the Early Writings of Maurice Blondel*, Unpublished doctoral dissertation, Pontificia Universitas Gregoriana (Vatican), 1988.

> Includes material on Spinoza.

De Vet, J. J. V. M., "Spinoza's Authorship of *Stelkonstige Reeckening van den Regenboog* and of *Reeckening van Kanssen* Once More Doubtful," in *Studia Spinozana*, Vol. 2 (1986), pp. 267-309.

Devine, Philip E., "On the Definition of Religion," *Faith and Philosophy*, Vol. 3 (July 1986), pp. 270-284.

> In *Philosopher's Index*, No. 144005, noting that the paper offers a definition of religion and attempts to apply it to several "complex borderline cases," including "Spinozism."

De Vries, Theun, "Spinoza and the Rise of Liberalism," *Science and Society*, Vol. 22 (1958), pp. 356-364.

De Vries, Theun, "Spinoza: State, Religion, Freedom," *Giornale critico della filosofia italiana*, Vol. 8 (October-December 1977), pp. 591-611.

Dewey, John, "The Pantheism of Spinoza," *Journal of Speculative Philosophy*, Vol. 16 (July 1882), pp. 249-257.

> Reprinted in *John Dewey: The Early Works, 1882-1898* (Carbondale and Edwardsville: Southern Illinois University Press; London and Amsterdam: Feffer & Simons, 1969), Vol. 1, pp. 9-18.

Diamond, D., "The Heretic and the Fanatic," *Jewish Affairs*, Vol. 37, No. 2 (1977), pp. 17-20.

> In Van der Werf (1984), No. 563.

Dienstag, Jacob I. (ed.), *Studies in Maimonides and Spinoza*, Texts, Studies, and Translations in Maimonidean Thought and Scholarship, Vol. 3 (Hoboken, NJ: Ktav Publishing Co., n. d.).

Dienstag, Jacob I., "The Relations of Spinoza to the Philosophy of Maimonides: An Annotated Bibliography," in *Studia Spinozana*, Vol. 2 (1986), pp. 375-416.

Dimou, N., "The Mind-Body Problem in Philosophy," in *Paleo Psychico* (New York: Plenum Press, 1987), pp. 27-34.

> In *Mental Health Abstracts*, No. 0543108, citing a discussion of the views of Plato, Aristotle, Descartes, Spinoza, Leibniz, T. H. Huxley, Ryle, Popper, and others.

Dodwell, H. The natural morality of humane souls. With a letter to J. Norris of Bemerton. And an expostulation, relating to the late insults of Mr. Clark and Mr. Chisull. London, 1708.

> In Hertzberger (1950), No. 799, citing references to Spinoza. *See* Clarke (1706).

Dombrowski, Daniel A., "McFarland, Pantheism and Panentheism," *History of European Ideas*, Vol. 9 (1988), pp. 569-582.

> In *Philosopher's Index*, No. 159595, citing discussion of Spinoza's influence on Coleridge, as seen by McFarland and Hartshorne.

Donagan, Alan, *Spinoza* (Chicago: University of Chicago Press, 1989).

> First published by Harvester/Wheatsheaf, 1988.

Donagan, Alan, *et al.* (eds.), *Human Nature and Natural Knowledge* (Dordrecht: D. Reidel Publishing Co., 1986).

> Includes essays by Harry G. Frankfurt, "Two Motivations for Rationalism: Descartes and Spinoza," pp. 47-62, and Ruth Barcan Marcus, "Spinoza and the Ontological Proof," pp. 153-186.

Donagan, Alan, "A Note on Spinoza, *Ethics, I, 10*," *The Philosophical Review*, Vol. 75, No. 3 (July 1965), pp. 380-382.

> A reply to Bennett (1965).

Donagan, Alan, "Spinoza and Descartes on Extension," *Midwest Studies in Philosophy*, Vol. 1 (1976), pp. 31-33.

Donagan, Alan, "Essence and the Distinction of Attributes in Spinoza's Metaphysics," in Grene (1979), pp. 164-181.

Donagan, Alan, "Spinoza's Proof of Immortality," in Grene (1979), pp. 241-258.

Donagan, Alan, "Spinoza's Dualism," in Kennington (1980), Chap. 6, pp. 89-102.

Donagan, Alan, *Homo Cogitat*: Spinoza's Doctrine and Some Recent Commentators," in Curley and Moreau (1990), pp. 102-112.

Doney, Willis, "Spinoza on Philosophical Skepticism," in Mandelbaum and Freeman (1975), pp. 139-158.

Originally in *The Monist*, Vol. 55 (1971), pp. 617-635.

Doney, Willis, "Spinoza's Ontological Proof," in Kennington (1980), Chap. 3, pp. 35-52.

Doney, Willis, "Rationalism," *The Southern Journal of Philosophy*, Vol. 21 (1983), pp. 1-14.

In *Philosopher's Index*, No. 119330, citing references to Descartes, Spinoza, and Leibniz.

Doney, Willis, "Gueroult on Spinoza's Proof of God's Existence," in Curley and Moreau (1990), pp. 32-38.

Donnelley, Strachen, "Human Selves, Chronic Illness, and the Ethics of Medicine," *Hastings Center Report*, Vol. 18 (April-May 1988), pp. 5-8.

In *Philosopher's Index*, No. 157884, citing discussion of the views of Spinoza and other philosophers on the self.

Dorter, Kenneth, "Ontology and Contingency," *Idealistic Studies*, Vol. 8 (May 1978), pp. 93-114.

In *Philosopher's Index*, No. 059279.

Dreher, John Paul, *The Metaphysical Bases of Spinoza's Ethical and Political Thinking*, Unpublished doctoral dissertation, University of Chicago, 1962.

Dresser, Horatio W., *Man and the Divine Order: Essays in the Philosophy of Religion and in Constructive Idealism* (New York: Putnam, 1903).

Includes a chapter, "Plotinus and Spinoza," pp. 201-222, and other references.

Dresser, Horatio W., *A History of Modern Philosophy* (New York: Thomas Y. Crowell Co., 1929).

Includes a chapter on Spinoza, pp. 39-50.

Drummond, James, *The Life and Letters of James Martineau*, With a survey of his philosophical work by C. B. Upton (New York: Dodd, Mead and Co., 1902). 2 vols.

> Includes a chapter on Martineau's study of Spinoza, Vol. 2, pp. 449-459.

DuBois de la Cour. *See* Filleau de la Chaise (1682).

Dubnov, Semen Markovich, *An Outline of Jewish History*, Authorized translation from the Russian (New York: M. N. Maisel, 1925). 3 vols.

> Includes a section, "The Netherlands — Acosta and Spinoza," Vol. 3, pp. 211-217.

Duff, Archibald, *History of Old Testament Criticism* (New York: G. P. Putnam's Sons, 1910).

> Includes a section, "The Old Testament Criticism of Baruch Spinoza," pp. 129-136. Hertzberger (1950), No. 83, cites a 1910 London edition with the section on Spinoza on pp. 101-106.

Duff, Robert A., *Spinoza's Political and Ethical Philosophy* (New York: Augustus M. Kelley, Publishers, 1970).

> A facsimile reprint of the original 1903 edition published in Glasgow by James Maclehose and Sons.

Dunham, Barrows, *Heroes and Heretics: A Political History of Western Thought* (New York: Alfred A. Knopf, 1964).

> Includes a section on Spinoza, pp. 330-342.

Dunham, James Henry, *Freedom and Purpose: An Interpretation of the Psychology of Spinoza* (Princeton: Princeton University Press, 1916).

> Also published in Lancaster, PA, by the Psychological Review Company as Philosophical Monograph No. 3 (March 1916). Based on the author's doctoral dissertation of the same title, University of Pennsylvania, 1913.

Dunham, James Henry, *The Religion of Philosophers* (Freeport, NY: Books for Libraries Press, 1969).

> Originally published by the University of Pennsylvania Press in 1947. Includes a chapter, "Spinoza," pp. 180-212.

Dunner, Joseph, *Baruch Spinoza and Western Democracy: An Interpretation of His Philosophical, Religious, and Political Thought* (New York: Philosophical Library, 1955).

Dunning, William Archibald, *A History of Political Theories: From Luther to Montesquieu* (New York: The Macmillan Co., 1923).

> Includes a section on Spinoza, pp. 309-317.

Duprat, Guilliaume Leonce, *Morals: A Treatise on the Psycho-Sociological Bases of Ethics*, Translated by W. J. Greenstreet (London and Newcastle-on-Tyne: W. Scott Publishing Co., 1903).

> Includes a section on Spinoza, pp. 117-120.

Durant, Will, *Philosophy and the Social Problem* (New York: Macmillan, 1917).

> Published under the same title in London by Allen & Unwin, 1928. Both editions include a chapter, "Spinoza and the Social Problem," pp. 90-116.

Durant, Will, *A Guide to Spinoza*, Little Blue Book, No. 520 (Girard, KA: Haldeman-Julius Company, 1924) 96 pp.

Durant, Will, *The Story of Philosophy: The Lives and Opinions of the Greater Philosophers* (New York: Simon and Schuster, 1926).

> Includes a chapter on Spinoza, pp. 161-217.

Durant, Will, *The Mansions of Philosophy: A Survey of Human Life and Destiny* (New York: Simon and Schuster, 1929).

> Includes many references to Spinoza.

Durant, Will, "Spinoza: My Paean," in Hessing (1977), pp. 143-144.

Dutka, J., "Spinoza and the Theory of Probability," *Scripta Mathematica*, Vol. 19 (1953), pp. 24-32.

> In Wetlesen (1968), p. 48.

Earbury, Matthias. Deism Examin'd and Confuted. In an answer to a book entitled, Tractatus Theologico Politicus. By Matthias Earbury, M. A. School-Master of Wye in Kent. London: Printed for Charles Brome, at the Gun, at the West End of St. Pauls. 1697.

In Van der Linde, No. 370, and in Oko (1964), p. 167. According to Oko, also appeared as: An answer to a book entitled, Tractatus theologico politicus. London, Printed for Charles Brome, 1697.

Earle, William A., *Mystical Reason* (Chicago: Regnery, 1980).

In *Philosopher's Index*, No. 112632.

Earle, William A., "The Ontological Argument in Spinoza," in Grene (1979), pp. 213-219.

Originally in *Philosophy and Phenomenological Research*, Vol. 11 (1950-1951), pp. 549-554.

Earle, William A., "The Ontological Argument in Spinoza: Twenty Years Later," in Grene (1979), pp. 220-226.

Eby, Louise S., *The Quest for Moral Law* (New York: Columbia University Press, 1944).

In Rice (1967), p. 292, citing a section on Spinoza, pp. 118-135.

Eckstein, Jerome, "On the Relationship Between Substance and Attribute in Spinoza's *Ethics*," *Philosophical Quarterly of India*, Vol. 29 (1956), pp. 1-16.

Eckstein, Walter, "Religious Element in Spinoza's Philosophy," *Journal of Religion*, Vol. 23 (1943), pp. 153-163.

Eckstein, Walter, "Rousseau and Spinoza: Their Political Theories and Their Conception of Ethical Freedom," *Journal of the History of Ideas*, Vol. 5, No. 3 (June 1944), pp. 259-291.

Edgar, William J., "Continuity and the Individuation of Modes in Spinoza's Physics," in Wilbur (1976), pp. 85-105.

Edman, Irwin, "Poetic Insight and Religious Truth," in *Septimana Spinozana* (1933), pp. 162-177.

Edwards, John. Some Thoughts Concerning the Several Causes and Occasions of Atheism, Especially in the Present Age, With some Brief Reflections on Socinianism, and on a late book entituled, *The reasonableness of Christianity as deliver'd in the Scriptures*. London, Printed for J. Robinson, 1695.

In Oko (1964), p. 388. A facsimile reprint was issued by Garland Publishing in New York as Vol. 4 in the Garland Series on the Philosophy of John Locke.

Edwards, Paul (ed.), *The Encyclopedia of Philosophy* (New York: Macmillan Publishing Co. and The Free Press, 1967). 8 vols. in four.

There are many references to Spinoza, sometimes lengthy discussions, throughout these volumes. Vol. 7 includes articles by Alasdair MacIntyre, "Spinoza," pp. 530-541, and Frederick M. Barnard, "Spinozism," pp. 541-544.

Ehrlich, Robert S., *Monarch Literature Notes on the Philosophy of Baruch Spinoza* (New York: Monarch, 1965).

In Curley (1975), p. 278.

Eisenberg, Paul D., "How To Understand *De Intellectus Emendatione*," *Journal of the History of Philosophy*, Vol. 9 (April 1971), pp. 171-191.

Eisenberg, Paul D., "Is Spinoza an Ethical Naturalist?" in Hessing (1977), pp. 145-164.

Also in *Philosophia* (Israel), Vol. 7 (March 1977), pp. 107-133.

Eisenberg, Paul D., "On the Attributes and Their Alleged Independence of One Another: A Commentary on Spinoza's *Ethics* IP10," in Curley and Moreau (1990), pp. 1-15.

Eisenberg, Paul D. *See* Spinoza, *Treatise on the Improvement of the Understanding* (1977).

Eldridge, Michael, *Philosophy as Religion: A Study in Critical Devotion*, Unpublished doctoral dissertation, University of Florida, 1985.

Discusses Socrates, Spinoza, and Dewey. Currently available from UMI (Order No. 85-23820).

Eliade, Mircea (ed.), *The Encyclopedia of Religion* (New York: Macmillan Publishing Co., 1987). 16 vols.

Includes an article by David Winston, "Barukh Spinoza," Vol. 14, pp. 7-11, as well as many other references.

[Eliot, George] *George Eliot's Life as Related in Her Letters and Journals,*
Arranged and edited by J. W. Cross (London: William Blackwood and Sons,
1885).

> Includes several references to Spinoza. A reprint was issued in Grosse
> Pointe, MI, by Scholarly Press, 1968.

Eliot, George. *See* Spinoza, *Ethics* (1981).

Elmendorf, John J., *Outlines of Lectures on the History of Philosophy* (New
York: G. P. Putnam's Sons, 1876).

> Includes a section on Spinoza, pp. 181-189.

Elovaara, Raili, "Spinoza and Finnish Literature," in *Studia Spinozana*, Vol. 5
(1989), pp. 59-80.

Elwes, R. H. M. *See* Spinoza, *passim.*

[Enelow, Hyman Gerson] *Selected Works of Hyman G. Enelow*, With a memoir
by Dr. Felix A. Levy (Kingsport, TN: Kingsport Press, 1935). 4 vols.

> Includes a sermon, "The Spiritual Value of Spinoza," Vol. 2, pp. 186-190.

Enfield, William. The history of philosophy, from the earliest times to the
beginning of the present century; drawn up from Brucher's Historia critica
philosophiae. In two volumes. Dublin, Printed for P. Wogan, 1792. 2 vols.

> In Oko (1964), p. 135, citing a section on Spinoza in Vol. 2. Later
> editions — 1819, 1837, 1839 — apparently include the same section.

Epstein, Fanny, "On the Definition of Moral Goodness," *Iyyun*, Vol. 19 (1968),
pp. 153-169.

> In Curley (1975), p. 299; in Grene (1979), p. 390.

Erdmann, Johann Eduard, *A History of Philosophy*, 3rd Edition Translated and
edited by Williston S. Hough (London: Swan Sonnenschein & Co.; New York:
Macmillan & Co., 1892). 3 vols.

> Includes sections on Spinoza, Vol. 2, pp. 52-91, and many other references.
> Reprinted in London by Allen & Unwin, 1924.

Erdmann, Johann Edward, "About Spinoza's Influence in Holland," *History of
Philosophy*, Vol. 2, pp. 88-89.

> In Melamed (1933), p. 381.

Ericson, Edward L., *The Free Mind Through the Ages* (New York: Frederick Ungar Publishing Co., 1985).

> Includes a chapter, "Eternal Nature Is God: Benedict Spinoza," pp. 65-74.

Esposito, Joseph L., *Schelling's Idealism and Philosophy of Nature* (Lewisburg: Bucknell University Press; Cranbury, NJ: Associated University Presses, 1977).

> Includes many references to Spinoza.

Esposito, Joseph L., "God and the Possibility of Philosophy," *International Journal for Philosophy of Religion*, Vol. 3 (Summer 1972), pp. 103-115.

> In *Philosopher's Index*, No. 037896.

Eucken, Rudolf, *The Problem of Human Life as Viewed by the Great Thinkers from Plato to the Present Time*, Translated by Williston S. Hough and W. R. Boyce Gibson, Revised and enlarged edition (New York: Charles Scribner's Sons, 1924).

> Includes a section on Spinoza, pp. 362-380.

Evans, J. L., "Error and the Will," *Philosophy*, Vol. 38 (April 1963), pp. 136-148.

> In *Philosopher's Index*, No. 063590, citing references to Spinoza and Descartes. Curley (1975), p. 299, cites O'Hear (1972) as a reply.

Everett, Katherine, *Mechanism and Teleology in the Philosophy of Spinoza*, Unpublished doctoral dissertation, Cornell University, 1912.

Fackenheim, Emil L., *To Mend the World: Foundations of Future Jewish Thought* (New York: Schocken Books, 1982).

> Considers the impact of the Holocaust on the character of post-Holocaust thought; Spinoza, Rosenzweig, Hegel, and Heidegger are discussed (*Philosopher's Index*, No. 116663).

Fairbairn, Andrew Martin, *Studies in the Philosophy of Religion and History* (New York: Lovell, Adam, Werson, 1876).

> In Oko (1964), p. 256, citing a section on Spinoza, pp. 346-348.

Falckenberg, Richard, *A History of Modern Philosophy from Nicolas of Cusa to the Present Time,* Translated by A. C. Armstrong, Jr. (New York: Henry Holt and Co., 1893).

> Includes a chapter on Spinoza, pp. 116-142.

Farid, Arifa, "Spinoza's Deterministic Ethics," *Pakistan Philosophical Congress,* Vol. 12 (1965), pp. 305-313.

> This citation is based on *Philosopher's Index,* No. 067796.

Farrar, Adam Storey, *A Critical History of Free Thought in Reference to the Christian Religion,* Eight lectures preached before the University of Oxford in the year M.DCCC.LXII (London: J. Murray; New York: D. Appleton and Co., 1863).

> Includes a section on Spinoza, pp. 106-114, and other references.

Faurot, Jean H., *The Philosopher and the State: From Hooke to Popper* (San Francisco: Chandler, 1971).

> In *Philosopher's Index,* No. 019463.

Faurot, Jean H., "Santayana's Philosophy of Religion," *Hibbert Journal,* Vol. 58, pp. 258-267.

> In *Philosopher's Index,* No. 071193; date not given.

Feehan, Stephen S., *Substance, Reason and Intuition in Spinoza,* Unpublished doctoral dissertation, St. Louis University, 1970.

> Currently available from UMI (Order No. 71-21386).

Feibleman, James K., "Was Spinoza a Nominalist?" *The Philosophical Review,* Vol. 60 (July 1951), pp. 386-389.

Feld, E., "Spinoza the Jew: Jewish Mysticism and the Enlightenment," *Modern Judaism,* Vol. 9, No. 1 (1989), pp. 101-119.

Feldman, Seymour. *See* Spinoza, *Ethics* (1982).

[Fénélon, François de Salignac de la Mothe] A demonstration of the existence and attributes of God, drawn from the knowledge of nature, from proofs purely intellectual, and from the idea of the Infinite himself. Harrisburgh, W. Gillmor, 1811.

In Oko (1964), p. 414. Includes "A refutation of the principles of Spinoza," pp. 190-240, and "The reflections of Father Tournemine, a Jesuite upon atheism; upon my lord of Cambray's Demonstration, and upon Spinoza's system," pp. 242-263. Earlier (p. 204), Oko cites the second London edition, 1769. Here (p. 414) he also cites editions of 1713 and 1754. Hertzberger (1950), No. 803, cites a London edition of 1821, with S. Boyse as the translator.

Ferm, Vergilius (ed.), *A History of Philosophical Systems* (New York: The Philosophical Library, 1950).

Includes a section on Spinoza on pp. 244-246 of Albert G. Ramsperger's essay, "Early Modern Rationalism," and many other references.

Ferstler, Howard W., Jr., "Skeleton Key to Spinoza," *Man and World*, Vol. 8 (November 1975), pp. 424-435.

Feuer, Lewis S., *Spinoza and the Rise of Liberalism* (Boston: Beacon Press, 1958).

Feuer, Lewis S., "The Social Motivation of Spinoza's Thought," *Proceedings of the XI International Congress of Philosophy*, Vol 13 (1953), pp. 36-42.

In Oko (1964), p. 107, and Walther (1991), p. 50, who cites the French journal title and identifies the publisher as North Holland, with E. Nauwelaerts as editor.

Feuer, Lewis S., "The Dream of Benedict de Spinoza," *American Imago*, Vol. 25 (1957), pp. 225-242.

In Walther (1976), p. 424.

Feuer, Lewis S., "Spinoza's Thought and Modern Perplexities: Its American Career," in Kogan (1979), pp. 36-79.

Feuer, Lewis S., "Spinoza's Political Philosophy: The Lessons and Problems of a Conservative Democrat," in Kennington (1980), Chap. 9, pp. 133-154.

Feuer, Lewis S., "Einstein and the Prague Circle," *Midstream*, Vol. 28, No. 6 (1982), pp. 36-39.

Includes a brief comparison of Einstein's metaphysical views with those of Spinoza.

Fichte, Johann Gottlieb, *The Way Towards the Blessed Life; or, The Doctrine of Religion*, Translated by William Smith (London: J. Chapman, 1849).

In Oko (1964), p. 330.

[Filleau de la Chaise, Jean] An excellent discourse proving the divine original and authority of the five books of Moses. Written originally in French by Monsieur Du Bois de la Cour [pseud.] ... To which is added a second part, or an examination of ... Pere Simon's Critical history of the Old Testament, wherein all his objections, with the weightiest of Spinosa's, against Moses's being the author of the first five books of the Bible are answered ... By W. L[orimer]. London, Printed for Tho. Parkhurst, 1682.

> In Oko (1964), p. 395. Hertzberger (1950), No. 642, attributes this book to Du Bois de la Cour.

Findlay, J. N., *The Transcendance of the Cave*, Gifford Lectures Given at the University of St. Andrews, December 1965 - January 1966 (London: George Allen & Unwin; New York: Humanities Press, 1967).

> Includes many references to Spinoza. This volume is a sequel to the author's *The Discipline of the Cave*, Gifford Lectures Given at the University of St. Andrews, December 1964 – February 1965 (London: George Allen & Unwin; New York: Humanities Press, 1970), which itself contains several references.

Findlay, J. N., *Ascent to the Absolute: Metaphysical Papers and Lectures* (London: George Allen & Unwin; New York: Humanities Press, 1970).

> Includes many references to Spinoza.

Fisch, Max H. (ed.), *Classic American Philosophers* (New York: Appleton-Century-Crofts, 1951).

> Includes George Santayana's essay, "Ultimate Religion," pp. 317-326.

Fischer, Kuno, *Descartes and His School*, Translated by J. P. Gordy from the 3rd and revised German edition of the author's *History of Modern Philosophy*, edited by Noah Porter (London: T. Fisher Unwin; New York: Charles Scribner's Sons, 1887).

> Includes many references to Spinoza. Currently available from UMI Out-of-Print Books on Demand (Order No. OP57988).

Fischer, Kuno, "The Life and Character of Baruch Spinoza," Translated by Frida Schmidt, in Knight (1882), pp. 75-127.

Fishler, Max, *What the Great Philosophers Thought about God* (Los Angeles: Universe Books, 1958).

> In *Philosopher's Index*, No. 018356.

Fix, Andrew C., *Prophecy and Reason: The Dutch Collegiants in the Early Enlightenment* (Princeton: Princeton University Press, 1991).

> Includes discussion of Spinoza's influence on Bredenburg, pp. 219-227, and on Collegiant thought generally, pp. 240-246, along with many other references. From the author's doctoral dissertation of essentially the same title, Indiana University, 1984. Van Bunge (1989), p. 229, cites what appears to be a substantially longer discussion of Spinoza and Bredenburg on pp. 325-374 of the dissertation.

Flage, Daniel E., "The Essences of Spinoza's God," *History of Philosophy Quarterly*, Vol. 6, No. 2 (April 1989), pp. 147-160.

Flemming, Arthur Henry, *Egoism in Spinoza*, Unpublished doctoral dissertation, University of California, Los Angeles, 1975.

> Currently available from UMI (Order No. 76-08991).

Flint, Robert, *Anti-Theistic Theories*, Being the Baird Lectures for 1877, 6th Edition (Edinburgh and London: W. Blackwood and Sons, 1899).

> Includes a section on Spinoza, pp. 358-375, with an appendix on pp. 546-551.

Floistad, Guttorm (ed.), *Contemporary Philosophy: A New Survey* (The Hague: Martinus Nijhoff, 1983).

> Includes an essay by G. H. R. Parkinson, "Spinoza's Philosophy of Mind," Vol 4, pp. 105-131.

Floistad, Guttorm, "The Knower and the Known," *Man and World*, Vol. 3 (May 1970), pp. 3-25.

> In *Philosopher's Index*, No. 030120, citing a discussion of Spinoza's "view on the knower, or the mind, as an agent."

Floistad, Guttorm, "Spinoza's Theory of Knowledge Applied to the *Ethics*," in Kashap (1972), pp. 249-275.

> Also under the title, "Spinoza's Theory of Knowledge in the *Ethics*," in Grene (1979), pp. 101-127. Originally in *Inquiry*, Vol. 12, No. 1 (1969), pp. 41-65.

Floistad, Guttorm, "Experiential Meaning in Spinoza," in Van der Bend (1974), pp. 51-60.

Floistad, Guttorm, "Reality or Perfection," in Hessing (1977), pp. 165-169.

Floistad, Guttorm, "Mind and Body in Spinoza's *Ethics*," in Wetlesen (1978), pp. 36-50.

> Also in *Synthèse*, Vol. 37 (January 1978), pp. 1-14; originally in *Giornale critico della filosofia italiana*, Vol. 8 (October-December 1977), pp. 345-357.

Floistad, Guttorm, "Reality as Perfection: Some Remarks on Spinoza's Concept of a Lifeworld," in *Studia Spinozana*, Vol. 2 (1986), pp. 233-246.

Floistad, Guttorm, "*The Source*: Spinoza in the Writings of Gabriel Scott," in *Studia Spinozana*, Vol. 5 (1989), pp. 185-201.

Force, James E., "Spinoza's *Tractatus Theologico-Politicus*: A New Way of Looking at the World," *The Southern Journal of Philosophy*, Vol. 12 (Fall 1974), pp. 343-355.

Forster, Charles, *Spinoza Redivivus; or, The Reappearance of His School and Spirit in the Volume Entitled "Essays and Reviews,"* A sermon delivered in Canterbury Cathedral on Monday, May 6, 1861 (London: Spottiswood, 1861).

> In Oko (1964), p. 349. *See* Hedge (1861).

Forsyth, T. M., *God and the World* (London: Allen & Unwin, 1952).

> In *Philosopher's Index*, No. 072868.

Forsyth, T. M., "Spinoza's Doctrine of God in Relation to His Conception of Causality," in Kashap (1972), pp. 3-15.

> Originally in *Philosophy*, Vol. 23, No. 87 (October 1948), pp. 291-301.

Foss, Lawrence, "Hegel, Spinoza and a Theory of Experience as Closed," *The Thomist*, Vol. 35 (July 1971), pp. 435-446.

Foti, Veronique M., "Spinoza's Doctrine of Immortality and the Unity of Love," *The Southern Journal of Philosophy*, Vol. 17, No. 4 (1979), pp. 437-442.

Foti, Veronique M., "Thought, Affect, Drive and Pathogenesis in Spinoza and Freud," *History of European Ideas*, Vol. 3, No. 2 (1982), pp. 221-236.

Foucher de Careil, Louis Alexandre, *A Refutation Recently Discovered of Spinoza by Leibnitz*, Translated with prefatory remarks and introduction by the Rev. Octavius Freire Owen (Edinburgh: T. Constable, 1855).

Currently available from UMI Out-of-Print Books on Demand (Order No. OP34004 or OP41206).

Fradkin, H. G., "The Separation of Religion and Politics: The Paradoxes of Spinoza," *Review of Politics*, Vol. 50, No. 4 (1988), pp. 603-627.

Franck, Isaac, "Spinoza's Onslaught on Judaism," *Judaism*, Vol. 28 (1979), pp. 177-193.

Franck, Isaac, "Was Spinoza a 'Jewish' Philosopher?" *Judaism*, Vol. 28 (1979), pp. 345-352.

Franck, Isaac, "Spinoza's Logic of Inquiry: Rationalist or Experimentalist?" in Kennington (1980), Chap. 14, pp. 247-272.

Francks, Richard, "Omniscience, Omnipotence and Pantheism," *Philosophy*, Vol. 54 (July 1979), pp. 395-399.

> "Attempts to justify Spinoza's pantheism by showing it as the necessary consequence of the belief that God is perfect" — *Philosopher's Index*, No. 082754.

Francks, Richard, "Caricatures in the History of Philosophy: The Case of Spinoza," in Holland (1985), pp. 179-197.

Frank, Joseph, Helmut Minkowski, and Ernest J. Sternglass, *Horizons of a Philosopher: Essays in Honor of David Baumgardt* (Leiden: E. J. Brill, 1963).

> In *Philosopher's Index*, No. 074136.

Frank, Waldo, *The Rediscovery of Man: A Memoir and a Methodology of Modern Life* (New York: George Braziller, 1958).

> Includes many references to Spinoza.

Frankena, William K., "Spinoza's 'New Morality': Notes on Book IV," in Mandelbaum and Freeman (1975), pp. 85-100.

Frankena, William K., "Spinoza on the Knowledge of Good and Evil," *Philosophia* (Israel), Vol. 7 (March 1977), pp. 15-44.

Frankfurt, Harry G. (ed.), *Leibniz: A Collection of Critical Essays* (Garden City, NY: Doubleday, 1972).

Reprinted by the University of Notre Dame Press (Notre Dame, 1976). Includes papers by Martha Kneale, "Leibniz and Spinoza on Activity," pp. 215-238, and Arthur O. Lovejoy, "Plenitude and Sufficient Reason in Leibniz and Spinoza," pp. 281-334.

Frankfurt, Harry G., "Two Motivations for Rationalism: Descartes and Spinoza," in Donagan (1986), pp. 47-62.

Fraser, Alexander Campbell, *Philosophy of Theism*, Being the Gifford Lectures delivered before the University of Edinburgh in 1894-96, 2nd Edition, amended (Edinburgh: William Blackwood and Sons, 1899).

Includes a lecture, "Pantheistic Unity and Necessity: Spinoza," pp. 89-103.

Fraser, Alexander Campbell, "M. Saisset and Spinoza," *The North British Review* (Edinburgh), Vol. 38 (1863), pp. 454-489.

In Oko (1964), p. 258.

Freehof, Solomon B., *Stormers of Heaven* (New York and London: Harper & Brothers, 1931).

Includes a section on Spinoza, pp. 112-118.

Freehof, Solomon B., "Spinoza and Religion," in Schaub (1933).

Freeman, James B., and Charles B. Daniels, "Maximal Propositions and the Coherence Theory of Truth," *Dialogue* (Ottawa), Vol. 17 (1978), pp. 56-71.

In *Philosopher's Index*, No. 058865, citing references to Spinoza, Wittgenstein, and Blanshard.

Freudenthal, Jacob, "On the History of Spinozism," *The Jewish Quarterly Review*, Vol. 8, No. 29 (October 1895), pp. 17-70.

Also published separately by Macmillan in 1895 in London.

Friedlander, Michael, *Spinoza: His Life and Philosophy*, Two papers read before the Jews' College Literary Society, June 5, 1887, and April 22, 1888 (London: Office of the *Jewish Chronicle*, 1888).

32 pp.; paper cover. Originally in Jews' College Literary Society, *Papers...* (1887), pp. 163-177.

Friedman, Joel I., "Some Set Theoretical Partition Theorems Suggested by the Structure of Spinoza's God," *Synthèse*, Vol. 27 (May-June 1974), pp. 199-209.

Friedman, Joel I., "The Universal Class Has a Spinozistic Partitioning," *Synthèse*, Vol. 32 (April 1976), pp. 403-418.

Friedman, Joel I., "An Overview of Spinoza's *Ethics*," *Synthèse*, Vol. 37 (January 1978), pp. 67-106.

Friedman, Joel I., "Spinoza's Denial of Free Will in Man and God," in Wetlesen (1978), pp. 51-84.

Friedman, Joel I., "The Mystic's Ontological Argument," *American Philosophical Quarterly*, Vol. 16 (1979), pp. 73-78.

> In Van der Werf (1984), No. 699.

Friedman, Joel I., "Was Spinoza Fooled by the Ontological Argument?" *Philosophia* (Israel), Vol. 11, No. 3-4 (July 1982), pp. 307-344.

> An abstract was published in *The Journal of Philosophy*, Vol. 75, No. 10 (1978), p. 565.

Friedman, Joel I., "Spinoza's Problem of 'Other Minds,'" *Synthèse*, Vol. 57, No. 1 (October 1983), pp. 99-126.

Friedman, Joel I., "How the Finite Follows from the Infinite in Spinoza's Metaphysical System," *Synthèse*, Vol. 69, No. 3 (December 1986), pp. 371-407.

Friedrich, Carl Joachim, *Constitutional Reason of State: The Survival of Constitutional Order* (Providence, RI: Brown University, 1957).

> In *Philosopher's Index*, No. 016592 (repeated at No. 073930), citing references to Spinoza and other philosophers.

Friedrich, Carl Joachim, *The Philosophy of Law in Historical Perspective* (Chicago: University of Chicago Press, 1958).

> Includes a chapter, "Law as the Expression of 'Pure Reason': From Spinoza to Wolff," pp. 110-121.

Froude, James Anthony, *Essays in Literature and History* (London: Dent, 1908).

> In Hertzberger (1950), No. 1014, citing an essay on Spinoza, pp. 224-272.

Froude, James Anthony, *A Short Account of Spinoza's Thought* (1845).

> This incomplete (and improbable) citation is in Wolfson (1969), p. 333.

Froude, James Anthony, *Short Studies on Great Subjects* (New York: Charles Scribner and Co., 1871).

> Includes a chapter on Spinoza, pp. 274-323. Hertzberger (1950), No. 1015, cites a two-volume edition published in London (1867) with the chapter on Spinoza in Vol. II, pp. 1-60. Wolfson (1969), p. 333, cites an 1867 edition, Vol. I, pp. 339-400. Walther (1991), p. 46, cites the original publication, "The Life of Spinoza," *Oxford and Cambridge Review*, Vol. 5 (1847), pp. 387-427.

Fu, Charles Wei-hsun, "Lao Tzu's Conception of Tao," *Inquiry*, Vol. 16 (Winter 1973), pp. 367-391.

> In *Philosopher's Index*, No. 042346, citing "a brief comparison of Lao Tzu and Spinoza...to emphasize the non-conceptual and non-propositional nature of Lao Tzu's metaphysical language."

Fuller, B. A. G., "Spinozistic Fancy: The Infinity of Attributes," *The Journal of Philosophy*, Vol. 29 (June 1932), pp. 355-358.

Fullerton, George Stuart, *On Spinozistic Immortality*, University of Pennsylvania Publications, Series in Philosophy, No. 3 (Philadelphia: University of Pennsylvania, 1899).

> Also published in Boston by Ginn in 1899. Currently available from UMI Out-of-Print Books on Demand (Order No. OP51914).

Fullerton, George Stuart. *See* Spinoza, *The Philosophy of Spinoza as Contained in ... the "Ethics"* (1894).

Funke, G., "Anonymous Presuppositions in Spinoza's Philosophy," in Rotenstreich and Schneider (1983), pp. 53-70.

Funkenstein, Amos, *Theology and the Scientific Imagination from the Middle Ages to the Seventeenth Century* (Princeton: Princeton University Press, 1986).

> Includes a section, "Hobbes, Spinoza, and Malebranche," pp. 80-89, and many other references.

Funkenstein, Amos, "Natural Science and Social Theory: Hobbes, Spinoza and Vico," in Tagliacozzo and Verene (1976), pp. 187-212.

Furlan, Augusto, "Logic According to Spinoza," in Van der Bend (1974), pp. 61-68.

Gabriel, Richard Mason, *Spinoza and Schelling*, Unpublished doctoral dissertation, New York University, n.d.

> In Feuer (1979), p. 77.

Gadd, Christopher D., *The Pre-Eminence of Spinoza's Third Kind of Knowledge*, Unpublished doctoral dissertation, Queen's University at Kingston (Canada), 1975.

Galik, M., "Two Modern Chinese Philosophers on Spinoza: Some Remarks on a Sino-German Spinoza *Festschrift*," *Oriens Extremus* (Germany), Vol. 22, No. 1 (1975), pp. 29-43.

Gane, M., "Borges, Menard, Spinoza," *Economy and Society*, Vol. 9, No. 4 (1980), pp. 404-419.

> In *Arts and Humanities Search*, No. 093879.

Gannon, Mary Ann Ida, "'Knowledge' and 'Free Man' in Spinoza's *Ethics*," *Proceedings of the American Catholic Philosophical Association*, Vol. 30 (1956), pp. 191-204.

Garber, Daniel, "Does History Have a Future? Some Reflections on Bennett and Doing Philosophy Historically," in Hare (1988), pp. 27-43.

Garber, Daniel, "Spinoza's Worlds: Reflections on Balibar on Spinoza," in Curley and Moreau (1990), pp. 77-81.

> Comments on Étienne Balibar's "Causalité, individualité, substance: Réflexions sur l'ontologie de Spinoza," in Curley and Moreau, pp. 58-76.

Garelick, Herbert M., *Spinoza's Absolute Presupposition*, Unpublished doctoral dissertation, Yale University, 1958.

Garrett, Don, "Spinoza's 'Ontological' Argument," *The Philosophical Review*, Vol. 88, No. 2 (April 1979), pp. 198-223.

Garrett, Don, "Truth and Ideas of Imagination in the *Tractatus de Intellectus Emendatione*," in *Studia Spinozana*, Vol. 2 (1986), pp. 61-92.

Garrett, Don, "'A Free Man Always Acts Honestly, Not Deceptively': Freedom and the Good in Spinoza's *Ethics*," in Curley and Moreau (1990), pp. 221-238.

Garrett, Don, "Truth, Method, and Correspondence in Spinoza and Leibniz," in *Studia Spinozana* (1990), pp. 13-43.

Garrett, Don, "Spinoza's Necessitarianism," in Yovel (1990).

Garver, N., "Pantheism and Ontology in Wittgenstein's Early Work," *Idealistic Studies*, Vol. 7 (September 1977), pp. 269-277.

> In *Philosopher's Index*, No. 033879.

Geach, P. T., "Spinoza and Divine Attributes," in Vesey (1972), pp. 15-27.

Gehring, Albert, *The Religion of Thirty Great Thinkers, Together with Miscellaneous Essays on Religious Subjects* (Boston: Marshall Jones Co. [1925?]).

> Includes a section on Spinoza, pp. 14-17.

Geisler, Norman L., *Miracles and Modern Thought* (Grand Rapids, MI: Zondervan, 1982).

> In *Philosopher's Index*, No. 121255, noting arguments against Spinoza and several later philosophers that "miracles are both possible and actual."

Gerrish, B. A., "The Secret Religion of Germany: Christian Piety and the Pantheism Controversy," *The Journal of Religion*, Vol. 67 (October 1987), pp. 437-455.

> In *Humanities Index*, No. 871230.

Gerstein, Israel and Carl L. Manello (eds.), *Obel Moed: A Volume of Essays in Jewish Studies*, Issued by the Hebrew Theological College of Chicago (St. Louis: Moinester Printing Co., 1927).

> Includes an essay by Simon G. Kramer, "Judaism and Spinoza's Philosophy."

Getchev, G. S., "Some of Malebranche's Reactions to Spinoza as Revealed in His Correspondence with Dourtons de Mairan," *The Philosophical Review*, Vol. 41 (July 1932), pp. 385-394.

Gettell, Raymond G., *History of Political Thought* (London, 1924).

> In Hertzberger (1950), No. 106. A second edition, edited by Lawrence C. Wanlass, was published in New York by Appleton-Century-Crofts, 1953.

Giancotti, Boscherini, Emilia, *Lexicon Spinozanum* (The Hague: Martinus Nijhoff, 1970). 2 vols.

The preface and introduction are presented in both English and Italian, pp. x-xxxvii.

Giancotti Boscherini, Emilia (ed.), *Proceedings of the First Italian International Congress on Spinoza* (Naples: Bibliopolis, 1985).

Includes papers in English by M. Bertman, E. Curley, H. De Dijn, E. Harris, H. Hubbeling, W. Klever, G. Kline, R. McShea, and Y. Yovel.

Giancotti Boscherini, Emilia, "Necessity and Freedom: Reflections on Texts by Spinoza," in Hessing (1977), pp. 90-107.

Giancotti Boscherini, Emilia, "Man as a Part of Nature," in Wetlesen (1978), pp. 85-96.

Giancotti Boscherini, Emilia. See *Studia Spinozana*, Vol. 1 (1985).

Gierke, Otto von, *The Development of Political Theory*, Translated by Bernard Freyd (New York: Norton, 1939).

In Oko (1964), p. 448.

Gilbert, George Holley, *Interpretation of the Bible: A Short History* (New York: Macmillan, 1980).

Includes a section on Spinoza, pp. 241-244.

Gilbert, Katherine E., "Hegel's Criticisms of Spinoza," in *Philosophical Essays in Honor of ... Creighton* (1917), pp. 26-41.

Gilden, Hilail, *The Problem of Political Liberty in Mill and Spinoza*, Unpublished doctoral dissertation, University of Chicago, 1963.

Gilden, Hilail, "Spinoza and the Political Problem," in Grene (1979), pp. 377-387.

Gilden, Hilail, "Notes on Spinoza's Critique of Religion," in Kennington (1980), Chap. 10, pp. 155-172.

Gildon, Charles. The deist's manual: or, A rational enquiry into the Christian religion. With some considerations on Mr. Hobbs, Spinosa ... &c. To which is prefix'd a letter, from the author of The method with the Deists. London, Printed for A. Roper, Fran. Coggan [etc.], 1705.

In Oko (1964), p. 401; in Hertzberger (1950), No. 810.

Gilead, Amihud, "Spinoza's 'Principium-Individuationis' and Personal Identity," *International Studies in Philosophy*, Vol. 15, No. 1 (Spring 1983), pp. 41-58.

Gilead, Amihud, "The Problem of Immediate Evidence: The Case of Spinoza and Hegel," *Hegel-Studien*, Vol. 20 (1985), pp. 145-162.

Gilead, Amihud, "The Order and Connection of Things: Are They Constructed Mathematically-Deductively According to Spinoza?" *Kant-Studien*, Vol. 76, No. 1 (1985), pp. 72-78.

Gillett, Ezra Hall, *God in Human Thought; or, Natural Theology Traced in Literature, Ancient and Modern, to the Time of Bishop Butler* (New York: Scribner, Armstrong, 1874). 2 vols.

Includes a section on Spinoza, pp. 537-544.

Gilson, Étienne, *The Unity of Philosophical Experience* (New York: Charles Scribner's Sons, 1937).

Includes many references to Spinoza.

Gilson, Étienne, and Thomas Langan, *Modern Philosophy: Descartes to Kant* (New York: Random House, 1963).

Includes a chapter on Spinoza, pp. 127-144.

Ginsburg, Benjamin, *The Doctrine of Essence in the Philosophy of Spinoza*, Unpublished doctoral dissertation, Harvard University, 1926.

Ginsburg, Benjamin, "Spinoza and the Jewish Tradition," *The Menorah Journal*, Vol. 13, No. 1 (February 1927), pp. 1-19.

Glouberman, M., "Conceptuality: An Essay in Retrieval," *Kant-Studien*, Vol. 70 (1979), pp. 383-408.

In *Philosopher's Index*, No. 084903.

Glouberman, M., "Causation, Cognition and Historical Typology," *Dialectica*, Vol. 34 (1980), pp. 221-228.

In *Philosopher's Index*, No. 107788.

Glouberman, M., "Structure and the Interpretation of Classical Modern Metaphysics," *Metaphilosophy*, Vol. 18 (July-October 1987), pp. 270-287.

In *Philosopher's Index*, No. 153471, noting that this paper focuses on Bennett (1984) as an example of "negligent interpretation."

[Goethe, J. W. von] *Goethe's Autobiography: Poetry and Truth from My Own Life*, Translated by R. O. Moon (Washington, DC: Public Affairs Press, 1949).

Includes a section on Spinoza, pp. 591-595.

Goldblatt, David, *Is the Jewish Race Pure? An Examination of the Evidence Against and a Statement of Facts in Its Favor* (New York: The Goldblatt Publishing Co., 1933).

In Oko (1964), p. 367, citing a section on Spinoza, pp. 278-281.

Goldin, Judah (ed.), *The Jewish Expression* (New York: Bantam Books, 1974).

In Dienstag (1986), p. 407, citing a reprint of the preface in Strauss (1965).

Goldman, Solomon, *The Jew and the Universe* (New York: Arno Press, 1973).

Includes several sections on Spinoza—e.g., pp. 68-75—and many other references. This volume is a reprint of the 1936 edition issued in New York by Harper & Brothers.

Goldshur, David, *Cognitive Domains in the Philosophies of Descartes and Spinoza*, Unpublished doctoral dissertation, University of California, Los Angeles, 1941.

Goldwater, Raymond (ed.), *Jewish Philosophy and Philosophers* (London: Hillel Foundation, 1962).

Includes chapters on Spinoza by L. Jocobs and by D. D. Raphael.

Golomb, J., "Freud and Spinoza: Reconstruction," *Israel Annals of Psychiatry and Related Disciplines*, Vol. 16, No. 4 (1978), pp. 275-288.

Goncalves, Joaquin Cerqueira, "Individuality and Society in Spinoza's Mind," in Hessing (1977), pp. 174-182.

Goodheir, Albert, *Founded on a Rock: The Philosophy of Spinoza after Three Centuries* (Glasgow, 1978).

> In Van der Werf (1984), No. 792.

Goodman, Lenn E., "Equality and Human Rights: The Lockean and Judaic Views," *Judaism*, Vol. 25 (July 1976), pp. 357-362.

> In *Philosopher's Index*, No. 015014.

Goodman, Lenn E., "Determinism and Freedom," in Schoeman (1988), pp. 107-164.

[Goodwin, Timothy] The life and character of that eminent and learned prelate, the late Dr. Edw. Stillingfleet ... together with some account of the works he has publish'd. London, Morlock, 1710.

> In Oko (1964), p. 350, who notes that Goodwin is the supposed author.

Gore, William Clark, *The Imagination in Spinoza and Hume: A Comparative Study in the Light of Some Recent Contributions to Psychology* (Chicago: The University of Chicago Press, 1902).

> University of Chicago Contributions to Philosophy, Vol. II, No. 4. From the author's doctoral dissertation, University of Chicago, 1901.

Gossett, H. A. *See* Spinoza, *Chief Works* ... (1883-1884).

Gotthelf, Ezra Gerson, "Spinoza and the Moreh Nebuchim," *Jewish Institute Quarterly*, Vol 5, No. 1 (1928), pp. 6-11.

Gottschalk, Alfred, "Maimonides, Spinoza and Ahad Ha-Am," *Judaism*, Vol. 21, No. 1 (Winter 1972), pp. 303-310.

Gottschalk, Alfred, "Spinoza — A Three Hundred Year Perspective," in Kogan (1979), pp. 1-4.

Gouinlock, James, "The Moral Value of a Philosophic Education," *Teaching Philosophy*, Vol. 3 (Spring 1979), pp. 37-49.

> In *Philosopher's Index*, No. 086653, noting that the author uses Spinoza and several other philosophers to discuss the notion that philosophies "can function as maps of reality" to help people to form a world view.

Gould, R., "Spinoza and Lavater in *Dichtung und Wahrheit* and the Paradoxical Nature of Autobiography," *Seminar: A Journal of Germanic Studies*, Vol. 24, No. 4 (1988), pp. 310-343.

Grabo, Carl Henry, "Spinoza and Shelley," *Chicago Jewish Forum*, Vol. 1, No. 1 (Fall 1942), pp. 43-50.

> In Oko (1964), p. 261.

Graetz, Heinrich, "Baruch Spinoza: A Biographical Sketch," *The Israelite*, Vol. 14 (1868). 6 parts.

> In Oko (1964), p. 48, identifying this essay as being from the author's *Geschichte der Juden*, Bd. 10 (Leipzig, 1868).

Gram, Moltke S., "Spinoza, Substance and Predication," *Theoria*, Vol. 34 (1968), pp. 222-244.

Grange, Joseph, "Being, Feeling, and Environment," *Environmental Ethics*, Vol. 7 (Winter 1985), pp. 351-364.

> In *Philosopher's Index*, No. 138322, noting the author's comparison of Spinoza and Heidegger on the unity of reality, and his argument that this view provides a basis for ecology.

Grange, Joseph, "Spinoza's Scientia Intuitiva," *Philosophy and Theology*, Vol. 2 (Spring 1988), pp. 241-257.

Gray, Edward Dundas McQueen, *Old Testament Criticism: Its Rise and Progress from the Second Century to the End of the Eighteenth: A Historical Sketch* (New York: Harper, 1923).

> Includes a chapter on Spinoza, pp. 86-100.

Grayeff, Felix, *A Short Treatise on Ethics* (London: Duckworth, 1980).

> Includes a section on Spinoza, pp. 17-20, and other references.

Green, Thomas Hill, *Works*, Edited by R. L. Nettleship (London and New York: Longmans, Green and Co., 1908-1911). 3 vols.

> Sixth printing of the 1885-1888 edition. Includes a discussion of Spinoza's theory of the state, Vol. 2, pp. 355-365.

Green, Thomas Hill, *Lectures on the Principles of Political Obligation*, With preface by Bernard Bosanquet (New York: Longmans, Green and Co., 1937).

Reprints on pp. 49-59 the sections on Spinoza in Green's *Works*, Vol. 2, pp. 355-365.

Greene, Jesse A., *Spinoza's Conception of the Physical World*, Unpublished doctoral dissertation, University of Rochester, 1983.

Currently available from UMI (Order No. 83-21670).

Gregory, Brad S. *See* Spinoza, *Tractatus Theologico-Politicus* (1989).

Gregory, T. C. *See* Spinoza, *Ethics* (1959).

Grene, Marjorie (ed.), *Spinoza: A Collection of Critical Essays* (Notre Dame, IN: University of Notre Dame Press, 1979).

Reprint of the 1973 Doubleday (and Anchor Book) edition. Includes papers by R. Blair, E. Curley, A. Donagan, W. Earle, G. Floistad, H. Gilden, M. Gueroult, H. Hallett, S. Hampshire, M. Kneale, L. Kolaskowski, G. Parkinson, D. Savan, M. Wartofsky, and H. Wolfson.

Grene, Marjorie, and Debra Nails (eds.), *Spinoza and the Sciences*, Boston Studies in the Philosophy of Science, Vol. 91 (Dordrecht: D. Reidel Publishing Co., 1986).

In addition to the introduction by Grene, pp. xi-xix, includes papers by J. Agassi, J. Cook, H. Jonas, A. Lecrivain, G. Lloyd, A. Matheron, N. Maull, D. Nails, M. Paty, R. Popkin, D. Savan, H. Siebrand, and J. van Zandt.

Grew, Nehemiah. Cosmologia sacra: or a discourse of the universe as it is the creature and kingdom of God. Chiefly written, to demonstrate the truth and excellency of the Bible; which contains the laws of his kingdom in this lower world. In five books. ... London, Printed for W. Rogers, S. Smith, and B. Walford, 1701.

In Oko (1964), p. 396, who notes references to Spinoza on pp. 179-180 and 203.

Griffin, Edward Herrick, "A Comparison of Spinoza's *Ethics* and Spencer's *First Principles*," *The Psychological Bulletin*, Vol. 5 (1908), pp. 101-102 [sic].

In Oko (1964), p. 261.

Griffith, Gwilym O., *Makers of Modern Thought* (London: Butterworth Press, 1948).

In *Philosopher's Index*, No. 074439.

Groen, J. J., "Spinoza: 'Philosopher and Prophet," in Van der Bend (1974), pp. 69-81.

Groen, J. J., "Spinoza's Theory of Affects and Modern Psychobiology," in Wetlesen (1978), pp. 98-118.

Gruen, W., "Determinism, Fatalism, and Historical Materialism," *The Journal of Philosophy*, Vol. 33 (November 1936), pp. 617-628.

> A discussion of this article followed in Vol. 34 (January 1937), pp. 53-55.

Grunder, K., and W. Schmidt-Biggemann (eds.), *Spinoza in der Frühzeit seiner religiösen Wirkung* (Heidelberg, 1984).

> In Van der Werf (1984), No. 1820, citing three papers in English: Michael J. Petry, "Behmenism and Spinozism in the Religious Culture of the Netherlands, 1660-1730," pp. 111-147; S. Hutton, "Reason and Revelation in the Cambridge Platonists, and Their Reception of Spinoza," pp. 181-200; and J. D. Woodbridge, "Richard Simon's Reaction to Spinoza's *Tractatus Theologico-Politicus*," pp. 201-226.

Gruntfest, J., "Spinoza as Linguist," *Israel Oriental Studies*, Vol. 9 (1979), pp. 103-128.

> In Van der Werf (1984), No. 811.

Gueroult, Martial, *Descartes' Philosophy Interpreted According to the Order of Reasons*, Translated by Roger Ariew, with the assistance of Robert Ariew and Alan Donagan (Minneapolis: University of Minnesota Press, 1984). 2 vols.

> Translation of the second edition of *Descartes selon l'ordre des raisons* (1968). Vol. I is entitled, *The Soul and God*; Vol. II, *The Soul and the Body*. Includes many references to Spinoza throughout.

Gueroult, Martial, "Spinoza's Letter on the Infinite," in Grene (1979), pp. 182-212.

> Translated by Kathleen McLaughlin from the author's "La lettre de Spinoza sur l'infini," *Revue de métaphysic et de morale*, Vol. 71 (1966), pp. 385-411.

Gullvag, Ingemund and Jon Wetlesen (eds.), *In Sceptical Wonder: Inquiries into the Philosophy of Arne Naess on the Occasion of His 70th Birthday* (Oslo: Universitetsforlaget, 1982).

Includes papers by Einar Jahr, "Some Problems Concerning the Application of Modern Logic to the Philosophy of Spinoza," pp. 207-211 (with a reply by Arne Naess, pp. 211-212), and Ragnar Naess, "The Snout Beetles," pp. 213-219.

Gunn, J. Alexander, *Benedict Spinoza* (Melbourne: Macmillan & Co., in association with Melbourne University Press, 1925).

University of Melbourne Publications, No. 5. Kashap (1972), p. 352, cites an edition published in New York in 1925.

Gunn, J. Alexander, *The Problem of Time: An Historical and Critical Study* (London, 1929).

In Hertzberger (1950), No. 110, citing "numerous interesting references to Spinoza."

Gunn, J. Alexander, "Spinoza and the Present-Day Politics," *Contemporary Review*, Vol. 120 (1921), pp. 83-92.

Gunn, J. Alexander, "Spinoza," *Australasian Journal of Psychology and Philosophy*, Vol. 2, No. 1 (March 1924), pp. 23-42.

Gunton, Colin, "Rejection, Influence, and Development: Hartshorne in the History of Philosophy," *Process Studies*, Vol. 6 (Spring 1976), pp. 32-42.

In *Philosopher's Index*, No. 050877, noting a comparison of Hartshorne's ontology with that of Spinoza.

Gupta, Bina, "Brahman, God, Substance and Nature: Sankara and Spinoza," *Indian Philosophical Quarterly*, Vol. 11 (July 1984), pp. 265-284.

In *Philosopher's Index*, No. 129466.

Gupta, Bina, and W. C. Wilcox, "Are All Names of the Absolute Synonymous? Advaita Vedanta and Spinoza in Light of Frege and Quine," *Philosophy East and West*, Vol. 33, No. 3 (1983), pp. 285-293.

Gurdon, B. The pretended difficulties in natural and reveal'd religion no excuse for infidelity. 16 Sermons preach'd at the Lecture founded by Rob. Boyle. London, 1723.

In Hertzberger (1950), No. 816.

Gutmann, James. *See* Spinoza, *Ethics* (1949).

Guttmann, Julius, *Philosophies of Judaism: The History of Jewish Philosophy from Biblical Times to Franz Rosenzweig*, Translated by David W. Silverman, with introduction by Zwi Werblowsky (New York: Holt, Rinehart and Winston, 1964).

> Includes a chapter, "The Influence of Jewish Philosophy on Spinoza," pp. 265-284.

Hall, A. Rupert, and Marie Ross Hall, "Philosophy and Natural Philosophy: Boyle and Spinoza, " in *L'aventure de l'esprit: Mélanges Alexandre Koyré ...* (1964), Vol. II, pp. 241-256.

Hallett, H. F., *Aeternitas: A Spinozistic Study* (Oxford: Clarendon Press, 1930).

> Currently available from UMI Out-of-Print Books on Demand (Order No. OP49890).

Hallett, H. F., *Benedict de Spinoza: The Elements of His Philosophy* (London: The Athlone Press, University of London, 1957).

> Reprinted in Bristol by Thoemmes, 1989. Also currently available from UMI Out-of-Print Books on Demand (Order No. OP52976).

Hallett, H. F., *Creation, Emanation, and Salvation: A Spinozistic Study* (The Hague: Martinus Nijhoff, 1962).

Hallett, H. F., "Spinoza's Conception of Eternity," *Mind*, Vol. 37, No. 147 (July 1928), pp. 283-303.

Hallett, H. F., "Benedict Spinoza," in *Septimana Spinozana* (1933), pp. 296-305.

Hallett, H. F., "On Things in Themselves," *Philosophy*, Vol. 14 (1939), pp. 155-179.

Hallett, H. F., "Knowledge, Reality, and Objectivity," *Mind*, Vol. 49 (1940), Part I, pp. 170-188; Part II, pp. 303-332.

Hallett, H. F., "Some Recent Criticisms of Spinoza," *Mind*, Vol. 51 (1942), Part I (April), pp. 134-159; Part II (July), pp. 223-243; Part III (October), pp. 319-342; Vol. 52 (1943), Part IV (January), pp. 1-23.

Hallett, H. F., "Dr. Johnson's Refutation of Bishop Berkeley," *Mind*, Vol. 56 (1947), pp. 132-147.

In Rice (1967), p. 301.

Hallett, H. F., "On a Reputed Equivoque in the Philosophy of Spinoza," in Kashap (1972), pp. 168-188.

Originally in *The Review of Metaphysics*, Vol. 3 (1949-1950), pp. 189-212.

Hallett, H. F., "Substance and Its Modes," in Grene (1979), pp. 131-163.

A reprint of Hallett (1957), Chaps I-III, pp. 9-43.

Hamlyn, D. W., *A History of Western Philosophy* (New York: Viking, 1987).

Includes a section on Spinoza, pp. 148-157, in Chapter 10, "Rationalism."

Hammacher, Klaus (ed.), *Der transzendentale Gedanke* (Hamburg, 1981).

In Van der Werf (1984), No. 882, citing an essay by Errol E. Harris, "Fichte and Spinozism," pp. 407-420.

Hammacher, Klaus, "Spinoza's Conclusions Drawn from Systematic Reflection on the Affections: A Critical Review," in Van der Bend (1974), pp. 82-96.

Hammacher, Klaus, "The Cosmic Creed and Spinoza's Third Mode of Knowledge," in Hessing (1977), pp. 183-196.

Hammacher, Klaus, "Ambition and Social Engagement in Hobbes' and Spinoza's Political Thought," in De Deugd (1984), pp. 56-62.

Hammond, Albert L., *Ideas about Substance* (Baltimore: Johns Hopkins Press, 1969).

Includes a section on Spinoza, pp. 81-85, and other references.

Hampshire, Stuart, *Spinoza*, With a new introduction and revisions (Harmondsworth: Penguin Books, 1987).

Originally published in 1951 by Penguin Books and, in hardcover, by Faber and Faber.

Hampshire, Stuart, *The Age of Reason: The 17th Century Philosophers* (New York: A Mentor Book, The New American Library, 1956).

Includes an essay on Spinoza, pp. 99-105, followed by selections from his works.

Hampshire, Stuart, *Spinoza and the Idea of Freedom* (London: Oxford University Press, 1961).

> 21 pp. Originally in *Proceedings of the British Academy*, Vol. 46 (1960), pp. 195-215. Also reprinted in Strawson (1968), pp. 48-70; Kashap (1972), pp. 310-331; Hampshire (1972); and Grene (1979), pp. 297-317.

Hampshire, Stuart, *Freedom of Mind and Other Essays* (Princeton: Princeton University Press, 1971; Oxford: Oxford University Press, 1972).

> Includes Hampshire (1961) and Hampshire (1970).

Hampshire, Stuart, *Two Theories of Morality* (Oxford: Oxford University Press, 1977).

> Contrasts the moral philosophies of Aristotle and Spinoza.

Hampshire, Stuart, *Morality and Conflict* (Cambridge: Harvard University Press, 1983).

> Chapter 2, pp. 10-68, presents an amended version of the preceding book; pp. 45-68 focus on Spinoza.

Hampshire, Stuart, "A Kind of Materialism," *Proceedings and Addresses of the American Philosophical Association*, Vol. 43 (September 1970), pp. 5-23.

> Reprinted in Hampshire (1972). *See* Magill (1982).

Hampshire, Stuart, "Spinoza's Theory of Human Freedom," in Mandelbaum and Freeman (1975), pp. 35-48.

> Originally in *The Monist*, Vol. 55, No. 4 (October 1971), pp. 554-566.

Hampshire, Stuart, "The Political and Social Philosophy of Spinoza," in Rotenstreich and Schneider (1983), pp. 132-141.

> *See* Ben-Shlomo (1983) for a reply.

Hanak, Moroslav J., "The Enlightenment as Secularization of Baroque Eschatology in France and England," *International Studies in Philosophy*, Vol. 3 (Autumn 1971), pp. 83-109.

> In *Philosopher's Index*, No. 034314, citing references to Spinoza, Leibniz, and Locke.

Handyside, John, *The Historical Method in Ethics and Other Essays* (Liverpool: Liverpool University Press, 1920).

> Includes a section on Spinoza, pp. 40-45.

Hankins, James, John Monfasani, and Frederick Purnell, Jr. (eds.), *Supplementum Festiuum: Studies in Honor of Paul Oskar Kristeller* (Binghamton, NY: Center for Medieval and Early Renaissance Studies, State University of New York at Binghamton, 1987).

> Includes an essay by Thomas Carson Mark, "Spinoza on the Power and Eternity of the Intellect," pp. 589-610.

Hansen, Oskar, "Spinoza's Proof of an External World," in Van der Bend (1974), pp. 97-102.

Hardin, C. L., "Spinoza on Immortality and Time," in Shahan and Biro (1978), Chap. 6, pp. 129-138.

> Originally in the *Southwestern Journal of Philosophy*, Vol. 8 (Fall 1977), pp. 129-138.

Hardin, William J., *Free Will, Determinism, and the Nature of Education: The Philosophical Viewpoints of Benedict Spinoza and John Dewey*, Unpublished doctoral dissertation, St. Louis University, 1971.

> Currently available from UMI (Order No. 72-23946).

[Hare, Francis] The difficulties and discouragements which attend the study of the Scriptures in the way of private judgment ... In a letter to a young clergyman. By a presbyter of the Church of England. The second edition. London, Printed for John Baker, 1714.

> 47 pp. In Oko (1964), p. 350.

Hare, Peter H. (ed.), *Doing Philosophy Historically* (Buffalo, NY: Prometheus Books, 1988).

> Includes three papers focusing on Bennett (1984): Daniel Garber, "Does History Have a Future? Some Reflections on Bennett and Doing Philosophy Historically," pp. 27-43; Jonathan Ree, "History, Philosophy, and Interpretation: Some Reactions to Jonathan Bennett's *Study of Spinoza's Ethics*," pp. 44-61; and Jonathan Bennett, "Response to Garber and Ree," pp. 62-69.

Harris, Errol E., *Nature, Mind and Modern Science* (London: George Allen & Unwin, 1954).

> In Bowman (1966), p. 392, and in Greene (1983), p. 213.

Harris, Errol E., *Salvation from Despair: A Reappraisal of Spinoza's Philosophy*, International Archives of the History of Ideas, No. 59 (The Hague: Martinus Nijhoff, 1973).

Harris, Errol E., *Is There an Esoteric Doctrine in the Tractatus Theologico-Politicus?* Mededelingen XXXVIII vanwege het Spinozahuis (Leiden: E. J. Brill, 1978).

Harris, Errol E., "Comment on Watt," *Canadian Journal of Philosophy*, Vol. 2, No. 2 (December 1972), pp. 191-197.

> *See* Watt (1973) for a reply.

Harris, Errol E., "The Order and Connection of Ideas," in Van der Bend (1974), pp. 103-113.

Harris, Errol E., "Spinoza's Theory of Human Immortality," in Mandelbaum and Freeman (1975), pp. 245-262.

> Originally in *The Monist*, Vol. 55, No. 4 (October 1971), pp. 668-685. A version of the 1971 paper also appeared as Chap. 11 in the author's *Salvation from Despair* (1972).

Harris, Errol E., "The Body-Mind Problem," in Wilbur (1976), pp. 13-28.

Harris, Errol E., "Atheism and Theism," *Tulane Studies in Philosophy*, Vol. 26 (1977), pp. 1-157.

Harris, Errol E., "Finite and Infinite in Spinoza's System," in Hessing (1977), pp. 197-211.

Harris, Errol E., "The Infinity of the Attributes and *Idea Ideae*," *Neue Hefte für Philosophie*, Vol. 12 (1977), pp. 9-20.

Harris, Errol E., "The Essence of Man and the Subject of Consciousness," in Wetlesen (1978), pp. 119-135.

Harris, Errol E., "Fichte and Spinozism," in Hammacher (1981), pp. 407-420.

Harris, Errol E., "Spinoza's Treatment of Natural Law," in De Deugd (1984), pp. 63-72.

Harris, Errol E., "The Concept of Substance in Spinoza and Hegel," in Giancotti Boscherini (1985), pp. 51-70.

Harris, Errol E., "Method and Metaphysics in Spinoza," in *Studia Spinozana*, Vol. 2 (1986), pp. 129-150.

Harris, Errol E., "Schelling and Spinoza: Spinozism and Dialectic," in Curley and Moreau (1990), pp. 359-372.

Harris, John. The atheistical objections, against the being of a God, and His attributes, fairly considered, and fully refuted. In eight sermons, preach'd in the Cathedral-Church of St. Paul, London, 1698. Being the seventh year of the lecture founded by the Honourable Robert Boyle, Esq; By John Harris ... London, Printed by J. L. for Richard Wilkin, 1698.

> In Oko (1964), p. 388; in Hertzberger (1950), No. 817.

Harris, Maurice Henry, *Modern Jewish History from the Renaissance to the World War* (New York, 1910).

> Includes a section, "Spinoza and His Contemporaries," pp. 63-70.

Hart, Alan, *Spinoza's Ethics, Part I and II: A Platonic Commentary* (Leiden: E. J. Brill, 1983).

Hart, Alan, "Leibnitz on Spinoza's Concept of Substance," *Studia Leibnitiana*, Vol. 14, No. 1 (1982), pp. 73-86.

Hart, Alan, "Melville and Spinoza," in *Studia Spinozana*, Vol. 5 (1989), pp. 43-58.

Harte, Frederick Edward, *The Philosophical Treatment of Divine Personality from Spinoza to Hermann Lotze*, With a foreword by Herbert L. Stewart (London: C. E. Kelly, 1913).

> Includes a section on Spinoza and Leibniz, pp. 29-59.

Hartnack, Justus, *History of Philosophy* (Odense, Denmark: Odense University Press, 1976).

> Includes the sections, "Spinoza's Naturalism," pp. 96-104, and "Spinoza's Moral Philosophy," pp. 105-110.

Hartshorne, Charles, *Anselm's Discovery: A Re-Examination of the Ontological Proof for God's Existence* (LaSalle, IL: Open Court, 1965).

> Includes a section on Spinoza, pp. 173-176, and many other references.

Hartshorne, Charles, *Creative Synthesis and Philosophic Method* (London: SCM Press, 1970).

> Includes many references to Spinoza.

Hartshorne, Charles, *Aquinas to Whitehead: Seven Centuries of Metaphysics of Religion* (Milwaukee, WI: Marquette University Press, 1976).

> In *Philosopher's Index*, No. 016209.

Hartshorne, Charles, *Insights and Oversights of Great Thinkers: An Evaluation of Western Philosophy* (Albany, NY: State University of New York Press, 1983).

> Includes a chapter, "Spinoza: First of the Moderns or Last of the Medievals?" on pp. 118-126.

Hartshorne, Charles, "Theism in Asian and Western Thought," *Philosophy East and West*, Vol. 28 (1978), pp. 401-412.

> In Van der Werf (1984), No. 889.

Hartshorne, Charles, and William L. Reese, *Philosophers Speak of God* (Chicago: University of Chicago Press, 1953).

> Includes a section on Spinoza, pp. 189-197, and many other references.

Harvey, Warren Zev, "A Portrait of Spinoza as a Maimonidean," *Journal of the History of Philosophy*, Vol. 19, No. 2 (April 1981), pp. 151-172.

Harvey, Warren Zev, "Maimonides and Spinoza on the Knowledge of Good and Evil," in Dan (1989), Vol. II.

Haserot, Francis S., *Essays on the Logic of Being* (New York: Macmillan, 1932).

> In Greene (1983), p. 214.

Haserot, Francis S., "Spinoza's Definition of Attribute," in Kashap (1972), pp. 28-42.

> Originally in *The Philosophical Review*, Vol. 62 (October 1953), pp. 499-513.

Haserot, Francis S., "Spinoza and the Status of Universals," in Kashap (1972), pp. 43-67.

Originally in *The Philosophical Review*, Vol. 59 (October 1950), pp. 469-492.

Hassing, R. F., "The Use and Non-Use of Physics in Spinoza's Ethics," *Southwestern Journal of Philosophy*, Vol. 11, No. 2 (Summer 1980), pp. 41-70.

Hastings, James (ed.), *Encyclopedia of Religion and Ethics* (New York: Charles Scribner's Sons, 1928). 13 vols.

Includes an article on Spinoza by E. E. Kellett, Vol. XI, pp. 768-784, as well as many other references.

Hauser, Helen A., "Spinozan Philosophy in *Pierre*," *American Literature*, Vol. 49, No. 1 (March 1977), pp. 49-56.

Hawton, Hector, *Philosophy for Pleasure* (London: Watts & Co., 1949).

Includes a section on Spinoza, "The Monistic Solution," pp. 41-44, and other references.

Hayes, Frank A., *Platonic Elements in Spinoza's Theory of Method*, Unpublished doctoral dissertation, Indiana University, 1957.

Currently available from UMI (Order No. 00-22687).

Hayes, Frank A. *See* Spinoza, *Earlier Philosophical Writings* (1963).

Haynes, E. S. P., *Religious Persecution: A Study in Political Psychology* (London, 1904).

In Hertzberger (1950), No. 114, citing a discussion of the *Tractatus Theologico-Politicus.*

Hazard, Paul, *European Thought in the Eighteenth Century: From Montesquieu to Lessing* (New Haven, CT: Yale University Press, 1954).

Includes many references to Spinoza.

Headstrom, B. R., "Spinoza and the Cartesian Physics," *The Open Court*, Vol. 43 (September 1929), pp. 571-575.

Hearnshaw, F. J. C. (ed.), *The Social and Political Ideas of Some Great Thinkers of the Sixteenth and Seventeenth Centuries* (London: George G. Harrap & Co., 1926).

Includes a chapter, "Benedict Spinoza," by A. D. Lindsay, pp. 204-220. Barnes & Noble published an edition of this work in New York in 1949.

Hecker, Julius F., *Moscow Dialogues: Discussions on Red Philosophy*, With a foreword by John MacMurray (London: Chapman and Hall, 1933).

> Includes a discussion of the relationship of Spinoza's philosophy and dialectical materialism, pp. 55-63, and other references.

Hedge, Frederic Henry (ed.), *Recent Inquiries in Theology, By Eminent English Churchmen*, Being "Essays and Reviews," 2nd American Edition (Boston: Walker, Wise, 1861).

> In Oko (1964), p. 466. *See* Forster (1861).

Hedman, Carl G., "Toward a Spinozistic Modification of Skinner's Theory of Man," *Inquiry*, Vol. 18, No. 3 (Autumn 1975), pp. 325-335.

Hegel, G. W. F., *Lectures on the History of Philosophy*, Translated by E. S. Haldane and F. H. Simson (New York: The Humanities Press, 1955). 3 vols.

> Includes a section on Spinoza, Vol. 3, pp. 252-289, and many other references.

Heine, Heinrich, *Religion and Philosophy in Germany*, Translated by John Snodgrass, with a new introduction by Ludwig Marcuse (Boston: Beacon Press, 1959).

> Includes a section on Spinoza, pp. 69-80.

Heinekamp, A. (ed.), *Leibniz et la Renaissance*, Colloque à Domaine de Seillac (France), 17-21 June 1981 (Wiesbaden: Franz Steiner, 1983).

> Includes an essay by H. G. Hubbeling, "The Understanding of Nature in Renaissance Philosophy: Leibniz and Spinoza," pp. 210-220.

Heinekamp, A. See *Studia Spinozana*, Vol. 6 (1990).

Heinemann, Fritz, "An Unknown Manuscript of the Oldest Biography of Spinoza," *Tijdschrift voor Filosofie*, Vol. 1 (1939), pp. 378-386.

> In Walther (1991), p. 12.

Heller, Bernard, *Is Spinozism Compatible with Judaism?* (New York: Bloch, 1927).

> 40 pp. Reprinted from the *Yearbook* of the Central Conference of American Rabbis, Vol. XXXVII. Probably also the same as the author's "Spinoza and Judaism," a paper read at the 38th Conference of American Rabbis and published in *American Israelite*, Vol. 74, No. 7 (1927).

Heller, Bernard, *Stoic Elements in the Philosophy of Spinoza*, Unpublished doctoral dissertation, University of Michigan, 1932.

Heller, Bernard, "Spinoza and the Kabbalah," *Jewish Institute Quarterly*, Vol. 4 (1926), pp. 9-15.

> In Oko (1964), p. 380.

Heller, Bernard, "Spinoza and the Enlightenment," *Michigan Alumnus Quarterly Review*, Vol 54, No. 16 (March 1948), pp. 139-147.

> In Oko (1964), p. 332.

Hendel, Charles W., "Goethe's *Faust* and Philosophy," *Philosophy and Phenomenological Research*, Vol. 10 (December 1949), pp. 157-171.

> In *Philosopher's Index*, No. 001734.

Henle, Mary, "Psychological Concept of Freedom: Footnote to Spinoza," *Social Research*, Vol. 27 (1960), pp. 359-374.

Henrard, R. See *Studia Spinozana*, Vol. 5 (1989).

Henry, Caleb Sprague, *An Epitome of the History of Philosophy: Being the Work Adopted by the University of France for the Instruction in the Colleges and High Schools*, Translated with additions, and a continuation of the history from the time of Reid to the present day (New York: Harper & Brothers, 1842). 2 vols.

> In Oko (1964), p. 140, citing a section on Spinoza, Vol. 2, pp. 72-76.

Hensley, Michael L., *Holism as Expressed in the Philosophy of Jan C. Smuts and the Psychology of Abraham Maslow*, Unpublished doctoral dissertation, United States International University, 1973.

> Includes a discussion of the monism of Spinoza, Leibniz, Hegel, and Schelling, and their influence on Smuts and Maslow. Currently available from UMI (Order No. 73-22670).

Herschel, J. F. W., *A Preliminary Discourse on the Study of Natural Philosophy* (London, 1830).

> In Hertzberger (1950), No. 117.

Hertzberger (1950). *See* Wolf (1950).

Hessing, Siegfried (ed.), *Speculum Spinozanum, 1677-1977*, With foreword by Huston Smith (London: Routledge & Kegan Paul, 1977).

Includes four papers by Hessing— "Prologue with Spinozana: Parallels via East and West," pp. 1-62; "Freud's Relation with Spinoza," pp. 224-239; "*Proton axioma kai proton pseudos*," pp. 240-322; and "Epilogue: Ban Invalid after Death," pp. 572-580 (which was also published under the title, "Spinoza: Ban Invalid after Death," *Giornale critico della filosofia italiana*, Vol. 10 [1979], pp. 158-167). This volume also includes papers in English by W. Bernard, L. Bickel, W. Brann, J. Collins, E. Curley, W. Durant, P. Eisenberg, G. Floistad, E. Giancotti Boscherini, J. Goncalves, K. Hammacher, E. Harris, H. Hubbeling, Hu-Shih, G. Kline, R. Misrahi, A. Naess, A. Offenberg, H. Saito, G. van Suchtelen, J. Wetlesen, P. Wienpahl, and C. Wilson.

Hessing, Siegfried, "A New Look at Maimonides," *Giornale critico della filosofia italiana*, Vol. 8 (October-December, 1977), pp. 383-389.

Includes references to Spinoza.

Hicks, G. Dawes, *Critical Realism: Studies in the Philosophy of Mind and Nature* (London: Macmillan and Co., 1938).

Includes the author's essay, "The 'Modes' of Spinoza and the 'Monads' of Leibniz," pp. 305-338; originally in the *Proceedings of the Aristotelian Society*, Vol. 18 (1918), pp. 329-362.

Hicks, G. Dawes, "Benedictus de Spinoza," *Nature*, Vol. 119 (March 5, 1927), pp. 357-360.

Hickes, George. Two treatises, one of the Christian priesthood, the other of the dignity of the episcopal order. Formerly written, and now published to obviate the erroneous opinions, fallacious reasonings, and bold and false assertations, in a late book, entituled, The rights of the Christian church. With a large prefatory discourse, wherein is contained an answer to the said book. All written by George Hickes, D. D. London, Printed by W. B. for Richard Sare, 1707.

In Oko (1964), p. 350. *See* Carroll (1709).

Hill, J. Thoughts concerning God and Nature. In answer to Lord Bolingbroke's philosophy. London, 1755.

In Hertzberger (1950), No. 822, citing sections on Spinoza, pp. 245-260 and pp. 376 ff., and other references.

Himmelfarb, Milton, "Spinoza and the Colonel," *Commentary*, Vol. 57, No. 3 (1974), pp. 67-70.

[Hitchcock, Ethan Allan] *The Doctrines of Spinoza and Swedenborg Identified; In So Far as They Claim a Scientific Ground.* In four letters. By *.*.*., United States Army. (Boston: Munroe & Francis; New York: C. S. Francis & Co., 1846).

> 36 pp. In Van der Linde, No. 331; in Oko (1964), p. 236. Nails (1986), p. 309, cites *Four Letters* (Boston, 1846), pp. 187-192.

[Hitchcock, Ethan Allan] Swedenborg, a Hermetic Philosopher. Being a sequel to Remarks on alchemy and the alchemists. Showing that Emanuel Swedenborg was a hermetic philosopher and that his writings may be interpreted from the point of view of hermetic philosophy. With a chapter comparing Swedenborg and Spinoza. By the author of Remarks on alchemy and the alchemists. (New York: D. Appleton, 1858).

> In Oko (1964), p. 236. An 1865 edition, published in New York by James Miller, is currently available from UMI Out-of-Print Books on Demand (Order No. OP67749.)

Hittell, John S., *A Plea for Pantheism* (New York: C. Blanchard, 1857).

> In Oko (1964), p. 442.

Hocking, William Ernest, *Types of Philosophy* (New York: Charles Scribner's Sons, 1929).

> Includes many references to Spinoza.

Hoffding, Harald, *A History of Modern Philosophy: A Sketch of the History of Philosophy from the Close of the Renaissance to Our Own Day*, Translated by B. E. Meyer (New York: Dover Publications, 1955). 2 vols.

> Reprint of the 1900 translation from the Danish edition of 1894-1895. Includes a chapter on Spinoza, Vol. l, pp. 292-331.

Hoffheimer, Michael H., "The Four Equals: Analyzing Spinoza's Idea of Equality," *Philosophia* (Israel), Vol. 15, No. 3 (December 1985), pp. 237-249.

Hoffheimer, Michael H., "Locke, Spinoza, and the Idea of Political Equality," *History of Political Thought*, Vol. 7, No. 2 (Summer 1986), pp. 341-360.

Hoffmann, S. M., *The Mind-Body Problem in Spinoza's Ethics*, Unpublished doctoral dissertation, St. Louis, MO, 1971.

> In Van der Werf (1984), No. 930.

Holland, A. J. (ed.), *Philosophy, Its History and Historiography* (Dordrecht: D. Reidel Publishing Co., 1985).

> Includes a paper by Richard Francks, "Caricatures in the History of Philosophy: The Case of Spinoza," pp. 179-197, and other references.

Hollingworth, Harry Lewis, *Psychology and Ethics: A Study of the Sense of Obligation* (New York: Ronald Press, 1949).

> In *Philosopher's Index*, No. 021294, citing references to Spinoza and W. McDougall.

Holmes, Edmond, *All Is One: A Plea for the Higher Pantheism* (New York: E. P. Dutton [192?]).

> In Oko (1964), p. 442.

Holyoake, George Jacob. *See* Spinoza, *Treatise on Politics* (1853).

Holz, H., and E. Wolf-Gazo (eds.), *Whitehead und der Prozessbegriff/Whitehead and the Idea of Process: Proceedings of the First International Whitehead Symposium, 1981* (Freiburg: Karl Alber, 1984).

> Includes an essay by H. G. Hubbeling, "Whitehead and Spinoza," pp. 375-385.

Honderich, Ted (ed.), *Philosophy Through Its Past* (Harmondsworth: Penguin Books, 1984).

> Includes an essay by T. L. S. Sprigge, "Spinoza: His Identity Theory."

Hooker, Michael, "The Deductive Character of Spinoza's Metaphysics," in Kennington (1980), Chap. 2, pp. 17-34.

Horn, W. M., *Substance and Mode: A Spinozistic Study*, Unpublished doctoral dissertation, Providence, RI, 1978.

> In Van der Werf (1984), No. 939.

Horn, Walter, "A New Proof for the Physical World," *Philosophy and Phenomenological Research*, Vol. 44 (June 1984), pp. 531-538.

> In *Philosopher's Index*, No. 125424.

Hoslett, Schuyler Dean, "Spinoza and Lucretius," *The Personalist*, Vol. 22 (Spring 1941), pp. 159-168.

Hosmer, James Kendall, *The Story of the Jews, Ancient, Medieval, and Modern* (New York and London: G. P. Putnam's Sons, 1887).

> Includes a chapter primarily on Spinoza, pp. 215-231.

Howe, John. The living temple: or, A designed improvement of that notion that a good man is the temple of God ... by John Howe ... London, Printed by J. H. for R. Clavell, J. Robinson, and A. and J. Churchill, 1702. 2 vols.

> In Oko (1964), p. 332. Van der Linde (No. 340), whose citation is somewhat different, cites the titles of each "part" (i.e., volume): I. Concerning God's Existence, and his conversibleness with man. Against Atheisme, or the Epicurian Deism. II. Containing animadversions on Spinoza, and a french writer pretending to confute him. Both Kellett in Hastings (1928) and Hertzberger (1950), No. 661, give 1675 as the date of this book.

[Howe, John] The works of ... J. H. ... With his funeral sermon by Mr. Spademan. To which are prefix'd, Memoirs of the life of the author, collected by E. Calamy. London, 1724. 2 vols.

> In Oko (1964), p. 507.

Howe, John, *Works*, With a preface by H. Rogers (London, 1862-1863). 6 vols.

> In Hertzberger (1950), No. 660, noting that Vol. III, pp. 221-271, presents "The living temple, part II. Containing Animadversiones on Spinoza and a French writer pretending to confute him." The French writer is identified as Noel Aubert de Versé in his *L'impie convaincu ou dissertation contre Spinoza* (Amsterdam, 1684); also in Hertzberger (1950), No. 737.

Hubbard, Elbert, *Little Journeys to the Homes of the Great Philosophers: Spinoza*, Vol. 14, No. 5 (East Aurora, NY: The Roycrofters, May 1904).

> This self-contained soft-cover publication numbers the pages on Spinoza as pp. 119-151.

Hubbeling, H. G., *Spinoza's Methodology*, 2nd Edition (Assen, The Netherlands: Van Gorcum & Co., 1967).

Hubbeling, H. G., *Principles of the Philosophy of Religion* (Assen, The Netherlands: Van Gorcum & Co., 1987).

Hubbeling, H. G., "The Application of Spinoza's Methodology in Theology," *Acta Spinozana*, Vol. 3 (1964), pp. 7-13; Vol. 4 (1964), pp. 11-16.

> In Rice (1967), p. 302.

Hubbeling, H. G., "Logic and Experience in Spinoza's Mysticism," in Van der Bend (1974), pp. 126-143.

Hubbeling, H. G., "The Discussions at the Spinoza Symposium in Amersfoort, September 10-13, 1973," in Van der Bend (1974), pp. 184-188.

Hubbeling, H. G., "The Development of Spinoza's Axiomatic (Geometric) Method: The Reconstructed Geometric Proof of the Second Letter of Spinoza's Correspondence and Its Relation to Earlier and Later Versions," *Revue internationale de philosophie*, Vol. 31 (1977), pp. 53-68.

Hubbeling, H. G., "The Logical and Experiential Roots of Spinoza's Mysticism: An Answer to Jon Wetlesen," in Hessing (1977), pp. 323-329.

Hubbeling, H. G., "Spinoza's Life: A Synopsis of Sources and Some Documents," *Giornale critico della filosofia italiana*, Vol. 8 (October-December 1977), pp. 390-409.

Hubbeling, H. G., "Short Survey of Recent Spinoza Research," in Wetlesen (1978), pp. 7-18.

Hubbeling, H. G., "The Understanding of Nature in Renaissance Philosophy: Leibniz and Spinoza," in Heinekamp (1983), pp. 210-220.

Hubbeling, H. G., "Whitehead and Spinoza," in Holz and Wolf-Gazo (1984), pp. 375-385.

Hubbeling, H. G., "Today's Western Spinozism," in De Deugd (1984), pp. 7-13.

Hubbeling, H. G., "Philopater: A Dutch Materialistic Interpretation of Spinoza in the Seventeenth Century," in Giancotti Boscherini (1985), pp. 489-514.

Hubbeling, H. G., "The Third Way of Knowledge (Intuition) in Spinoza," in *Studia Spinozana*, Vol. 2 (1986), pp. 219-231.

Hubbeling, H. G., "Spinozism and Spinozistic Studies in the Netherlands Since World War II," in Curley and Moreau (1990), pp. 381-394.

[Huber, Marie] The world unmask'd: or, The philosopher the greatest cheat; in twenty-four dialogues ... To which is added, The state of souls separated from their bodies ... In answer to ... An enquiry into origenism ... Translated from the French [by B. Mandeville]. London, Printed for A. Millar, 1736.

> In Oko (1964), p. 351.

Humber, James M., "Spinoza's Proof of God's Necessary Existence," *The Modern Schoolman*, Vol. 49 (March 1972), pp. 221-233.

Hunt, John, *Pantheism and Christianity* (London: Isbister, 1884).

> In Hertzberger (1950), No. 248, citing a section on Spinoza, pp. 219-242, as well as many other references. Wetlesen (1968), p. 11, cites an 1866 edition, with pp. 214-240 on Spinoza.

Hunter, Graeme (ed.), *Spinoza: The Enduring Questions*, Essays in Honor of David Savan (Toronto: University of Toronto Press, 1991).

> In addition to Hunter's "Spinoza on the Origin of Societies," includes papers by L. Byrne, E. Curley, J. Morrison, D. Nesher, D. Odegard, D. Savan, and M. Walther.

Hurst, John Fletcher, *History of Rationalism: Embracing a Survey of the Present State of Protestant Theology*, With an appendix of literature, revised and enlarged from the 3rd American edition (London: Trübner, 1867).

> Includes a section on Spinoza, pp. 84-91.

Hu-Shih, "Spinoza and Chuang Tzu," in Hessing (1977), pp. 330-332.

Husik, Isaac, *Philosophical Essays: Ancient, Medieval and Modern*, Edited by Milton C. Nahm and Leo Strauss (Oxford: B. Blackwell, 1952).

> Includes a chapter, "Maimonides and Spinoza on the Interpretation of the Bible," pp. 141-159, originally in Supplement No. 1, *Journal of the American Oriental Society*, Vol. 55 (September 1935), pp. 22-40. This book is currently available from UMI Out-of-Print Books on Demand (Order No. OP54085).

Husik, Isaac, "Spinoza, Apostle of Freedom," in *Baruch Spinoza* (Spinoza Institute of America, 1933).

Husted, James H., "Spinoza's Conception of the Attributes of Substance," *Proceedings of the Catholic Philosophical Association*, Vol. 61 (1987), pp. 121-131.

> In *Philosopher's Index*, No. 160986.

[Hutcheson, Francis] An Essay on the Nature and Conduct of the Passions and Affections. London, 1728.

> In Hertzberger (1950), No. 826. The third edition, published in London by
> A. Ward in 1742, is currently available from UMI Out-of-Print Books on
> Demand (Order No. OP22658).

[Hutchinson, J.] The religion of Satan, or Antichrist, delineated ... The use of reason recovered, by the data in Christianity. London, 1736.

> In Hertzberger (1950), No. 827.

Hutton, S., "Reason and Revelation in the Cambridge Platonists, and Their Reception of Spinoza," in Grunder and Schmidt-Biggemann (1984), pp. 181-200.

Hutton, S., "The Prophetic Imagination: A Comparative Study of Spinoza and the Cambridge Platonist, John Smith," in De Deugd (1984), pp. 73-81.

Hyman, Arthur, "Spinoza's Dogmas of Universal Faith in the Light of Their Medieval Jewish Background," in Altmann (1963), pp. 183-195.

> An earlier version was presented under the same title at Congrès interna-
> tional de philosophie médiévale (Cologne, 1961) and published in P.
> Wilpert (ed.), *Die Metaphysik in Mittelalter* (Berlin, 1963), pp. 731-736.

Inwood, M. J., *Hegel* (London: Routledge & Kegan Paul, 1983).

> Includes many references to Spinoza.

Iverach, James, *Descartes, Spinoza and the New Philosophy* (Edinburgh: T. & T. Clark, 1904).

Jackson, Reginald, "The Doctrine of Substance in Descartes and Spinoza," *Australasian Journal of Philosophy*, Vol. 4 (1926).

> In Radner (1971), p. 350.

Jacob, Margaret C., *The Radical Enlightenment: Pantheists, Freemasons and Republicans* (London: Allen & Unwin, 1981).

> In Van der Werf (1984), No. 987.

Jacob, Margaret C., "Science and Social Passion: The Case of Seventeenth Century England," *Journal of the History of Ideas*, Vol. 43 (April-June 1982), pp. 331-339.

> In *Philosopher's Index*, No. 103794.

Jacobi, F. H. *See* Valleé (1988) and Willis (1870).

Jacobs, Joseph, *Jewish Contributions to Civilization: An Estimate* (Philadelphia: The Jewish Publication Society of America, 1919).

> In Hertzberger (1950), No. 219, citing many references to Spinoza. The preface identifies the contents as "studies which appeared in the *Journal of the Anthropological Institute* and were afterwards republished in *Jewish Statistics*, 1891."

Jahr, Einar, "Some Problems Concerning the Application of Modern Logic to the Philosophy of Spinoza," in Gullvag and Wetlesen (1982), pp. 207-211.

Janet, Paul, "French Thought and Spinozism," *The Contemporary Review*, Vol. 29 (1877), pp. 1072-1091.

> Melamed (1933), p. 381, cites Paul Janet, "History of Spinozism in France," *Review of Philosophy*, Vol. 13.

Janet, Paul, and Gabriel Seailles, *A History of the Problems of Philosophy*, Translated by Ada Monahan, edited by Henry Jones (London and New York: Macmillan and Co., 1902). 2 vols.

> In Oko (1964), p. 264, citing many references to Spinoza in Vol. 2.

Jarrett, Charles E., *A Study of Spinoza's Metaphysics*, Unpublished doctoral dissertation, University of California, Berkeley, 1974.

Jarrett, Charles E., "A Note on Spinoza's Ontology," *Philosophical Studies*, Vol. 29 (June 1976), pp. 415-418.

Jarrett, Charles E., "Spinoza's Ontological Argument," *Canadian Journal of Philosophy*, Vol. 6 (December 1976), pp. 685-692.

Jarrett, Charles E., "The Concepts of Substance and Mode in Spinoza," *Philosophia* (Israel), Vol. 7 (March 1977), pp. 83-105.

Jarrett, Charles E., "Some Remarks on the 'Objective' and 'Subjective' Interpretation of Attributes," *Inquiry*, Vol. 20 (Winter 1977), pp. 447-456.

Jarrett, Charles E., "The Logical Structure of Spinoza's *Ethics*, Part I," *Synthèse*, Vol. 37 (January 1978), pp. 15-65.

Jarrett, Charles E., "On the Rejection of Spinozistic Dualism in the *Ethics*," *The Southern Journal of Philosophy*, Vol. 20, No. 2 (Summer 1982), pp. 153-175.

Jaspers, Karl, *The Great Philosophers*, Edited by Hannah Arendt, translated by Ralph Manheim (New York: Harcourt, Brace & World, 1966).

> Includes a section on Spinoza, Vol. 2, pp. 273-387. A number of authors also cite Jaspers, Karl, *Spinoza*, Edited by Hannah Arendt, translated by Ralph Manheim (New York: Harcourt Brace Jovanovich, 1974).

Jessop, T. E. *See* Spinoza, *Spinoza On Freedom of Thought* (1962).

Joachim, Harold H., *A Study of the Ethics of Spinoza* (Oxford: Clarendon Press, 1901).

> Currently available from UMI Out-of-Print Books on Demand (Order No. OP29256).

Joachim, Harold H., *The Nature of Truth*, 2nd Edition (Oxford: Clarendon Press, 1939).

> Includes a discussion of Spinoza's theory of error, pp. 148-163.

Joachim, Harold H., *Spinoza's Tractatus de Intellectus Emendatione: A Commentary* (Oxford: Clarendon Press, 1958).

Jocobs, L., "Spinoza," in Goldwater (1962).

Johnston, W., "The Present Position of the Philosophy of Spinoza," *Critical Review*, Vol. 13 (1906), pp. 3 ff.

Jonas, Hans, *Philosophical Essays: From Ancient Creed to Technological Man* (Englewood Cliffs, NJ: Prentice Hall, 1974).

Includes a chapter, "Spinoza and the Theory of Organism," pp. 206-223. Originally in the *Journal of the History of Philosophy* Vol. 3, No. 1 (April 1965), pp. 43-58; reprinted in Spicker (1970) and in Grene (1979), pp. 259-278.

Jonas, Hans, *The Phenomenon of Life* (New York: Dell, 1966).

In Greene (1983), p. 214.

Jonas, Hans, "Parallelism and Complementarity: The Psycho-Physical Problem in the Succession of Niels Bohr," in Kennington (1980), Chap. 8, pp. 121-130.

Also published under the title, "Parallelism and Complementarity: The Psycho-Physical Problem in Spinoza and in the Succession of Niels Bohr," in Grene and Nails (1986), pp. 237-247.

[Jones, Stephen] A new biographical dictionary; or, Pocket compendium: containing a brief account of the lives and writings of the most eminent persons in every age and nation ... London, Printed for G. G. and J. Robinson, J. Wallis, J. Scatcherd, and E. Newberry, 1794.

Includes a paragraph on Spinoza. This book went through many editions; Oko (1964), p. 49, cites this edition, as well as the third (London: Printed by T. Bensley, for G. G. and J. Robinson, etc., 1799) and the seventh (London: Printed for Longman, Hurst, Rees, Orme, and Brown, etc., 1822).

Jones, William Thomas, *A History of Western Philosophy*, 2nd Edition (New York: Harcourt, Brace and World, 1969). 4 vols.

Includes a chapter on Spinoza, Vol. 3, pp. 192-218.

Jongeneelen, Gerrit H., "The Translator of Spinoza's *Short Treatise*," in *Studia Spinozana*, Vol. 2 (1986), pp. 249-264.

Jongeneelen, Gerrit H., "An Unknown Pamphlet of Adriann Koerbagh," in *Studia Spinozana*, Vol. 3 (1987), pp. 405-415.

Jouffroy, Theodore Simon, *Introduction to Ethics, Including a Critical Survey of Moral Systems*, Translated by William H. Chenning (Boston: Hilliard, Gray, 1840). 2 vols.

Reprinted under the same title in Boston by J. Monroe and Company, 1848. Includes two lectures on Spinoza.

Jowett, Benjamin, *Sermons, Biographical and Miscellaneous*, Edited by W. H. Fremantle (New York: Dutton, 1899).

Includes a sermon, "John Bunyan and Benedict Spinoza," pp. 44-64.

Kahn, Joseph, *Spinoza's Idea of God*, Unpublished doctoral dissertation, New York University, 1904.

Kajanto, Iiro, "Aspects of Spinoza's Latinity," *Arctos* (Helsinki), Vol. 13 (1979), pp. 49-83.

Kallen, Horace Meyer, "Appreciation of Spinoza," *The Spinoza Quarterly*, Tercentenary Issue, Vol. 2, No. 2 (November 1932).

In Feuer (1979), p. 77.

Kallen, Horace Meyer, "Spinoza: Three Hundred Years After," *The Menorah Journal*, Vol. 21 (April 1933), pp. 1-6.

Kallisch, M. M., *Path and Goal: A Discussion on the Elements of Civilization and the Conditions of Happiness* (London: Longmans, Green and Co., 1880).

In Oko (1964), p. 443, citing references to Spinoza in Chap. IX, "Pantheism," pp. 377-417.

Kalmar, Martin, *Some Collision Theories of the Seventeenth Century: Mathematicism vs. Mathematical Physics*, Unpublished doctoral dissertation, Johns Hopkins University, 1981.

Includes material on Spinoza. Currently available from UMI (Order No. 81-06618).

[Kames, Henry Home, Lord] Essays on the principles of morality and natural religion. In two parts. Edinburgh, Printed by R. Fleming, for A. Kincaid and A. Donaldson, 1751.

In Oko (1964), p. 206.

Kane, R., "Prima Facie Good," *The Journal of Value Inquiry*, Vol. 22 (October 1988), pp. 279-297.

In *Philosopher's Index*, No. 160909, noting a discussion of the views of Spinoza and some 20th century value theorists.

Kantor, H. R., and J. R. Kantor, "Some Humanistic Elements in Spinoza's Thinking," *Biosophical Review*, Vol. 4, No. 1 (1934), pp. 14-23.

> In Oko (1964), p. 111.

Kaphagawani, Didier N., *Leibniz on Freedom and Determinism in Relation to His Predecessors*, Unpublished doctoral dissertation, University of Leeds (UK), 1987.

> Currently available from UMI (Order No. DX-80023).

Kaplan, Abraham, *The New World of Philosophy* (New York: Random House, 1961).

> Includes many references to Spinoza.

Kaplan, Abraham, "Spinoza and Freud," *Journal of the American Academy of Psychoanalysis*, Vol. 5, No. 3 (1977), pp. 299-326.

Kaplan, Yosef, "Spinoza Scholarship in Israel," in De Deugd (1984), pp. 19-22.

Kaplan, Yosef, "On the Relation of Spinoza's Contemporaries in the Portuguese Jewish Community of Amsterdam to Spanish Culture and the Marrano Experience," in De Deugd (1984), pp. 82-94.

Kashap, S. Paul, *Spinoza and Moral Freedom* (Albany, NY: State University of New York Press, 1987).

Kashap, S. Paul (ed.), *Studies in Spinoza: Critical and Interpretive Essays* (Berkeley: University of California Press, 1972).

> In addition to a paper by Kashap — "Thought and Action in Spinoza," pp. 332-350 (parts of which appear in Chap. 3 of Kashap [1987]) — includes essays by H. Barker, R. Demos, G. Floistad, T. Forsyth, H. Hallett, S. Hampshire, F. Haserot, G. Parkinson, D. Savan, R. Saw, A. Taylor, and A. Wolf.

Kashap, S. Paul, "Some Recent Works on Spinoza's Thought," *Journal of the History of Ideas*, Vol. 38, No. 3 (1977), pp. 541-548.

Kashap, S. Paul, "Spinoza's Use of 'Idea,'" in Shahan and Biro (1978), Chap. 3, pp. 57-70.

> Originally in *Southwestern Journal of Philosophy* Vol. 8, No. 3 (Fall 1977), pp. 57-70. Parts of this paper also appear in Chap. 2 of Kashap (1987).

Kasher, Asa, and Shlomo Biderman, "When Was Spinoza Banned?" *Studia Rosenthaliana*, Vol. 12, Nos. 1-2 (1978), pp. 108-111.

Kasher, Asa, and Shlomo Biderman, "Why Was Baruch de Spinoza Excommunicated?"" in Katz and Israel (1990), pp. 98-141.

Kastein, Joseph, *The Messiah of Ismir, Sabbatai Zevi*, Translated by Huntley Paterson (New York: The Viking Press, 1931).

> Includes several references to Spinoza.

Katz, David S., and Jonathan I. Israel (eds.), *Sceptics, Millenarians and Jews* (Leiden: E. J. Brill, 1990).

> Includes on pp. 98-141 an essay by Asa Kasher and Shlomo Biderman, "Why Was Baruch de Spinoza Excommunicated?"

Katz, J. *See* Spinoza, *On the Improvement of the Understanding* (1958).

Katz, Steven T. (ed.), *Jewish Philosophers* (New York: Bloch Publishing Co., 1975).

> Van der Werf (1984), No. 1008, cites a 1975 Jerusalem edition with a section on Spinoza, pp. 137-146.

Kaufmann, Fritz, "Spinoza's System as Theory of Expression," *Philosophy and Phenomenological Research*, Vol. 1 (September 1940), pp. 83-97.

Kaufmann, M., "Spinoza, Goethe, and the Moderns," *Quarterly Review*, Vol. 217, No. 433 (October 1912), pp. 390-412.

> In Oko (1964), p. 323.

Kaufmann, William, *From Shakespeare to Existentialism: Studies in Poetry, Religion and Philosophy* (Boston: Beacon Press, 1959).

> Includes many references to Spinoza.

Kaunitz, Maurice M., *A Popular History of Philosophy* (Cleveland: The World Publishing Company, 1943).

> Includes a section on Spinoza, pp. 205-215, and other references.

Kaye, A. S., "Spinoza as Linguist," *Hebrew Annual Review*, Vol. 4 (1980), pp. 107-125.

> In Van der Werf (1984), No. 1043.

Kayser, Rudolf, *Spinoza: Portrait of a Spiritual Hero*, Translated by A. Allen and M. Newmark, with preface by Albert Einstein (New York: Philosophical Library, 1946).

Reprinted in New York by Greenwood Press, 1968.

Kayser, Rudolf, *The Saints of Qumran: Stories and Essays on Jewish Themes*, Edited by Harry Zohn (Rutherford, NJ: Fairleigh Dickinson University Press, 1977).

Contains an essay, "Amor Dei: An Approach to Spinoza's Philosophy of Religion," pp. 161-174.

Keeler, Leo W., *The Problem of Error from Plato to Kant: A Historical and Critical Study*, Analecta Gregoriana, Vol. VI (Rome: Pontificia Universitas Gregoriana, 1934).

Includes a chapter, "Spinoza," pp. 178-204, and other references.

Keeling, S. V., *Descartes* (London: Oxford University Press, 1934).

Includes a section on Spinoza, pp. 221-226, and other references.

Kegley, Jacquelyn A. K., "Spinoza's God and Laplace's World Formula," in *Akten Des II. Internationalen Leibniz-Kongresses...*(1975), pp. 25-35.

Kelkar, Meena, "Naturalistic Fallacy: Does Spinoza Commit This Fallacy?" *Indian Philosophical Quarterly*, Vol. 10 (April 1983), pp. 303-308.

Kellett, E. E., "Spinoza," in Hastings (1928), Vol. XI, pp. 768-784.

Kellett, E. E., "Spinoza," *London Quarterly and Holborn Review*, No. 158 (April 1933), pp. 221-225.

Kellogg, Samuel Henry, *The Jews; or, Prediction and Fulfilment: An Argument for the Times* (New York: A. D. P. Randolph, 1883).

Includes a section, "The Jews and Modern Pantheistic Rationalism: Spinoza — Maimonides," pp. 190-199.

Kennington, Richard (ed.), *The Philosophy of Baruch Spinoza* (Washington, DC: The Catholic University of America Press, 1980).

In addition to a paper by Kennington — "Analytic and Synthetic Methods in Spinoza's *Ethics*," Chap. 16, pp. 293-318 — includes chapters by H. Allison, R. Beck, J. Benardete, A. Donagan, W. Doney, L. Feuer, I. Frank, H. Gilden, M. Hooker, H. Jonas, J. Morrison, K. Schmitz, S. Umphrey, P. Weiss, and M. Wilson.

Kessler, Warren L., *The Problem of Attributes in Spinoza*, Unpublished doctoral dissertation, University of Wisconsin, 1971.

> Currently available from UMI (Order No. 71-12694).

Kessler, Warren L., "A Note on Spinoza's Concept of Attribute," in Mandelbaum and Freeman (1975), pp. 191-194.

> Originally in *The Monist*, Vol. 55 (1971), pp. 636-639.

Kettner, Frederick, *Spinoza, The Biosopher*, Introduction by Nicholas Roerich (New York: Roerich Museum Press, 1932).

[King, William] A defence of Dr. Clarke's Demonstration of the being and attributes of God ... Being an answer to a ... book entitul'd, A translation of Dr. King's Origin of evil, and some other objections. Together with a compendium of a demonstration of the being and attributes of God. London, 1732.

> In Oko (1964), p. 206. *See* Clarke (1749).

Kingma, J., and A. K. Offenberg, *Bibliography of Spinoza's Works up to 1800*, Corrected and annotated reproduction [of the 1977 edition] (Amsterdam: Printed for the Amsterdam University Library by Van Gorcum & Co., 1985).

> 32 pp., plus 20 additional pages presenting photographic copies of the title pages of 27 editions cited. Originally in *Studia Rosenthaliana*, Vol. 11, No. 1 (1977), pp. 1-32.

Kischner, M. S., *Spinozism in the Novels of George Eliot: Adam Bede, The Mill on the Floss, and Silas Marner*, Unpublished doctoral dissertation, University of Washington, 1976.

Klausner, N. W., "Under the Aspect of Eternity," *Religion in Life*, Vol. 18 (1949), pp. 263-273.

Klein, D. B., *The Concept of Consciousness* (Lincoln: University of Nebraska Press, 1984).

In *Mental Health Abstracts*, No. 0529793, citing a discussion of the views of Aristotle, Descartes, Spinoza, and others as background to the author's own conclusions.

Klever, Wim. See *Studia Spinozana*, Vol. 2 (1986) and Vol. 5 (1989).

Klever, Wim, "Power: Conditional and Unconditional," in De Deugd (1984), pp. 95-106.

Klever, Wim, *"Quasi Aliquod Automa Spirituale,"* in Giancotti Boscherini (1985), pp. 249-257.

Klever, Wim, "Axioms in Spinoza's Science and Philosophy of Science," in *Studia Spinozana*, Vol. 2 (1986), pp. 171-195.

Klever, Wim, "A Neglected Document of Spinozism," in *Studia Spinozana*, Vol. 2 (1986), pp. 313-350.

Klever, Wim, "The Warning Note of a Spinoza Editor," in *Studia Spinozana*, Vol. 2 (1986), pp. 351-353.

Klever, Wim, "Spinoza's Naturalism: A Short Reply to De Dijn," in *Studia Spinozana*, Vol. 3 (1987), pp. 431-435.

Klever, Wim, "The Helvétius Affair or Spinoza and the Philosopher's Stone: A Document on the Background of *Letter 40*," in *Studia Spinozana*, Vol. 3 (1987), pp. 439-450.

Klever, Wim, "Burchard Devolder (1643-1709), a Crypto-Spinozist on a Leiden Cathedra," *Lias*, Vol. 15, No. 2 (1988), pp. 191-241.

Klever, Wim, "Moles in Motu: Principles of Spinoza's Physics," in *Studia Spinozana*, Vol. 4 (1988), pp. 165-194.

Klever, Wim, "Spinoza Interviewed by Willem van Blyenbergh," in *Studia Spinozana*, Vol. 4 (1988), pp. 317-320.

Klever, Wim, "Letters to and from Neercassel about Spinoza and Rieuwertsz," in *Studia Spinozana*, Vol. 4 (1988), pp. 329-338.

Klever, Wim, "Spinoza in Poetry," in *Studia Spinozana*, Vol. 5 (1989), pp. 81-102.

Klever, Wim, "Spinoza and Van den Enden in Borch's Diary in 1661 and 1662," in *Studia Spinozana*, Vol. 5 (1989), pp. 311-325.

Klever, Wim, "Hudde's Question on God's Uniqueness: A Reconstruction on the Basis of Van Limborch's Correspondence with John Locke," in *Studia Spinozana*, Vol. 5 (1989), pp. 327-357.

Klever, Wim, "Spinoza's Fame in 1667," in *Studia Spinozana*, Vol. 5 (1989), pp. 359-363.

Klever, Wim, "Anti-Falsification: Spinoza's Theory of Experience and Experiments," in Curley and Moreau (1990), pp. 124-135.

Klever, Wim, "Proto-Spinoza Franciscus van den Enden," in *Studia Spinozana*, Vol. 6 (1990), pp. 281-289.

Klever, Wim, "Steno's Statements on Spinoza and Spinozism," in *Studia Spinozana*, Vol. 6 (1990), pp. 303-313.

Klijnsmit, Anthony J., *Spinoza and Grammatical Tradition*, Mededelingen XLIX vanwege het Spinozahuis (Leiden: E. J. Brill, 1986).

Klijnsmit, Anthony J., "Amsterdam Sephardim and Hebrew Grammar in the Seventeenth Century," *Studia Rosenthaliana*, Vol. 22, No. 2 (1988), pp. 144-164.

    Discusses five Hebrew grammars of the 17th century, including Spinoza's.

Klijnsmit, Anthony J., "The Problem of Normativity Solved or Spinoza's Stand in the Analogy/Anomaly Controversy," in *Studia Spinozana*, Vol. 4 (1988), pp. 305-314.

Klimke, Werner Josef, *Herder's Contribution to the Acceptance of Spinoza in Germany*, Unpublished doctoral dissertation, University of Michigan, 1976.

    Currently available from UMI (Order No. 77-07957).

Kline, David A., "A Rejoinder to the Supposed Freedom-Determinism Quandary in Spinoza's *Ethics*," *Dialogue: Journal of Phi Sigma Tau*, Vol. 12 (May 1970), pp. 23-30.

Kline, George L. (ed.), *Spinoza in Soviet Philosophy*, A series of essays selected and translated, with an introduction (New York: The Humanities Press, 1952).

From the author's doctoral dissertation, Columbia University, 1950. Includes translations into English of papers by L. I. Akselrod, V. K. Brushlinski, A. M. Deborin, I. K. Luppol, D. Rakhman, I. P. Razumovski, and S. Y. Volfson.

Kline, George L., "Humanities and Cosmologies: The Background of Certain Humane Values," *Western Humanities Review*, Vol. 7 (1953), pp. 95-103.

In *Philosopher's Index*, No. 015208.

Kline, George L., "Review of Hallett's *Spinoza*," *The Journal of Philosophy*, Vol. 58 (1961), pp. 346-355.

Kline, George L., "Randall's Reinterpretation of the Philosophies of Descartes, Spinoza, and Leibniz," in Anton (1967), pp. 83-93.

Kline, George L., "On the Infinity of Spinoza's Attributes," in Hessing (1977), pp. 333-352.

Kline, George L., "Absolute and Relative Senses of *Liberum* and *Libertas* in Spinoza," in Giancotti Boscherini (1985), pp. 259-280.

Kline, George L., "Pierre Macherey's *Hegel ou Spinoza*," in Curley and Moreau (1990), pp. 373-380.

Kneale, Martha, "Leibniz and Spinoza on Activity," in Frankfurt (1972), pp. 215-238.

Kneale, Martha, "Eternity and Sempiternity," in Grene (1979), pp. 227-240.

Originally in *Proceedings of the Aristotelian Society*, Vol. 69, New Series (1968-1969), pp. 223-238.

Knight, Rachel, *The Founder of Quakerism: A Psychological Study of the Mysticism of George Fox* (London: The Swarthmore Press, 1929).

Includes a section on Spinoza, pp. 245-249.

Knight, William (ed.), *Spinoza: Four Essays* (London: Williams and Norgate, 1882).

Includes essays by J. Land, "In Memory of Spinoza"; K. Fischer, "The Life and Character of Baruch Spinoza"; J. Van Vloten, "Spinoza: An Oration"; and E. Renan, "Spinoza: 1677, and 1877."

Knight, William, "Worms in the Morals of Spinoza," *Critical Review*, Vol. 3 (1896), pp. 59 ff.

Knox, Clifford, *The Idiom of Contemporary Thought* (London: Chapman & Hall, 1956).

> "A Spinozistic interpretation of some of the themes central to contemporary philosophy" — *Philosopher's Index*, No. 075517.

Koenigsberger, H. G. (ed.), *Republiken und Republikanismus im Europa der Frühen Neuzeit* (Munich: Oldenbourg, 1988).

> Cited by Hans W. Blom in *Studia Spinozana*, Vol. 4 (1988), p. 299, as including his essay, "Virtue and Republicanism: Spinoza's Political Philosophy in the Context of the Dutch Republic," pp. 195-212.

Kogan, Barry S. (ed.), *Spinoza: A Tercentenary Perspective* (Cincinnati: Hebrew Union College Press, 1979).

> Papers presented at a conference of the same name on May 2-3, 1978, sponsored by the Hebrew Union College — Jewish Institute on Religion. In addition to Kogan's Preface, pp. ix-xiii, includes papers by L. Feuer, A. Gottschalk, E. Mihaly, R. Popkin, and D. Savan.

Kohlberg, Lawrence, and Clark Power, "Moral Development, Religious Thinking, and the Question of a Seventh Sage," *Zygon*, Vol. 16 (September 1981), pp. 203-259.

> In Van der Werf (1984), citing a discussion of "Spinoza's theory," pp. 246-250, and "commonalities in the theories of Spinoza and Teilhard," pp. 254-255.

Kolakowski, Leszek, "The Two Eyes of Spinoza," in Grene (1979), pp. 279-294.

> Translated by Oscar Swan from the author's 1966 paper (in Polish).

Konvitz, M. R., "On Spinoza and Maimonides," *The Open Court*, Vol. 43, No. 3 (March 1929), pp. 160-168.

Kors, Alan Charles, *Atheism in France, 1650-1729* (Princeton: Princeton University Press, 1990). 2 vols.

> Vol. I, *The Orthodox Sources of Disbelief* (1990), includes a section on Bayle and Spinoza, pp. 247-251, and many other references.

Kraemer, S., "A Note on Spinoza's Contribution to Systemic Therapy," *Family Process*, Vol. 21, No. 3 (1982), pp. 353-357.

Kramer, Simon G., "Judaism and Spinoza's Philosophy," in Gerstein and Manello (1927).

Oko (1964), p. 425, indicates that this paper was also published in the *Eighth Anniversary Banquet Journal of the Hebrew Theological College* (Chicago, 1930), pp. 19+.

Kristeller, Paul Oskar, "Stoic and Neoplatonic Sources of Spinoza's *Ethics*," *History of European Ideas*, Vol. 5, No. 1 (1984), pp. 1-15.

Kroeger, Adolf Ernest, "Spinoza," *Journal of Speculative Philosophy*, Vol. 9, No. 3 (July 1875), pp. 363-393.

In Oko (1964), pp. 111.

Kropotkin, P. A., *Ethics: Origin and Development*, Translated by Louis S. Friedland and Joseph R. Piroshnikoff, with introduction by N. Lebedev (New York: Benjamin Blom, 1968).

Reprint of the original 1924 edition. Includes a section on Spinoza, pp. 157-162, and many other references.

Kurlick, Bruce, "Seven Thinkers and How They Grew: Descartes, Spinoza, Leibniz; Locke, Berkeley, Hume; Kant," in Rorty *et al.* (1984), pp. 125-140.

Kvastad, Nils Bjorn, "Pantheism and Mysticism," *Sophia*, Vol. 14, No. 2 (July 1975), pp. 1-15; No. 3, pp. 19-30.

In *Philosopher's Index*, No. 048655, citing a discussion of the "validity of various views on pantheism, e.g., some of Spinoza" [sic].

Lachterman, David R., "The Physics of Spinoza's *Ethics*," in Shahan and Biro (1978), Chap. 4, pp. 71-111.

Originally in the *Southwestern Journal of Philosophy*, Vol. 8, No. 3 (Fall 1977), pp. 71-111.

Lai, Yuen-Ting, *Variations on the Theme of the Philosopher's God: Europe and China*, Unpublished doctoral dissertation, University of California, San Diego, 1982.

Includes material on Spinoza. Currently available from UMI (Order No. 82-24522).

Lai, Yuen-Ting, "The Linking of Spinoza to Chinese Thought by Bayle and Malebranche," *Journal of the History of Philosophy*, Vol. 23, No. 2 (April 1985), pp. 151-178.

Laird, John, *The Idea of Value* (Cambridge: Cambridge University Press, 1929).

Includes a chapter, "Spinoza's Account of Value," pp. 69-91, and other references.

Lake, John, "Spinozistic Partitions of Classes," *Synthèse*, Vol. 32 (April 1976), pp. 419-422.

[La Mothe, Claude Grostete] The inspiration of the New Testament asserted and explained, in answer to some modern writers. London, Printed for Tho. Bennet, 1694.

In Oko (1964), p. 396.

Lamprecht, Sterling P., *Our Philosophical Traditions: A Brief History of Philosophy in Western Civilization* (New York: Appleton-Century-Crofts, 1955).

In *Philosopher's Index*, No. 018287.

Land, J., "In Memory of Spinoza," Translated by Allan Menzies, in Knight (1882), pp. 1-74, preceded by a two-page preface.

Lang, B., "The Politics of Interpretation: Spinoza's Modernist Turn," *The Review of Metaphysics*, Vol 43, No. 2 (1989), pp. 327-356.

Lang, Helen S., "Philosophy as Text and Context," *Philosophy and Rhetoric*, Vol. 18 (1985), pp. 158-170.

In *Philosopher's Index*, No. 136615, citing references to Spinoza, Aristotle, and Aquinas.

Lascola, Russell A., "Spinoza's Super Attribute," *The Modern Schoolman*, Vol. 52 (January 1975), pp. 199-206.

Latta, Robert, "On the Relation Between the Philosophy of Spinoza and That of Leibniz," *Mind*, Vol. 8 (1899), pp. 333-356.

Latta, Robert, "*Spinoza: His Life and Philosophy*, by Sir Frederick Pollock, 2nd Edition," *International Journal of Ethics*, Vol. 10 (1900), pp. 241-252.

Lauterpacht, E. (ed.), *International Law: Collected Papers of Hersch Lauterpacht* (Cambridge: Cambridge University Press, 1975).

Includes an essay, "Spinoza and International Law," Vol. 2, pp. 366-384; originally in the *British Year Book of International Law* (1927), pp. 89-107.

Law, Edmund. An Enquiry into the Ideas of Space, Time, Immensity, and Eternity; As also the Self-existence, Necessary Existence, and Unity of the Divine Nature: In Answer to a Book lately Publish'd by Mr. Jackson, entitled, The Existence and Unity of God proved from his Nature and Attributes. ... To which is added, A Dissertation upon the Argument a Priori for proving the Existence of a First Cause. By a Learned Hand. Cambridge: Printed by W. Fenner and R. Beresford for W. Thurlbourn ... 1734.

> In Oko (1964), p. 456, who identifies the "learned hand" as Daniel Water-land. Reprinted in Bristol by Thoemmes, 1990.

Lazaron, Morris Samuel, *Seed of Abraham: Ten Jews of the Ages* (New York and London: The Century Co., 1930).

> Includes a chapter on Spinoza.

Lazerowitz, Morris, *Studies in Metaphilosophy* (New York: The Humanities Press, 1964).

> Includes a section on Spinoza's determinism, pp. 251-256, and other references.

Lazerowitz, Morris, *The Language of Philosophy: Freud and Wittgenstein*, Boston Studies in the Philosophy of Science, Vol. 55 (Dordrecht: D. Reidel Publishing Co., 1977).

> Includes a chapter, "The Semantics of a Spinozistic Proposition," pp. 127-140.

Leclerc, Ivor (ed.), *The Philosophy of Leibniz and the Modern World* (Nashville, TN: Vanderbilt University Press, 1973).

> Includes many references to Spinoza.

Leclerc, Ivor, "Being and Becoming in Whitehead's Philosophy," *Kant-Studien*, Vol. 46 (1955), pp. 427-437.

> In *Philosopher's Index*, No. 068148.

Lecrivain, André, "Spinoza and Cartesian Mechanics," in Grene and Nails (1986), pp. 15-60.

Lee, Arthur Bolles, "Spinoza: The Man and the Philosopher," *The Contemporary Review*, Vol. 29 (May 1877), pp. 567-602.

> Oko (1964), p. 112, cites a reprint in *Littell's Living Age* (April 1877), pp. 131-151.

Lee, Arthur Bolles, "Spinozism: The Religion of Gladness," *Fraser's Magazine for Town and Country*, Vol. 97 (1878), pp. 46-57.

Lee, William, *The Inspiration of Holy Scripture: Its Nature and Proof*, Eight discourses, preached before the University of Dublin, 4th Edition (Dublin: Hodges, Smith, 1865).

> In Oko (1964), p. 397.

Lefevre, André, *Philosophy, Historical and Critical*, Translated with an introduction by A. H. Keane (London: Chapman and Hall; New York: J. B. Lippincott and Co., 1879).

> Includes a section on Spinoza, pp. 317-324.

Lefkowitz, David, "The Relation of the Life and Philosophy of Spinoza to Judaism," *Kallah*, Vol. 1 (1928), pp. 30-36.

> In Oko (1964), p. 425.

Leibniz, G. W., *The Philosophical Works of Leibnitz*, Translated with notes by George Martin Duncan (New Haven: Tuttle, Morehouse & Taylor, 1890).

> Includes "Notes on Spinoza's Ethics," pp. 11-26, and "Refutation of Spinoza," pp. 175-184.

Leibniz, G. W., *Philosophical Papers and Letters*, A selection translated and edited with an introduction by Leroy E. Loemker (Chicago: University of Chicago Press, 1956). 2 vols.

> Includes "Two Notations for Discussion with Spinoza, 1676," Vol. 1, pp. 259-262; "On the Ethics of Benedict de Spinoza, 1678," Vol. 1, pp. 300-316; and many other references.

Leibniz, G. W. *See* Foucher De Careil (1855).

Leidecker, K. F., "Spinozism and Hinduism," *The Open Court*, Vol. 48 (October 1934), pp. 219-227.

Leifchild, John R., *The Great Problem: The Higher Ministry of Nature Viewed in the Light of Modern Science, and as an Aid to Advanced Christian Philosophy*, With an introduction by Howard Crosby (New York: Putnam, 1872).

> In Oko (1964), p. 268, citing references to Spinoza in two chapters, pp. 149-196.

Leighton, Joseph Alexander, *The Field of Philosophy: An Introduction to the Study of Philosophy*, 2nd Edition (Columbus, OH: R. G. Adams and Company, 1919).

> Includes a section, "The Spinozistic Conception of the Absolute," pp. 249-252, and many other references.

Leland, John, *A View of the Principal Deistical Writers*, British Philosophers and Theologians of the 17th and 18th Centuries, No. 33 (New York: Garland Publishing, 1978). 3 vols.

> A facsimile reprint of the 3rd edition, Vols. 1 and 2 of which were published in 1757, and Vol. 3 in 1756, all by Benjamin Dod in London. Spinoza is discussed in Vol. 1, pp. 76-78 (a passage repeated in Vol. 3, pp. 21-25). He is also mentioned in Vol. 1, p. 296. Oko (1964), p. 336, cites a two-volume edition published by R. Ogle in London in 1808; Hertzberger (1950), No. 840, cites the first edition (1754-1756), in 3 vols.

Lemon, M. C., *Politics and Salvation: A Study of the Relationship Between Political Society and the Human Good in the Writings of Spinoza*, Unpublished doctoral dissertation, London, 1975.

> In Van der Werf (1984), No. 1127.

[Lempriere, John] Lempriere's universal biography; containing a critical and historical account of the lives, characters, and labours of eminent persons, in all ages and countries. Together with selections of foreign biography from Watkin's dictionary, recently published, and about eight hundred original articles of American biography. By Eleazar Lord. New York, R. Lockwood, 1825. 2 vols.

> In Oko (1964), p. 51, citing an article on Spinoza, Vol. 2, p. 659.

Lennox, James G., "The Causality of Finite Modes in Spinoza's *Ethics*," *Canadian Journal of Philosophy*, Vol. 6 (Spring 1976), pp. 479-500.

Leo, Aileen, "On the Correlations Between Spinoza's Metaphysical System and the Main Principles of Holism," *De Philosophia* (Ottawa), Vol. 6 (1985-1986), pp. 1-22.

> In *Philosopher's Index*, No. 148939.

Lermond, Lucia, *The Form of Man: Human Essence in Spinoza's "Ethic"* (Leiden: E. J. Brill, 1988).

> From the author's doctoral dissertation, Columbia University, 1985, which is also currently available from UMI (Order No. 85-23193).

Le Rossignol, James Edward, "Spinoza as a Biblical Critic," *Canadian Methodist Quarterly*, Vol. 7 (1895), pp. 52-60.

>   In Oko (1964), p. 397.

Leslie, Charles. A short and easie method with the deists. Wherein the certainty of the Christian religion is demonstrated ... In a letter to a friend. The sixth edition, corrected and enlarg'd, with a letter from the author to a deist ... To which is added a second part to the Jews; and also The truth of Christianity vindicated; and a defence of the short method with the deists prefix'd. By Mr. Charles Leslie. London, Printed for Geo. Strahan [1727?].

>   In Oko (1964), p. 352.

Lessing, Abba, "Spinoza and Merleau-Ponty on Human Existence," *Proceedings of the New Mexico-West Texas Philosophical Society* (April 1972), pp. 20-24.

Lessing, Abba, "Inability To Exist Is Impotence: Ability To Exist Is Power," *Human Context*, Vol. 7 (1975), pp. 458-462.

>   In *Philosopher's Index*, No. 049465, citing references to Spinoza, Sartre, and Merleau-Ponty.

Lessing, Gotthold Ephrain. *See* particularly Valleé (1988) and Willis (1870).

Letsome, Sampson. A defence of natural and revealed religion: being a collection of the sermons preached at the lecture founded by the Hon. Robert Boyle esq. (from the year 1691 to the year 1732). With the additions and amendments of the several authors, and general indexes. London, Printed for D. Midwinter, 1739.

>   In Oko (1964), p. 456.

Levin, Dan, *Spinoza: The Young Thinker Who Destroyed the Past* (New York: Weybright and Talley, 1970).

Levine, Israel, *Faithful Rebels: A Study in Jewish Speculative Thought* (London: The Soncino Press, 1936).

>   Includes a chapter on Spinoza, pp. 59-78.

Levy, Ze'ev, *Baruch or Benedict: On Some Jewish Aspects of Spinoza's Philosophy* (New York: Peter Lang Publishing, 1989).

Levy, Ze'ev, "On Spinoza's and Mendelssohn's Conceptions of the Relationship Between Religion and State," in De Deugd (1984), pp. 107-116.

Levy, Ze'ev, "The Problem of Normativity in Spinoza's *Hebrew Grammar*," in *Studia Spinozana*, Vol. 3 (1987), pp. 351-390.

Levy, Ze'ev, "The Relation of Spinoza's Concept of Substance to the Concept of Ultimate Reality," *Ultimate Reality and Meaning*, Vol. 10, No. 3 (September 1987), pp. 186-201.

> In *Philosopher's Index*, No. 152778.

Levy, Ze'ev, "On Some Early Responses to Spinoza's Philosophy in Jewish Thought," in *Studia Spinozana*, Vol. 6 (1990), pp. 251-278.

Lewes, George Henry, *The History of Philosophy from Thales to Comte*, 3rd Edition (London: Longmans, Green, and Co., 1867). 2 vols.

> Includes a chapter on Spinoza, Vol. 2, pp. 160-225.

Lewes, George Henry, *The Biographical History of Philosophy from Its Origin in Greece Down to the Present Day* (New York: D. Appleton and Co., 1885).

> Includes a chapter on Spinoza, pp. 458-492. Hertzberger (1950), No. 133, cites an 1891 edition with this chapter on pp. 409-438.

Lewes, George Henry, "Spinoza," and "Spinozism," articles in *The Penny Cyclopaedia of the Society for the Diffusion of Useful Knowledge*, Vol. 22 (1842), pp. 350-353.

> In Oko (1964), p. 126.

Lewes, George Henry, "Spinoza," *Fortnightly Review*, Vol. 4, No. 22 (April 1866), pp. 385-406.

Lewis, Christopher E., "Baruch Spinoza: A Critique of Robert Boyle on Matter," *Dialogue: Journal of Phil Sigma Tau*, Vol. 27, No. 1 (October 1984), pp. 11-22.

Lewis, Douglas, "Spinoza on Extension," *Midwest Studies in Philosophy*, Vol. 1 (1976), pp. 26-30.

Lewis, Douglas, "On the Aims and Method of Spinoza's Philosophy," in Shahan and Biro (1978), Chap. 11, pp. 217-234.

> Originally in the *Southwestern Journal of Philosophy*, Vol. 8, No. 3 (1977), pp. 217-234.

Liccione, Michael James, *The Concept of Mystery: A Philosophical Investigation*, Unpublished doctoral dissertation, University of Pennsylvania, 1988.

Includes material on Spinoza. Currently available from UMI (Order No. 88-27424).

Lichtgenstein, Isaac, *Spinoza: Eight Plates* (New York: Machmadim Art Editions [1946?]).

Presents eight portraits; in portfolio.

Lichtigfeld, A., "Spinoza: A Tercentenary Reflection Based on the Philosophy of Karl Jaspers," *Kant-Studien*, Vol. 71, No. 1 (1980), pp. 117-121.

Liddell, A. F., *The Logical Relationship of the Philosophy of Hegel to the Philosophies of Spinoza and Kant*, Unpublished doctoral dissertation, University of North Carolina, 1924.

In Van der Werf (1984), No. 2209.

Lilly, William Samuel, *Many Mansions: Being Studies in Ancient Religions and Modern Thought* (London: Chapman & Hall, 1907).

Includes a chapter, "Spinoza and Modern Thought," pp. 155-187, which also appeared in *Fortnightly Review*, Vol. 81 (1907), pp. 43-61.

Lindsay, A. D., "Benedict Spinoza," in Hearnshaw (1926), pp. 204-220.

Lindsay, James, *Studies in European Philosophy* (Edinburgh and London: Blackwood, 1909).

Includes a chapter, "The Philosophy of Spinoza," pp. 154-170.

Lindsay, James, "Some Criticisms of Spinoza's Ethics," *Archiv für Geschichte der Philosophie*, Vol. 18 (1905), pp. 496-506.

Linter, J. E., *Spinoza* (London, 1873).

Cited in the entry on Spinoza in S. M. Jackson (ed.), *The New Schaff-Herzog Encyclopedia of Religious Knowledge* (Grand Rapids, MI: Baker Book House, 1953), Vol. XI, p. 49. Also in Wetlesen (1968), p. 8.

Litman, Alexander, "Man's Value and Destiny: Moral Atheism in Spinoza," *American Scholar*, Vol. 41 (January 1935), pp. 77-85.

Little, Ivan, "Freedom, Determinism, and Reason," *Proceedings of the New Mexico-West Texas Philosophical Society* (April 1974), pp. 21-27.

> In *Philosopher's Index*, No. 047564, citing references to Spinoza, Descartes, and Leibniz on the rationality of determinism.

Lloyd, Genevieve, "Spinoza's Environmental Ethics," *Enquiry*, Vol. 23, No. 3 (September 1980), pp. 293-311.

> *See* Naess (1980) for a reply.

Lloyd, Genevieve, "Spinoza's Version of the Eternity of the Mind," in Grene and Nails (1986), pp. 211-233.

Lloyd, Genevieve, "Spinoza on the Distinction Between Intellect and Will," in Curley and Moreau (1990), pp. 113-123.

Lodge, Rupert Clendon, *The Great Thinkers* (Port Washington, NY: Kennikat Press, 1968).

> Reprint of the 1949 edition. Contains a section on Spinoza.

Loeb, Louis E., *From Descartes to Hume: Continental Metaphysics and the Development of Modern Philosophy* (Ithaca: Cornell University Press, 1981).

> Includes a chapter, "Spinoza's Denial of Causal Interaction Between Modes of Distinct Attributes," pp. 157-190, and frequent references to Spinoza in the chapter, "Seventeenth-Century Continental Metaphysics," pp. 320 ff.

Loemker, Leroy E., *Struggle for Synthesis: The Seventeenth Century Background of Leibniz's Synthesis of Order and Freedom* (Cambridge: Harvard University Press, 1972).

> Includes many references to Spinoza.

Loewe, Raphael (ed.), *Studies in Rationalism, Judaism, and Universalism* (London: Routledge & Kegan Paul, 1966).

> Includes an essay by Alexander Altmann, "Moses Mendelssohn on Leibniz and Spinoza," pp. 15-45.

Loptson, Peter, "Spinozistic Monism," *Philosophia* (Israel), Vol. 18, No. 1 (April 1988), pp. 19-38.

Lorimer, George Claude, *Isms Old and New*, Winter Sunday Evening Sermon Series for 1880-1881 Delivered in the First Baptist Church, Chicago (Chicago: S. C. Griggs, 1881).

In Oko (1964), p. 304, citing a section on Spinoza, pp. 65-70, and other references.

Lossky, N. O., *The Intuitive Basis of Knowledge*, Translated by N. Duddington (1919).

This citation is based on Wetlesen (1968), p. 20.

Love, Howard, "The Stages of Knowledge in Plato and Spinoza," *The Philosophical Forum*, Vol. 6 (Spring 1948), pp. 14-21.

Lovejoy, Arthur O., *The Great Chain of Being: A Study of the History of an Idea*, The William James lectures delivered at Harvard University, 1933 (Cambridge: Harvard University Press, 1950).

Includes a chapter, "Plenitude and Sufficient Reason in Leibniz and Spinoza," pp. 144-182, and other references. This chapter also appears in Frankfurt (1972), pp. 281-334.

Lovejoy, Arthur O., "The Dialectic of Bruno and Spinoza," in E. D. McGilvary *et al.* (1904), pp. 141-174.

Lowenthal, Marvin Marx, "Comparative Study of Spinoza and Neo-Realism as Indicated in Holt's *Concept of Consciousness*," *Journal of Philosophy, Psychology, and Scientific Methods*, Vol. 12, No. 25 (December 1915), pp. 673-682; No. 26, pp. 701-713.

In Oko (1964), p. 269.

Lowth, William. A vindication of the divine authority and inspiration of the writings of the Old and New Testament. In answer to a treatise lately translated out of French, entituled, Five letters concerning the inspiration of the Holy Scriptures [by Jean Le Clerc]. Oxford, Printed at the Theater, 1692.

In Oko (1964), p. 397.

Luby, Barry J., *Maimonides and Spinoza: Their Sources, Cosmological Metaphysics, and Impact on Modern Thought and Literature* (New York: Las Americas Publishing Co., 1973).

In Van der Werf (1984), No. 1171; in Dienstag (1986), p. 393.

Lucas, George R., Jr. (ed.), *Hegel and Whitehead: Contemporary Perspectives on Systematic Philosophy* (Albany, NY: State University of New York Press, 1986).

> Includes an essay by Hans Christian Lucas, "Spinoza, Hegel, Whitehead: Substance, Subject, and Superject," pp. 39-57.

Lucas, Hans Christian, "Spinoza, Hegel, Whitehead: Substance, Subject, and Superject," in Lucas (1986), pp. 39-57.

Lucas, Jean Maximilien. *See* Wolf (1927).

Lucash, Frank, "On the Finite and the Infinite in Spinoza," *The Southern Journal of Philosophy*, Vol. 20, No. 1 (Spring 1982), pp. 61-73.

Lucash, Frank, "The Mind's Body: The Body's Self-Awareness," *Dialogue* (Ottawa), Vol. 23 (December 1984), pp. 619-633.

> In *Philosopher's Index*, No. 132770, citing discussion of Spinoza's views on the mind/body relationship and on true/false, adequate/inadequate ideas.

Lucash, Frank, "What Spinoza's View of Freedom Should Have Been," *Philosophy Research Archives*, Vol. 10 (1985), pp. 491-499.

Lucash, Frank, "Ideas, Images, and Truth," *History of Philosophy Quarterly*, Vol. 6, No. 2 (April 1989), pp. 161-170.

> Discusses Spinoza's view of what constitutes the object of an idea and the origin and nature of false ideas.

Lucks, Henry A., "Natura Naturans — Natura Naturata," *The New Scholasticism*, Vol. 9 (1935), pp. 1-24.

Luppol, I. K., "The Historical Significance of Spinoza's Philosophy," in Kline (1952), pp. 162-176.

Luzzatti, Luigi, *God in Freedom: Studies in the Relations Between Church and State*, Translated by Alfonso Arbib-Costa, with American supplementary chapters by William H. Taft, Irving Lehman, and others (New York: The Macmillan Co., 1930).

> Includes a section, "Spinoza and the Precursors of Freedom of Conscience," pp. 115-125.

Lynch, Kelly, "'Die Inkonsequenz Spinozas': Notes on Nietzsche and Spinoza: Short Commentary on *Beyond Good and Evil*, Chap. 1, Sec. 13," *De Philosophia* (Ottawa), Vol. 3 (1982), pp. 45-53.

In *Philosopher's Index*, No. 126920.

Lyons, William E., *Emotion* (Cambridge: Cambridge University Press, 1980).

Includes a section on Spinoza's theory of emotion, pp. 37-40.

Maccall, William, *Foreign Biographies* (London: Tinsley, 1875). 2 vols.

Includes a section on Spinoza, Vol. 1, pp. 299-320.

Maccall, William. *See* Spinoza, *Treatise on Politics* (1854).

MacGregor, Phillip S., *Spinoza and Religious Philosophy*, Unpublished doctoral dissertation, Fordham University, 1952.

MacIntosh, J. J., "Spinoza's Epistemological Views," in Vesey (1972), pp. 28-48.

MacIntyre, Alasdair, *A Short History of Ethics: A History of Moral Philosophy from the Homeric Age to the Twentieth Century* (London: Routledge & Kegan Paul, 1967).

Includes a section on Spinoza, pp. 140-145.

MacIntyre, Alasdair, *After Virtue: A Study in Moral Theory*, 2nd Edition (Notre Dame: University of Notre Dame Press, 1984).

In Coers (1988), p. 186.

MacIntyre, Alasdair, "Spinoza," in Edwards (1967), Vol. 7, pp. 530-541.

MacKinnon, Flora Isabel, "The Treatment of Universals in Spinoza's *Ethics*," *The Philosophical Review*, Vol. 33 (July 1924), pp. 345-359.

MacLaurin, Charles, *Mere Mortals: Medico-Historical Essays*, Second Series (New York: George H. Doran Co., 1925).

Includes an essay on Spinoza, pp. 255 ff.

MacQuesten, Rockwood, *Higher Criticism the Philosophical Outgrowth of Spinozism*, Unpublished doctoral dissertation, New York University, 1893.

Madigan, Patrick, *The Modern Project to Rigor: Descartes to Nietzsche* (Lanham, MD: University Press of America, 1986).

> Discusses Spinoza in Chap. 8, "The Classical Enlightenment Solution," pp. 130-160.

Magee, Bryan, *The Great Philosophers: An Introduction to Western Philosophy* (New York: Oxford University Press, 1988).

Magill, Frank N. (ed.), *World Philosophy: Essay-Reviews of 225 Major Works* (Englewood Cliffs, NJ: Salem Press, 1982). 5 vols.

> Includes a review of the *Ethics* by Frederick Sontag, Vol. 2, pp. 886-893. This is followed by Wallace I. Matson's reviews on pp. 893-897 of Wolfson (1934), Curley (1969), and Stuart Hampshire, "A Kind of Materialism" (1970).

Magnus, Katie, *Outlines of Jewish History, from B.C. 586 to C.E. 1890*, Revised by M. Friedlander (Philadelphia: The Jewish Publication Society of America, 1890).

> Includes a chapter on Spinoza. Reprinted under the same title for the Council of the Jewish War Memorial (London: Myers, 1924).

Magnus, Laurie, *The Jews in the Christian Era, from the First to the Eighteenth Century, and Their Contribution to Its Civilization* (London: E. Benn, 1929).

> Includes a section on Spinoza, pp. 330-364.

Maland, David, *Europe in the Seventeenth Century* (London: Macmillan; New York: St. Martin's Press, 1968).

> Includes a section, "The Cartesian Revolution: Spinoza and Leibniz," pp. 62-67, and other references.

Malebranche, Nicolas, *Dialogue Between a Christian Philosopher and a Chinese Philosopher*, Translated with an introduction by Dominick A. Iorio (Lanham, MD: University Press of America, 1980).

> In *Philosopher's Index*, No. 089565, but without the title.

Mandelbaum, Maurice, "The Determinants of Choice," *Philosophy Research Archives*, Vol. 11 (1985), pp. 355-377.

> In *Philosopher's Index*, No. 143013, citing a comparison of Spinoza's views on human choice with those of many other philosophers.

Mandelbaum, Maurice, and Eugene Freeman (eds.), *Spinoza: Essays in Interpretation* (LaSalle, IL: Open Court, 1975).

Includes papers by F. Copleston, E. Curley, W. Doney, W. Frankena, S. Hampshire, E. Harris, W. Kessler, W. Matson, R. McShea, D. Odegard, G. Parkinson, L. Rice, W. Sacksteder, and R. Saw.

[Mandeville, B. de] The fable of the bees: or, private vices, publick benefits. With an essay on charity and charity-schools and a search into the nature of society. 5th ed. Added vindication of the book. London, 1728. 2 vols.

In Hertzberger (1950), No. 854.

Mangey, T. Remarks upon Nazerenus. Wherein the falsity of Mr. Toland's Mahometan Gospel, and his misrepresentation of Mahometan sentiments, in respect of Christianity, are set forth, the history of the old Nazareans clear'd up, and the whole conduct of the first Christians in respect of the Jewish law, explain'd and defended. London, Printed for W. and J. Innys, 1718.

In Oko (1964), p. 228; in Hertzberger (1950), No. 932. *See* Toland (1718 and 1720).

Mangum, Donald, "Spinoza's Method," *Auslegung*, Vol. 3 (June 1976), pp. 174-181.

Manning, Jacob Merrill, *Half Truths and the Truth: Lectures on the Origin and Development of Prevailing Forms of Unbelief* (Boston: Lee & Shepard, 1872).

Includes a section, "Spinoza and Other Masters," pp. 39-73.

Mara, Gerald M., "Liberal Politics and Moral Excellence in Spinoza's Political Philosophy," *Journal of the History of Philosophy*, Vol. 20, No. 2 (April 1982), pp. 129-150.

Marcus, John T., "East and West: Phenomenologies of the Self and the Existential Bases of Knowledge," *International Philosophical Quarterly*, Vol. 11 (March 1971), pp. 5-48.

In *Philosopher's Index*, No. 031691.

Marcus, Ralph, "Spinoza on Judaism: Notes on the *Tractatus Theologico-Politicus*, Chapters I-III," *Jewish Institute Quarterly*, Vol. 2, No. 4 (March 1926), pp. 16-21.

In Oko (1964), p. 168.

Marcus, Ruth Barcan, "Spinoza and the Ontological Proof," in Donagan (1986), pp. 153-186.

Marias, Julian, *History of Philosophy*, Translated by Stanley Appelbaum and Clarence C. Strawbridge (New York: Davis Publications, 1967).

> Translation of the 22nd Spanish edition (1966). Includes a section on Spinoza, pp. 231-235, and other references.

Mark, Thomas Carson, *Spinoza's Theory of Truth* (New York: Columbia University Press, 1972).

> From the author's doctoral dissertation of the same title, Columbia University, 1970. The book edition is currently available from UMI Out-of-Print Books on Demand (Order No. 2006117).

Mark, Thomas Carson, "A Unique Copy of Spinoza's *Nagelate schriften*," *Journal of the History of Philosophy*, Vol. 13 (January 1975), pp. 81-83.

Mark, Thomas Carson, "*Ordine geometrica demonstrata*: Spinoza's Use of the Geometric Method," *The Review of Metaphysics*, Vol. 29 (December 1975), pp. 263-286.

Mark, Thomas Carson, "The Spinozistic Attributes," *Philosophia* (Israel), Vol. 7, No. 1 (March 1977), pp. 55-82.

Mark, Thomas Carson, "Truth and Adequacy in Spinozistic Ideas," in Shahan and Biro (1978), Chap. 1, pp. 11-34.

> Originally in the *Southwestern Journal of Philosophy*, Vol. 8, No. 3 (Fall 1977), pp. 11-34.

Mark, Thomas Carson, "Spinoza's Concept of Mind," *Journal of the History of Philosophy*, Vol. 17, No. 4 (October 1979), pp. 401-416.

Mark, Thomas Carson, "Spinoza on the Power and Eternity of the Intellect," in Hankins, Monfasani, and Purnell (1987), pp. 589-610.

Martens, Stanley C., "Spinoza on Attributes," *Synthèse*, Vol. 37 (January 1978), pp. 107-111.

Martin, Jean-Pierre, "Edwards' Epistemology and the New Science," *Early American Literature*, Vol. 7, No. 3 (1973), pp. 247-255.

In the *America: History and Life* database, No. 220069, citing a discussion of Jonathan Edwards' differences from Descartes, Spinoza, and others on the metaphysical basis of epistemology.

Martin, Rex, "Green on Natural Rights in Hobbes, Spinoza and Locke," in Vincent, pp. 104-126.

Martineau, James, *A Study of Spinoza* (London: Macmillan and Co., 1882).

The second edition (1883) is currently available from UMI Out-of-Print Books on Demand (Order No. BH05538). An 1895 edition was reprinted by Ayer Company Publications.

Martineau, James, *A Study of Religion: Its Sources and Contents* (Oxford: The Clarendon Press, 1888). 2 vols.

Includes a section on Spinoza and pantheism, Vol. II, pp. 161-166, and other references. An American edition, revised by the author, was published in New York by Macmillan in 1888, with the section on Spinoza in Vol. II, pp. 152-157.

Martineau, James, *Types of Ethical Theory*, 3rd Edition, revised (Oxford: The Clarendon Press, 1901). 2 vols.

Includes a chapter on Spinoza, Vol. 1, pp. 247-393.

Marx, Werner, "Reply to Professor Yovel," in Rotenstreich and Schneider (1983), pp. 91-98.

See Yovel (1983) for a reply.

Mason, Gabriel Richard, *Spinoza and Schelling: An Inquiry into the Relation of the God of Spinoza to the Absolute of Schelling*, Unpublished doctoral dissertation, New York University, 1911.

Currently available from UMI (Order No. 73-20759).

Mason, Gabriel Richard, "Living in Accordance with the Philosophy of Spinoza," in *Baruch Spinoza* (Spinoza Institute of American, 1933).

Mason, H. T., *Pierre Bayle and Voltaire* (London: Oxford University Press, 1963).

Includes a chapter, "Spinoza and Agnosticism," pp. 104-127, and other references.

Mason, R., "Spinoza on the Causality of Individuals," *Journal of the History of Philosophy*, Vol. 24, No. 2 (April 1986), pp. 197-210.

Mason, R., "Spinoza on Modality," *The Philosophical Quarterly*, Vol. 36, No. 144 (July 1986), pp. 313-342.

Massumi, Brian, *Annotated Translation with Critical Introduction of "Mille Plateaux," by Giles Deleuze and Fritz Guattari*, Unpublished doctoral dissertation, Yale University, 1987. 3 vols.

> The introduction discusses the influence of Spinoza, Nietzsche, and Bergson on Deleuze and Guattari. Currently available from UMI (Order No. 87-29112).

Matheron, Alexandre, "Spinoza and Euclidean Arithmetic: The Example of the Fourth Proportional," in Grene and Nails (1986), pp. 125-150.

Matheron, Alexandre. See *Studia Spinozana*, Vol. 1 (1985).

Mathews, Freya, "Some Reflections on Spinoza's Theory of Substance," *Philosophia* (Israel), Vol. 19, No. 1 (May 1989), pp. 1-21.

Matson, Wallace I., "Spinoza's Theory of Mind," in Mandelbaum and Freeman (1975), pp. 49-60.

> Originally in *The Monist*, Vol. 55 (1971), pp. 567-578.

Matson, Wallace I., "Death and Destruction in Spinoza's *Ethics*," *Inquiry*, Vol. 20 (Winter 1977), pp. 403-417.

Matson, Wallace I., "Steps Toward Spinozism," *Revue internationale de philosophie*, Vol. 31 (1977), pp. 69-83.

Matson, Wallace I., "Body Essence and Mind Eternity in Spinoza," in Curley and Moreau (1990), pp. 82-95.

> *See* Allison (1990) for a reply.

Mattern, Ruth M., "An Index of References to Claims in Spinoza's *Ethics*," *Philosophy Research Archives*, Vol. 5 (1979), pp. 259-274.

Maudalay, Henry, *Body and Mind: An Inquiry into Their Connection and Mutual Influence, Especially in Reference to Mental Disorders*, Enlarged and revised edition (New York: D. Appleton and Co., 1874).

> In Oko (1964), p. 453.

Maull, Nancy, "Spinoza in the Century of Science," in Grene and Nails (1986), pp. 3-13.

Maurice, Frederick Denison, *Modern Philosophy, or, A Treatise of Moral and Metaphysical Philosophy from the Fifteenth Century to the French Revolution, with a Glimpse into the Nineteenth Century* (London: Griffin, Bohn, and Co., 1862).

> In Van der Linde, No. 148, Monograph XXXII, with additional detail from Oko (1964), p. 145, whose citation differs somewhat. Includes a section on Spinoza, pp. 372-432.

Maverick, Lewis A., "Possible Chinese Source of Spinoza's Doctrine," *Revue de Litérature Comparée*, Vol. 19 (1939), pp. 417-428.

Maxwell, Douglas V., *Substance and A Priori Knowledge: A Spinozan Epistemology*, Unpublished doctoral dissertation, University of Toronto, 1974.

Maxwell, Vance, "The Philosophical Method of Spinoza," *Dialogue* (Ottawa), Vol. 27, No. 1 (Spring 1988), pp. 89-110.

May, Rollo, *The Meaning of Anxiety*, 2nd Edition (New York: Norton, 1977).

> In *Mental Health Abstracts*, No. 0308510, citing a discussion of the interpretation of anxiety by philosophers such as Spinoza, Pascal, and Kierkegaard. See also the same author's discussion of Spinoza's views on the capacity of reason to overcome fear, presented in the course of his chapter in *Psychology and the Human Dilemma* (Princeton: Van Nostrand, 1967), pp. 53-83.

Mayer, Frederick, *Man, Morals, and Education* (New Haven, CT: College and University Press Service, 1962).

> In *Philosopher's Index*, No. 018321, citing references to Spinoza, Jefferson, Tolstoy, and Dewey.

Mayo, C. *See* Amyrc (1898).

Mays, Morley, *The Attributes of Spinoza's Treatment of God*, Unpublished doctoral dissertation, University of Virginia, 1949.

Mazierski, S., "Albert Einstein on the Role of Philosophy in Natural Science," *Roczniki filozoficzne* (Lublin), Vol. 28 (1980), pp. 71-87.

> In Van der Werf (1984), No. 1259.

McCall, Raymond J., *Necessity, Analogy and the Historical Position of Spinoza*, Unpublished doctoral dissertation, Fordham University, 1941.

McCall, Raymond J., "The Teleological Approach to Spinoza," *The New Scholasticism*, Vol. 17 (April 1943), pp. 134-155.

McCracken, David John, *Thinking and Valuing: An Introduction, Partly Historical, to the Study of the Philosophy of Value* (London: Macmillan, 1950).

   In *Philosopher's Index*, No. 072817, and in Wetlesen (1968), p. 50.

McEachran, Frank, *The Life and Philosophy of Johann Gottfried Herder* (Oxford: The Clarendon Press, 1939).

   Includes a section on Spinoza, pp. 74-80, and other references.

McFarland, Thomas, *Coleridge and the Pantheist Tradition* (Oxford: The Clarendon Press, 1969).

   In *Philosopher's Index*, No. 077073.

McGahagan, T. A., *Cartesianism in the Netherlands: The New Science and the Calvinist Counter-Reformation*, Unpublished doctoral dissertation, Philadelphia, 1976.

   In Van der Werf (1984), No. 1185.

McGann, Thomas F., *A History of Philosophy in the West: A Synopsis from Descartes to Nietzsche* (Lanham, MD: University Press of America, 1979).

   In *Philosopher's Index*, No. 089108.

McGiffert, Arthur Cushman, "The God of Spinoza as Interpreted by Herder," *Hibbert Journal*, Vol. 3, No. 4 (July 1906), pp. 706-726.

McGilvary, E. B., *et al.* (eds.), *Studies in Philosophy Prepared in Commemoration of the Seventieth Birthday of Professor George Holmes Howison*, University of California Publications, Philosophy, Vol. 1 (Berkeley: The University Press, November 29, 1904).

   Includes a chapter by Arthur O. Lovejoy, "The Dialectic of Bruno and Spinoza," pp. 141-174.

McIntyre, James Lewis, *Giordano Bruno* (London and New York: Macmillan, 1903).

   Includes a section on Bruno's influence on Spinoza, pp. 337-343.

McKee, David Rice, *Simon Tyssot de Patot and the Seventeenth-Century Background of Critical Deism* (London: Oxford University Press, 1941).

> In *Philosopher's Index*, No. 072785.

McKenzie, Earl, "Time in European and African Philosophy: A Comparison," *Caribbean Quarterly* (Jamaica), Vol. 19, No. 3 (1973), pp. 77-85.

> In *Historical Abstracts* database, No. 1110031, citing a summary of the views of Parmenides, Plato, St. Augustine, Spinoza, Kant, and Hegel.

McKeon, Richard, *The Philosophy of Spinoza: The Unity of His Thought* (Woodbridge, CT: Ox Bow Press, 1987).

> From the author's doctoral dissertation, Columbia University, 1928. The original edition, published in New York by Longmans, Green and Co. in 1928, is currently available from UMI Out-of-Print Books on Demand (Order No. OP17880).

McKeon, Richard, "Spinoza and Medieval Philosophy," *The Open Court*, Vol. 42, No. 3 (March 1928), pp. 129-145.

McKeon, Richard, "Causation and the Geometric Method in the Philosophy of Spinoza," *The Philosophical Review*, Vol. 39, No. 2 (March 1930), pp. 178-189; No. 3 (May 1930), pp. 275-296.

McKeon, Richard, "Discussion and Resolution in Political Conflicts," *Ethics*, Vol. 54 (July 1944), pp. 235-262.

> In *Philosopher's Index*, No. 004519, citing references to Plato, Aristotle, and Spinoza.

McKeon, Richard, "Philosophic Differences and the Issues of Freedom," *Ethics*, Vol. 61 (January 1951), pp. 105-135.

> In *Philosopher's Index*, No. 004671, citing references to Plato, Aristotle, Spinoza, Rousseau, and Mill.

McKeon, Richard, "Spinoza on the Rainbow and on Probability," in Wolfson, *Wolfson Jubilee Volume...*(1965), Vol. II, pp. 533-559.

McKeon, Richard, "The Background of Spinoza," in Rotenstreich and Schneider (1983), pp. 24-46.

McMinn, J. B., "A Critique of Hegel's Critique of Spinoza's God," *Kant-Studien*, Vol. 51 (1959-1960), pp. 294-314.

McNeill, John J., "The Relationship Between Philosophy and Religion in Blondel's Philosophy of Action," *Proceedings of the Catholic Philosophical Association*, Vol. 44 (1970), pp. 220-231.

> In *Philosopher's Index*, No. 032388, citing references to Spinoza, Kant, Fichte, Schelling, and Hegel.

McNiven Hine, E., *A Critical Study of Condillac's "Traité des systèmes"* (The Hague, 1979).

> In Van der Werf (1984), No. 1194, citing a section on Spinoza and Leibniz, pp. 83-121.

McPhail, Robyn, and David E. Ward, *Morality and Agency* (Lanham, MD: University Press of America, 1988).

> In *Philosopher's Index*, No. 163439, citing discussion of the views of Spinoza and Kant.

McRae, Robert, "'Idea' as a Philosophical Term in the Seventeenth Century," *Journal of the History of Ideas*, Vol. 26 (April-June 1965), pp. 175-190.

> In *Philosopher's Index*, No. 008335.

McRae, Robert, "The Mind, Simple or Composite: Leibniz versus Spinoza," *The Southern Journal of Philosophy*, Vol. 21 (1983), pp. 111-120.

McShea, Robert J., *The Political Philosophy of Spinoza* (New York: Columbia University Press, 1968).

> From the author's doctoral dissertation, Columbia University, 1966. The latter is currently available from UMI (Order No. 67-00829).

McShea, Robert J., "Spinoza on Power," *Inquiry*, Vol. 12, No. 1 (Spring 1969), pp. 133-143.

McShea, Robert J., "Spinoza: Human Nature and History," in Mandelbaum and Freeman (1975), pp. 101-116.

> Originally in *The Monist*, Vol. 55 (1971), pp. 602-616.

McShea, Robert J., "Spinoza in the History of Ethical Theory," *Giornale critico della filosofia italiana*, Vol. 8 (October-December 1977), pp. 427-435.

> Also published under the same title in *The Philosophical Forum*, Vol. 8 (Fall 1976), pp. 59-67.

McShea, Robert J., "Spinoza's Human Nature Ethical Theory," in Giancotti Boscherini (1985), pp. 281-290.

Medicus, Fritz, and Fritz Marti, "The Work of Schelling," *Clio*, Vol. 13, No. 4 (1984), pp. 349-368.

> Memorial address delivered at the University of Zurich on June 11, 1954.
> Discusses the influence of Spinoza, Kant, and Fichte on Schelling.

Meerloo, Joost A. M., "Spinoza: A Look at His Psychological Concepts," *American Journal of Psychiatry*, Vol. 121 (1965), pp. 890-895.

> In Curley (1975), p. 306.

Meijer, W. *See* Spinoza, *Eigenhändigen Briefe ...* (1903).

Melamed, Samuel Max, *Spinoza and Buddha: Visions of a Dead God* (Chicago: University of Chicago Press, 1933).

> Currently available from UMI Out-of-Print Books on Demand (Order No. OP61721).

Melamed, Samuel Max, "Spinoza, the Jew: An Interpretation of His Philosophy," *The New Palestine*, Vol. 12 (1927), pp. 218-220.

> In Oko (1964), p. 373.

Melamed, Samuel Max, "Spinoza, the Jew: His Conception of the Jewish State," *The New Palestine*, Vol. 12 (1927), pp. 336-337.

> In Oko (1964), p. 460.

Mellone, S. H., *The Dawn of Modern Thought: Descartes, Spinoza, Leibniz,* With an introductory note by W. D. Ross (London: Oxford University Press, 1930).

> Includes a chapter on Spinoza, pp. 47-86, and many other references.
> Currently available from UMI Out-of-Print Books on Demand (Order No. OP54725).

Mendelssohn, Moses. *See* Valleé (1988) and Willis (1870).

Mendes-Flohr, Paul R., "Spinoza: Renegade or Meta-Rabbi," *Forum*, Vol. 27 (1977), pp. 54-63.

Mendes-Flohr, Paul R., and Stephen L. Weinstein, "The Heretic as Hero," *Jerusalem Quarterly* (Israel), Vol. 7 (1978), pp. 57-63.

Merz, John Theodore, *A History of European Thought in the Nineteenth Century* (Edinburgh: William Blackwood and Sons, MCML). 4 vols.

> Includes many references to Spinoza in Vols. III and IV.

Metzger, Lore, "Coleridge's Vindication of Spinoza: An Unpublished Note," *Journal of the History of Ideas*, Vol. 21 (April-June 1960), pp. 279-293.

Mignini, Filippo, "Theology as the Work and Instrument of Fortune," in De Deugd (1984), pp. 127-136.

Mignini, Filippo, "Spinoza's Theory on the Active and Passive Nature of Knowledge," in *Studia Spinozana*, Vol. 2 (1986), pp. 27-58.

Mignini, Filippo, "In Order To Interpret Spinoza's Theory of the Third Kind of Knowledge: Should Intuitive Science Be Considered *Per causam proximam* Knowledge?" in Curley and Moreau (1990), pp. 136-146.

Mignini, Filippo. See *Studia Spinozana*, Vol. 2 (1986) and Vol. 4 (1988).

Mihaly, Eugene, "Concluding Remarks," in Kogan (1979), pp. 104-106.

Mijnskovic, Ben, "Spinoza's Ontological Proof," *Sophia*, Vol. 12 (April 1973), pp. 17-24.

Miller, David Clark, *Religious Controversy and Enlightenment: A Study of French Biblical and Ecclesiastical Scholarship in the Age of Louis XIV, 1680-1715*, Unpublished doctoral dissertation, University of Kansas, 1984.

> Includes material on Spinoza. Currently available from UMI (Order No. 84-24380).

Miller, Hugh, *Historical Introduction to Modern Philosophy* (New York: Macmillan, 1947).

> In *Philosopher's Index*, No. 076600.

Miller, Samuel J. T., *A Study in Religious Reunion in the Seventeenth Century: Bossuet, Spinoza and Leibniz*, Unpublished doctoral dissertation, Brown University, 1952.

Millner, Simon L., *The Face of Benedictus Spinoza* (New York: Machmadim Art Editions, 1946).

Includes a 51-page introduction, followed by 42 plates.

Misrahi, Robert, "Spinoza and Christian Thought: A Challenge," in Hessing (1977), pp. 387-417.

Modak, M. S., *Spinoza and the Upanishads: A Comparative Study* (Nagpur: Nagpur University, 1970).

Perhaps from the author's doctoral dissertation, *Vedanta and Spinoza: A Comparative Study*, University of London, 1928. Paul Siwek, *Spinoza et la Panthéisme religieux* (Paris: Descleé De Brouwer, 1950), p. xxxi, cites *Spinozistic Substance and Upanishadic Self: A Comparative Study of Philosophy* (London, 1932). Kashap (1972), p. 354, and (1987), p. 191, cites a paper with the same title, *Philosophy*, Vol. 6 (1931), pp. 446-458.

Mollenhauer, Berhard, "Spinoza and the Borderland of Science," *The Personalist*, Vol. 22 (Winter 1941), pp. 64-72.

Molnar, Paul D., "Is God Essentially Different from His Creatures?" *The Thomist*, Vol. 51 (October 1987), pp. 575-631.

In *Philosopher's Index*, No. 152750, noting the author's argument that K. Rahner's theory of revelation "suffers from difficulties similar to those of Descartes and Spinoza in their attempts to reconcile reason and revelation."

Montague, Wm. Pepperell, *Great Visions of Philosophy: Varieties of Speculative Thought in the West from the Greeks to Bergson* (LaSalle, IL: The Open Court Publishing Co., 1950).

Includes a chapter, "Spinoza and the Monistic Vision of a Totalitarian Universe," pp. 262-269, and other references.

Moore, Asher, "Reason and Existence: Or, What Spinoza Was Doing Up In His Room," in Casey (1986), pp. 3-18.

Moreau, Joseph, "The Problem of Intentionality and Classical Thought," *International Philosophical Quarterly*, Vol. 1 (May 1961), pp. 215-234.

In *Philosopher's Index*, No. 004242, citing references to Plato, Descartes, Spinoza, and Malebranche.

Moreau, P. F. See *Studia Spinozana*, Vol. 4 (1988).

[Moreri, Louis]   The great historical, geographical and poetical dictionary; being a curious miscellany of sacred and profane history ... Collected from the best historians, chronologers, and lexicographers ... but more specially out of Lewis Morery, his 6th edition corrected and enlarged by Monsieur Le Clerk ... Now done into English ... London, Printed for H. Rhodes, 1694.

> In Oko (1964), p. 127, citing an article on Spinoza. A second edition – "rev., cor. and enl. to the year 1688; by Jer. Collier" – appeared in two vols. in 1701, also with an article (in Vol. 2) on Spinoza.

Morgan, Conwy Lloyd, *Life, Mind, and Spirit*, Being the Second Course of the Gifford Lectures, Delivered in the University of St. Andrews in the Year 1923 Under the General Title of Emergent Evolution (London: Williams and Norgate, 1926).

> Includes a section, "Back to Spinoza?" on pp. 26-30.

Morgan, M. L., "The Curse of Historicity: The Role of History in Leo Strauss's Jewish Thought," *The Journal of Religion*, Vol. 61 (1981), pp. 345-363.

> In Van der Werf (1984), No. 1356.

Morgan, M. L., "History and Modern Jewish Thought: Spinoza and Mendelssohn on the Ritual Law," *Judaism*, Vol. 30, No. 4 (1981), pp. 467-478.

Morgan, William Sacheus, *The Philosophy of Religion* (New York: Philosophical Library, 1950).

> In *Philosopher's Index*, No. 075521.

Morley, John, *Diderot and the Encyclopaedists* (London: Chapman and Hall, 1878). 2 vols.

> Includes a sketch of Diderot's essay on Spinoza in the *Encyclopedia*, Vol. I, pp. 223-226. A 1914 edition published in London by Macmillan includes this section in Vol. I, pp. 228-232.

Morrell, J. D., *An Historical and Critical View of the Speculative Philosophy of Europe in the Nineteenth Century*, From the last London edition [the 2nd] (New York: Robert Carter & Brothers, 1853).

> Includes a discussion of Spinoza, pp. 122-132. In the original two-volume version of the 2nd Edition (London: John Johnstone, 1847), this section is on pp. 181-195.

Morris, C. W., "Opening Remarks," in Schaub (1933).

Morris, George Sylvester, "Spinoza: A Summary Account of His Life and Teaching," *Journal of Speculative Philosophy*, Vol. 11, No. 3 (July 1877), pp. 278-299.

Morris, Henry D., "Interpretation and Reinterpretation in Maimonides and Spinoza," in Braune (1979), Vol. 1, pp. 75-88.

Morrison, James C., "Spinoza and History," in Kennington (1980), Chap. 11, pp. 173-198.

Morrison, James C., "Vico and Spinoza," *Journal of the History of Ideas*, Vol. 41, No. 1 (January-March 1980), pp. 49-68.

Morrison, James C., "The Ethics of Spinoza's *Ethics*," *The Modern Schoolman*, Vol. 63, No. 3 (1986), pp. 173-191.

Morrison, James C., "Why Spinoza Had No Aesthetics," *Journal of Aesthetics and Art Criticism*, Vol. 47, No. 4 (1989), pp. 359-365.

Morrison, James C., "Spinoza on the Self, Personal Identity and Immortality," in Hunter (1991).

Mosheim, Johann Lorenz, *Institutes of Ecclesiastical History, Ancient and Modern* ..., A new and literal translation from the original Latin, with copious additional notes, original and selected, by James Murdock, 3rd Edition (New York: Harper, 1845-1849). 3 vols.

> In Oko (1964), p. 305 (repeated on p. 353), citing references to Spinoza.

Moss, Arthur B., *Bruno and Spinoza* (London: Watts & Co., 1885).

> Cited in all editions of Boyle's translation of the *Ethics* (except Parkinson's). Also cited in the entry on Spinoza in S. M. Jackson (ed.), *The New Schaff-Herzog Encyclopedia of Religious Knowledge* (Grand Rapids, MI: Baker Book House, 1953), Vol. XI, p. 50, and in Wetlesen (1968), p. 68.

Motzkin, Aryeh L., "Spinoza and Luzzatto: Philosophy and Religion," *Journal of the History of Philosophy*, Vol. 17, No. 1 (January 1979), pp. 43-51.

Muirhead, John Henry, *Coleridge as Philosopher* (London: G. Allen & Unwin; New York: The Macmillan Co., 1930).

> In Oko (1964), p. 272, citing a section, "Berkeley and Spinoza," pp. 45-48, and other references.

Mukhopadhyaya, Aloka, "Is Spinoza an Acosmist?" *Philosophical Quarterly of India*, Vol. 23 (1950-1951), pp. 177-183.

Mungello, David E., "Malebranche and Chinese Philosophy," *Journal of the History of Ideas*, Vol. 41 (October-December 1980), pp. 551-578.

> In *Philosopher's Index*, No. 108303. Also in Van der Werf (1984), No. 1377, citing a discussion on pp. 561-563 of "Spinozism as a possible source and motivation."

Munitz, Milton K., *The Mystery of Existence: An Essay in Philosophical Cosmology* (New York: Appleton-Century-Crofts, 1965).

> In *Philosopher's Index*, No. 019654, citing references to Aquinas, Spinoza, and Kant.

Munitz, Milton K., *The Ways of Philosophy* (New York: Macmillan Publishing Co.; London: Collier Macmillan Publishers, 1979).

> Includes a chapter on Spinoza, "Nature and Man's Well-Being," pp. 231-262, and other references.

Muraskin, I. H., "Why Honor Spinoza?" in *Baruch Spinoza* (Spinoza Institute of America, 1933).

Murphy, Cornelius, F., Jr., "The Grotian Vision of World Order," *American Journal of International Law*, Vol. 76, No. 3 (1982), pp. 478-498.

> Compares the views of Hugo Grotius with those of Suarez, Spinoza, Hobbes, Pufendorf, and others.

Murphy, J. G., "Rationality and the Fear of Death," *The Monist*, Vol. 59 (April 1976), pp. 187-203.

> In *Philosopher's Index*, No. 051133.

Murray, J. Clark, "Idealism of Spinoza," *The Philosophical Review*, Vol. 5 (1896), pp. 473-488.

Murti, T. R. V., "Review of *The Philosophy of Spinoza*, by Harry A. Wolfson," *The Philosophical Quarterly*, Vol. 11 (1935), pp. 180-197.

> In Oko (1964), pp. 487.

Muska, Rudolph C., *Religious Conceptions in Kierkegaard and Spinoza*, Unpublished doctoral dissertation, Michigan State University, 1960.

Currently available from UMI (Order No. 61-01189).

Mutch, W. J., "Spinoza Three Centuries After," *Homiletic Review*, No. 104 (November 1932), pp. 347-351.

Myers, Henry Alonzo, *An Introduction to the Timely and Synoptic Elements of Metaphysics: Illustrated by the Logic (Synoptic Element) and the History (Timely Element) of the Conceptions of Perspectives and the Metaphysical Object Appearing in the Logos of Heraclitus, the Attributes and Substance of Spinoza, the Perspectival Monads of Leibniz, the Categories and Absolute of Hegel, and the Concepts and Intuition of Bergson*, Unpublished doctoral dissertation, Cornell University, 1933.

Myers, Henry Alonzo, *The Spinoza-Hegel Paradox: A Study of the Choice Between Traditional Idealism and Systematic Pluralism* (Ithaca, NY: Cornell University Press, 1944).

Myers, Henry Alonzo, *Systematic Pluralism: A Study in Metaphysics* (Ithaca, NY: Cornell University Press, 1961).

> Chap. I and major portions of Chaps. IV, VI, and X are from Myers (1944). Much of the rest is from Myers (1933). Chap. IV, pp. 63-84, is entitled, "Static Element: Spinoza and Hegel on the Nature of Systems." Chap. V, pp. 85-107, is entitled, "Dynamic Element: Time in Heraclitus, Spinoza, and Hegel." There are many references to Spinoza in other chapters.

Myers, Henry A., "Systematic Pluralism in Spinoza and Hegel," *The Monist*, Vol. 45 (July 1935), pp. 237-263.

Naess, Arne, *Equivalent Terms and Notions in Spinoza's Ethics* (Oslo, 1974).

> In Van der Werf (1984), No. 1388.

Naess, Arne, *Freedom, Emotion, and Self-Subsistence: The Structure of a Central Part of Spinoza's Ethics* (Oslo: Universitetsforlaget, 1975).

> An earlier version was published under the same title, *Inquiry*, Vol. 12, No. 1 (January 1969), pp. 66-104.

Naess, Arne, "Is Freedom Consistent with Spinoza's Determinism?" in Van der Bend (1974), pp. 6-23.

Naess, Arne, "Friendship, Strength of Emotion, and Freedom," *Algemeen Nederlands tijdschrift voor wijsbegeerte*, Vol. 69 (1977), pp. 11-19.

> In Van der Werf (1984), No. 1391.

Naess, Arne, "Spinoza and Ecology," in Hessing (1977), pp. 418-425.

> Also published under the same title in *Philosophia* (Israel), Vol. 7 (March 1977), pp. 45-54.

Naess, Arne, "Through Spinoza to Mahayana Buddhism or Through Mahayana Buddhism to Spinoza," in Wetlesen (1978), pp. 136-158.

> *See* Wetlesen (1978) for a reply.

Naess, Arne, "Environmental Ethics and Spinoza's Ethics: Comments on Genevieve Lloyd's Article," *Inquiry*, Vol. 23, No. 3 (Summer 1980), pp. 313-325.

> *See* Lloyd (1980).

Naess, Arne, "Spinoza's Finite God," *Revue internationale de philosophie*, Vol. 35, No. 135 (1981), pp. 120-126.

Naess, Arne, "Spinoza and Attitudes Toward Nature," in Rotenstreich and Schneider (1983), pp. 160-175.

Naess, Arne, "Einstein, Spinoza and God," in Van der Merwe (1983), pp. 683-687.

Naess, Arne, "Limited Definiteness of God in Spinoza's System: Answer to Heine Siebrand," *Neue Zeitschrift für Systematische Theologie und Religionsphilosophie*, Vol. 28, No. 3 (1986), pp. 275-283.

> *See* Siebrand (1986).

Naess, Arne, and Jon Wetlesen, *Conation and Cognition in Spinoza's Theory of Affects: A Reconstruction* (Oslo: University of Oslo, 1967).

> Currently available from UMI Out-of-Print Books on Demand (Order No. OP66805).

Naess, Ragner, "The Snout Beetles," in Gullvag and Wetlesen (1982), pp. 213-219.

Nagel, Thomas, *Mortal Questions* (New York, 1979).

> In Bennett (1984), p. 380, citing the chapter, "Panpsychism."

Naik, Ajaya D., *Absolute Theory*, Unpublished doctoral dissertation, University of Aberdeen (UK), 1987.

Includes material on Spinoza. Currently available from UMI (Order No. DX-81385).

Nails, Debra, "Some Implications of Spinoza's Doctrine of Determinism and Human Freedom," *Kinesis*, Vol. 9 (Fall 1978), pp. 11-22.

Nails, Debra, "Conatus versus Eros/Thanatos: On the Principles of Spinoza and Freud," *Dialogue: Journal of Phi Sigma Tau*, Vol. 21, Nos. 2-3 (April 1979), pp. 33-40.

Nails, Debra, "Of Children, Fools and Madmen: Spinoza's Scientific Method and the Constraint of Fact," *Southwest Philosophy Review*, Vol. 2 (1985), pp. 30-42.

Nails, Debra, "Annotated Bibliography of Spinoza and the Sciences," in Grene and Nails (1986), pp. 305-314.

Nails, Debra, "A Human Being Like Any Other: Like No Other," *Philosophical Forum*, Vol. 18 (Winter-Spring 1987), pp. 124-136.

> In *Philosopher's Index*, No. 146924, noting the author's argument that today's dominant concept of human nature can be used either to support or to oppose apartheid, whereas Spinoza's position undermines this concept.

Nasmith, David, *Makers of Modern Thought, or, Five Hundred Years' Struggle (1200 A.D. to 1699 A.D.) between Science, Ignorance and Superstition* (London: G. Philip & Son, 1892). 2 vols.

> Discusses Spinoza and includes a translation of part of the *Ethics*, Vol. 2, pp. 138-192.

Nathanson, Harvey B., *Spinoza's Metaphysics: A New Interpretation*, Unpublished doctoral dissertation, University of Nebraska, Lincoln, 1954.

Nathanson, Harvey B., "Spinoza's God: Some Special Aspects," *Man and World*, Vol. 3 (September-November 1970), pp. 200-223.

Nathanson, William, "Spinoza and Bergson: A Parallel," Translated by David Wollins, *Guardian* (Philadelphia), Vol. 1, No. 4 (February 1925), pp. 117-122.

> In Oko (1964), p. 272.

Nauen, F., "Hermann Cohen's Perceptions of Spinoza: A Reappraisal," *Association for Jewish Studies Review*, Vol. 4 (1979), pp. 111-124.

In Van der Werf (1984), No. 1406, and in Dienstag (1986), p. 395.

Naug, Sukrit Chandra, "Four Types of A Priori," *Indian Philosophical Quarterly*, Vol. 3 (January 1976), pp. 149-160.

In *Philosopher's Index*, No. 050624, citing a discussion of Spinoza's substance as an example of "ontological apriorities."

Neff, D. S., "Synge, Spinoza, and the 'Well of the Saints,'" *ANQ: A Quarterly Journal of Short Articles, Notes, and Reviews*, Vol. 2, No. 4 (1989), pp. 138-145.

Negri, Antonio, "Between Infinity and Community: Notes on Materialism in Spinoza and Leopardi," Translated by Michael Hardt, in *Studia Spinozana*, Vol. 5 (1989), pp. 151-176.

Nesher, Dan, *An Analysis of Spinoza's Political Philosophy*, Unpublished doctoral dissertation, Brandeis University, 1972.

Currently available from UMI (Order No. 72-32114).

Nesher, Dan, "Spinoza's Theory of Truth," in Hunter (1991).

Neu, Jerome, *Emotion, Thought and Therapy: A Study of Hume and Spinoza and the Relationship of Philosophical Theories of the Emotions to Psychological Theories of Therapy* (Berkeley: University of California Press, 1977).

Also published in London by Routledge & Kegan Paul, 1978.

Neu, Jerome, "Thought, Theory, and Therapy," *Psychoanalysis and Contemporary Science*, Vol. 4 (1975), pp. 103-143.

Emphasizes "the advantages of a Spinozistic theory of mind — particularly, the importance of thoughts in the classification and discrimination of emotional states and the subsequent importance of reflexive knowledge in changing those states — in understanding the role of thought and insight." — *PsychINFO Database*, No. 0781260-4.7800.

Neumann, H., "Torah or Philosophy: Jewish Alternatives to Modern Epicureanism," *The Journal of Value Inquiry*, Vol. 11 (Spring 1977), pp. 16-28.

In *Philosopher's Index*, No. 057006.

Neumark David, *The Philosophy of the Bible* (Cincinnati: Ark Publishing, 1918).

In Cohon's bibliography in Neumark (1971), p. 373.

Neumark, David, *Essays in Jewish Philosophy*, Edited, with a bibliography of the author's writings, by Samuel S. Cohon (Amsterdam: Philo Press, 1971).

Reprint of the 1929 edition published in Cincinnati by the Central Conference of American Rabbis. Includes an essay, "Crescas and Spinoza: A Memorial Paper in Honor of the Five Hundredth Anniversary of the *Or Adonoi*," pp. 301-346, which was first published in the *Yearbook of the Central Conference of American Rabbis*, Vol. 18 (1908), pp. 277-318.

Nevinson, H., *A Sketch of Herder and His Times* (London, 1884).

In Hertzberger (1950), No. 821, citing a section on Spinoza, pp. 336-350, and other references.

Newman, Jay, "The Compatibilist Interpretation of Spinoza," *The Personalist*, Vol. 55 (Autumn 1974), pp. 360-368.

Newman, Jay, "Exclusive Salvation," *Sophia*, Vol. 17 (October 1978), pp. 16-26.

In *Philosopher's Index*, No. 080281.

Newman, Jay, "Some Tensions in Spinoza's Ethical Theory," *Indian Philosophical Quarterly*, Vol. 7 (April 1980), pp. 357-374.

Newman, Jay, "Humility and Self-Realization," *The Journal of Value Inquiry*, Vol. 16 (1982), pp. 275-285.

In *Philosopher's Index*, No. 116278, noting the author's argument that both Spinoza and Nietzsche believed humility to be a barrier to self-realization and, hence, not a virtue.

Nicholson, D. N., *Spinoza* (Binghamton, NY: Ben Halevi, 1933).

In Bruder (1970), p. 316.

Nicolson, John A., *Philosophy of Religion* (New York: Ronald Press, 1950).

In *Philosopher's Index*, No. 018460, citing references to Pascal, Spinoza, Kant, Comte, and Bergson.

Niddich, P. H., "Spinoza," in O'Connor (1964), pp. 187-203.

Nierenstein, M., "Helvetius, Spinoza, and Transmutation," *Isis*, Vol. 17 (1932), pp. 408-411.

In Walther (1976), p. 426.

[Nieuwentijdt, Bernard] The religious philosopher: or, The right use of contemplating the works of the Creator ... designed for the conviction of atheists and infidels ... throughout which, all the late discoveries in anatomy, philosophy, and astronomy ... are most copiously handled by that learned mathematician, Dr. Nieuwentyt. Translated from the original by John Chamberlayne ... To which is prefix'd a letter to the translator, by the Reverend J. T. Desaguliers ... London, Printed for J. Senex [etc.] 1718-1719. 3 vols.

In Oko (1964), p. 390; in Hertzberger (1950), No. 895.

Nigg, Walter, *The Heretics: Heresy Through the Ages*, Edited and translated by Richard and Clara Winston (New York: Dorset Press, 1990).

Reprint of the translation published in 1962 by Alfred Knopf from the 1949 German edition. Includes a section on Spinoza, pp. 352-361.

Nisbet, Hugh Barr, *Herder and Scientific Thought* (Cambridge: Modern Humanities Research Association, 1970).

In *Philosopher's Index*, No. 074439.

Noire, Ludwig, *A Sketch of the Development of Philosophic Thought from Thales to Kant* (London, 1900).

In Rabenort (1972), p. 86.

Noone, John B., Jr., "Spinoza's World-View," *The Southern Journal of Philosophy*, Vol. 7 (Summer 1969), pp. 161-169.

Nordau, Max, *Morals and the Evolution of Man*, Translated by Marie A. Lewenz (London: Cassell and Co., 1922).

Includes a section on Spinoza, pp. 13-18, and other references.

Norton, Andrews. Remarks on a pamphlet entitled "'The latest form of infidelity' examined." Cambridge, J. Owen, 1839.

72 pp. In Oko (1964), p. 354. *See* Ripley (1840).

Nutkiewicz, Michael E., *The Impact of Mechanical Philosophy on Early Modern Political Theory: Hobbes, Spinoza, Pufendorf, and Vico*, Unpublished doctoral dissertation, University of California, Los Angeles, 1978.

Currently available from UMI (Order No. 79-06186).

Nutkiewicz, Michael E., "Samuel Pufendorf: Obligation as the Basis of the State," *Journal of the History of Philosophy*, Vol. 21 (January 1983), pp. 15-30.

In *Philosopher's Index*, No. 119618.

Nuzhat, [?], "Spinoza and Freedom," *Pakistan Philosophical Congress*, Vol. 12 (1965), pp. 314-317.

In *Philosopher's Index*, No. 067797.

Oakeley, H. D., "Is There a Higher Reason?" *Proceedings of the Aristotelian Society*, Vol. 43 (1943), pp. 37-58.

In *Philosopher's Index*, No. 066313, citing references to Spinoza, Plato, and Kant.

Oakes, Robert A., "Classical Theism and Pantheism: A Victory for Process Theism?" *Religious Studies*, Vol. 13 (1977), pp. 167-173.

See Quinn (1979) for a reply.

Oakes, Robert A., "Classical Theism and Pantheism: A Reply to Professor Quinn," *Religious Studies*, Vol. 16 (1980), pp. 353-356.

O'Brien, Robert C., *The Achievement of Selfhood and the Life of Reason in the "Ethics" of Spinoza*, Unpublished doctoral dissertation, Fordham University, 1968.

Currently available from UMI (Order No. 69-02602).

Ochs, Carol R. B., *The Ontological Argument in Descartes, Spinoza and Leibniz*, Unpublished doctoral dissertation, Brandeis University, 1968.

Currently available from UMI (Order No. 69-02059).

O'Connor, D. J. (ed.), *A Critical History of Western Philosophy* (New York: Free Press of Glencoe; London: Collier-Macmillan, 1964).

Includes an essay on Spinoza by P. H. Niddich, pp. 187-203.

Odegard, Douglas, "The Body Identical with the Human Mind: A Problem in Spinoza's Philosophy," in Mandelbaum and Freeman (1975), pp. 61-84.

> Originally in *The Monist*, Vol. 55, No. 4 (October 1971), pp. 579-601.

Odegard, Douglas, "Spinoza and Cartesian Scepticism," in Hunter (1991).

Offenberg, A. K., "Spinoza's Library: The Story of a Reconstruction," *Quaerendo* (Leiden), Vol. 3 (1973), pp. 309-321.

> In Van der Werf (1984), No. 1440.

Offenberg, A. K., "Letter from Spinoza to Lodewijk Meyer, 26 July 1663," in Hessing (1977), pp. 426-435.

> Also published under the title, "A Newly Found Letter from Spinoza to Lodewijk Meijer, 26 July 1663," *Philosophia* (Israel), Vol. 7 (March 1977), pp. 1-13.

Ogden, M. R., "*Amor Dei intellectualis*: Holderlin, Spinoza and St. John," *Deutsche Vierteljahrschrift für Literaturwissenschaft und Geistesgeschichte*, Vol. 63, No. 3 (1989), pp. 420-460.

> In *Arts and Humanities Search*, No. 1112261.

Ogg, David, *Europe in the Seventeenth Century* (London, 1928).

> In Hertzberger (1950), No. 29, citing references to Spinoza on pp. 9 and 26-28. An 8th Edition was published in 1961 in London by A. & C. Black.

O'Hear, Anthony, "Belief and the Will," *Philosophy*, Vol. 47 (1972), pp. 95-112.

> In Curley (1975), p. 299. *See* Evans (1963).

Oko, Adolph S., *The Spinoza Bibliography*, With preface by Dorothy Kuhn Oko and introduction by Horace M. Kallen (Boston: G. K. Hall & Co., 1964).

[Oko, Adolph S.] "Spinoza," by S. Baruch [pseud.], *Hebrew Union College Monthly* (November 1914-January 1915). 3 parts.

> In Oko (1964), p. 100.

Oko, Adolph S., "William Hale White," in *Chronicon Spinozanum*, Vol. II (1922), pp. 233-242.

Oldham, Alice, *An Introduction to the Study of Philosophy*, A Series of Lectures on Ethics, Metaphysics, and Psychology Delivered in Alexandria College, Dublin (Dublin: Hodges, Figgis & Co., 1909).

Includes a lecture on Spinoza, pp. 79-88.

Oppenheimer, Oscar, *God and Man* (Lanham, MD: University Press of America, 1979).

In *Philosopher's Index*, No. 089118.

Orenstein, Esther, *The Significance of Action in Spinoza's Philosophy*, Unpublished doctoral dissertation, New York University, 1983.

Currently available from UMI (Order No. 83-24839).

Osgood, Samuel, "The Centenary of Spinoza," *The North American Review*, Vol. 124 (1877), pp. 265-288.

In Oko (1964), p. 180.

Pacchi, A., "*Leviathan* and Spinoza's *Tractatus* on Revelation: Some Elements for a Comparison," *History of European Ideas*, Vol. 10, No. 5 (1989), pp. 577-593.

Papadementriou, George C., "Moses Maimonides' Doctrine of God," *Philosophia* (Athens), Vol. 4 (1974), pp. 306-329.

In *Philosopher's Index*, No. 048133.

Parker, D. H., "Philosopher-Saint: Spinoza," *American Scholar*, Vol. 2 (January 1933), pp. 43-57.

Parker, Francis Howard, *The Story of Western Philosophy* (London: Indiana University Press, 1967).

In *Philosopher's Index*, No. 071915.

Parkinson, G. H. R., *Spinoza's Theory of Knowledge* (Oxford: Clarendon Press, 1954).

Parkinson, G. H. R., *Spinoza: Reason and Experience* (London: Open University Press, 1983). 84 pp.

Parkinson, G. H. R., *Logic and Reality in Leibniz's Metaphysics* (New York: Garland Publishing, 1985).

> Facsimile reprint of the original edition published in Oxford by the Clarendon Press in 1965. Includes many references to Spinoza, especially in Chap. 4, "Logic and Theism."

Parkinson, G. H. R. *See* Spinoza, *Ethics* (1989).

Parkinson, G. H. R., "Truth and Falsity in Spinoza," in Kashap (1972), pp. 212-235.

> Originally in Parkinson (1954), Chap. VI, pp. 112-137.

Parkinson, G. H. R., "Being and Knowledge in Spinoza," in Van der Bend (1974), pp. 24-40.

Parkinson, G. H. R., "Spinoza on the Power and Freedom of Man," in Mandelbaum and Freeman (1975), pp. 7-34.

> Originally in *The Monist*, Vol 55, No. 4 (October 1971), pp. 527-553.

Parkinson, G. H. R., "Hegel, Pantheism, and Spinoza," *Journal of the History of Ideas*, Vol. 38, No. 3 (July-September 1977), pp. 449-459.

Parkinson, G. H. R., "Spinoza on Miracles and Natural Law," *Revue internationale de philosophie*, Vol. 31 (1977), pp. 145-157.

Parkinson, G. H. R., "Leibniz's Paris Writings in Relation to Spinoza," in *Leibniz à Paris...*(1978), Vol. 2, pp. 73-89.

Parkinson, G. H. R., "'Truth Is Its Own Standard': Aspects of Spinoza's Theory of Truth," in Shahan and Biro (1978), Chap. 2, pp. 35-55.

> Originally in the *Southwestern Journal of Philosophy*, Vol. 8, No. 3 (Fall 1977), pp. 35-55.

Parkinson, G. H. R., "Language and Knowledge in Spinoza," in Grene (1979), pp. 73-100.

> Originally in *Inquiry*, Vol 12, No. 1 (1969), pp. 15-40.

Parkinson, G. H. R., "Spinoza's Concept of the Rational Act," in *Theoria cum praxi* (1981), pp. 1-19.

Parkinson, G. H. R., "Spinoza's Philosophy of Mind," in Floistad (1983), Vol. 4, pp. 105-131.

Parsons, Howard L., "Spinoza's Concept of Human Fulfillment: Its Nature and Contemporary Fulfillment in Thought and Practice," in Wetlesen (1978), pp. 159-178.

Partridge, George E. (ed.), *A Reading Book in Modern Philosophy* (New York: Sturgis & Walton Co., 1913).

> Includes a chapter on Spinoza.

Pasotti, Robert N., "Spinoza: The Metaphysician as Healer," in Wilbur (1976), pp. 106-114.

Paterson, Antoinette Mann, *The Infinite Worlds of Giordano Bruno* (Springfield, IL: Charles C. Thomas Publisher, 1970).

> Includes many references to Spinoza.

[Paterson, James] Anti-Nazarenus. By way of answer to Mr. Toland; or, A treatise proving the divine original and authority of the Holy Scriptures against atheists, Jews, heathens, Mahometans, papists, Spinoza and other modern errors. London, S. Butler, 1718.

> In Oko (1964), p. 339; in Hertzberger (1950), No. 933. *See* Toland (1718, 1720).

Paty, Michel, "Einstein and Spinoza," in Grene and Nails (1986), pp. 267-302.

Paul, Wilford, "Whitehead on 'Substance,'" *Proceedings of the New Mexico-West Texas Philosophical Society* (April 1974), pp. 94-98.

> In *Philosopher's Index*, No. 047574.

Paulsen, Friedrich, *An Introduction to Philosophy*, Translated by Frank Thilly, 2nd American Edition (New York: Henry Holt and Company, 1895).

> Includes many references to Spinoza.

Pearson, Karl, *The Ethic of Freethought and Other Addresses and Essays*, 2nd Edition, revised (London: Adam and Charles Black, 1901).

> Includes a chapter, "Maimonides and Spinoza," pp. 125-142; originally published in *Mind*, Vol. 11, No. 41 (1883), pp. 335-353.

Perrin, Raymond St. James, *The Religion of Philosophy; or, The Unification of Knowledge*, A Comparison of the Chief Philosophical and Religious Systems of the World Made with a View To Reducing the Categories of Thought, or the Most General Terms of Existence to a Single Principle, Thereby Establishing a True Conception of God (London: Williams and Norgate, 1885).

> Includes a section on Spinoza, pp. 117-126.

Perrin, Raymond St. James, *The Evolution of Knowledge: A Review of Philosophy* (New York: Baker & Taylor, 1905).

> Includes a section on Spinoza, pp. 129-135.

Perry, Ralph Barton, *Present Philosophical Tendencies* (New York: George Braziller, 1955).

> Includes sections on Spinoza, pp. 115-117, and pp. 172-175.

Pessin, Deborah, *Giants on the Earth: Stories of Great Jewish Men and Women from the Time of the Discovery of America to the Present* (New York: Behrman House, 1961).

> This book for Jewish young people contains chapters on Manasseh ben Israel, pp. 20-27; Sabbatai Zevi, pp. 28-35; and Spinoza, pp. 36-41.

Peters, R. S. (ed.), *Nature and Conduct* (London: Macmillan, 1975).

> Includes an essay by J. W. N. Watkins, "Three Views Concerning Human Freedom," pp. 200-228.

Petry, Michael J., *Nieuwentijt's Criticism of Spinoza*, Mededelingen XL vanwege het Spinozahuis (Leiden: E. J. Brill, 1979).

Petry, Michael J., "Kuyper's Analysis of Spinoza's Axiomatic Method," in Cramer, Jacobs, and Schmidt-Biggemann (1981), pp. 1-18.

Petry, Michael J., "Behmenism and Spinozism in the Religious Culture of the Netherlands, 1660-1730," in Grunder and Schmidt-Biggemann (1984), pp. 111-147.

Petry, Michael J., "Hobbes and the Early Dutch Spinozists," in De Deugd (1984), pp. 150-170.

Petry, Michael, J. *See* Spinoza, *Algebraic Calculation ...* (1985).

Petry, Michael J., and Guido van Suchtelen, "Spinoza and the Military: A Newly-Discovered Document," in *Studia Spinozana*, Vol. 1 (1985), pp. 359-369.

Pfleiderer, Otto, *The Philosophy of Religion, On the Basis of Its History*, Translated by Alexander Stewart and Allan Menzies (London: Williams and Norgate, 1886-1888). 4 vols.

> Includes a chapter, "Benedict Spinoza," Vol. I, pp. 31-67, and many other references in Vols. I, III, and IV.

Phillips, T. M., "The Influence of Spinoza on Modern Literature," *Manchester Quarterly*, Vol. 40 (1921), pp. 49-57.

> In Oko (1964), p. 307.

Pick, Barnhard, "Spinoza and the Old Testament," *The Biblical World*, Vol. 2 (August 1893), pp. 112-122; (September 1893), pp. 194-203.

Picton, J. Allanson, *The Mystery of Matter and Other Essays* (London: Macmillan, 1873).

> In Oko (1964), p. 430, and in Hertzberger (1950), No. 262.

Picton, J. Allanson, *Pantheism: Its Story and Significance* (London: Archibald. Constable & Co., 1905).

> Includes a chapter on Spinoza and his influence on Fichte, Hegel, Goethe, and Schleiermacher, pp. 56-82.

Picton, J. Allanson, *Spinoza: A Handbook to the Ethics* (London: Archibald Constable & Co., 1907).

Pietersma, H., "Merleau-Ponty and Spinoza," *International Studies in Philosophy*, Vol. 20, No. 3 (1988), pp. 89-93.

Pines, Shlomo, "Spinoza's *Tractatus Theologico-Politicus*, Maimonides and Kant," in Segal (1968), pp. 3-54.

> According to Collins (1984), p. 323, also in *Scripta Hierosolymitana*, Vol. 20 (1968), pp. 3-54.

Pines, Shlomo, "The Jewish Religion after the Destruction of the Temple and State: The Views of Bodin and Spinoza," in Stein and Loewe (1979), pp. 215-234.

Pines, Shlomo, "On Spinoza's Conception of Human Freedom and of Good and Evil," in Rotenstreich and Schneider (1983), pp. 147-159.

Pines, Shlomo, and Yirmiyahu Yovel (eds.), *Maimonides and Philosophy*, Papers presented at the Sixth Jerusalem Philosophical Encounter (Dordrecht: Martinus Nijhoff Publishers, 1986).

> Includes a paper by Yirmiyahu Yovel, "God's Transcendence and Its Schematization: Maimonides in Light of the Spinoza-Hegel Dispute," pp. 269-282.

Pitts, Edward I., "Spinoza on Freedom of Expression," *Journal of the History of Ideas*, Vol. 47, No. 1 (January/March 1986), pp. 21-35.

[Plumptre, Constance E.] *General Sketch of the History of Pantheism* (London: Samuel Deacon & Co., 1878-1879). 2 vols.

> Reprinted under the same title (London: Trübner, 1881). In either case: Vol. I, *From the Earliest Times to the Age of Spinoza*, and Vol. II, *From the Age of Spinoza to the Commencement of the Nineteenth Century*. Includes a chapter on Spinoza, Vol II, pp. 3-69, and a summary of this discussion, Vol. II, pp. 321-323.

Pocock, J. G. A., "Spinoza and Harrington: An Exercise in Comparison," *Bijdragen en Mededelingen betreffende de Geschiendenis der Nederlanden*, Vol. 102, No. 3 (1987), pp. 435-449.

Polegnac, M. de. Anti-Lucretius of God and Nature. A poem, rendered into English by the translator of Paradise Lost. London, 1757.

> In Hertzberger (1950), No. 904, citing "useful" references to Spinoza and Spinozism, and identifying W. Dobson as the translator.

Pollak, Gustav, *International Perspectives in Criticism* (New York: Dodd, Mead, 1914).

> Includes a section, "Goethe on Spinoza," pp. 282-285.

Pollock, Frederick, *Spinoza: His Life and Philosophy*, 2nd Edition (London: Duckworth and Co.; New York: Macmillan, 1899).

> Chapter 1 in the first edition (London: C. Kegan Paul & Co., 1880) includes bibliographical detail not repeated in the second. *Verslag het Spinozahuis* (1922-1923), p. 23, cites a third edition (London, 1912); this version was reprinted in New York by American Scholar Publications in 1966.

Pollock, Frederick, *Spinoza*, Great Lives Series, No. 60 (London: Duckworth, 1935).

Pollock, Frederick, "Spinoza: The Scientific Character of His Philosophy," *The Fortnightly Review*, Vol. 19 (1873), pp. 567-585.

Pollock, Frederick, "Notes on the Philosophy of Spinoza," *Mind*, Vol. 3 (1878), pp. 195-212.

Pollock, Frederick, "Benedict de Spinoza," *Proceedings of the Royal Society of Great Britain*, Vol. 8 (1879), pp. 363-377.

> A paper read before the Royal Society on April 20, 1877. According to Oko (1964), p. 115, originally published in *The Nineteenth Century* (February 1878), pp. 330-354; also published in *Popular Science Monthly*, Supplement No. 11 (March 1878), pp. 444-458. Oko, p. 54, also notes its publication in *Littell's Living Age*, 5th Series, Vol. 21, No. 1765 (March 30, 1878), pp. 771-785.

Pollock, Frederick, "Lotsij's Exposition of the Philosophy of Spinoza," *Mind*, Vol. 4 (1879), pp. 431 ff.

Pollock, Frederick, "Manuscript Letters of Spinoza in the Royal Society Library," *The Atheneum* (October 30, 1880).

> In Walther (1976), p. 422.

Pollock, Frederick, "Spinoza as a Moral Teacher," *Time* (London), Vol. 18 (1888), pp. 416-419.

Pollock, Frederick, "Spinoza," in *Religious Systems...*(1911), pp. 709-723.

Pollock, Frederick, "Spinoza's Political Doctrine, With Special Regard to His Relation to English Publicists," in *Chronicon Spinozanum*, Vol. I (1921), pp. 45-57.

Pollock, Frederick, "Contemporary Appreciations of Spinoza," *The Spinoza Quarterly*, Vol. 2, No. 2 (1932).

> In Feuer (1979), p. 73.

Pollock, Frederick, "Address," in *Septimana Spinozana* (1933), pp. 8-12

Pool, John Paul, *The Reception of Spinoza by Nineteenth-Century British Writers*, Unpublished doctoral dissertation, University of Alabama, 1964.

> Currently available from UMI (Order No. 65-04066).

Pombo, Olga, "Comparative Lines Between Leibniz's Theory of Language and Spinoza's Reflexion of Language Themes," in *Studia Spinozana*, Vol. 6 (1990), pp. 147-177.

Popkin, Richard H., *The History of Skepticism from Erasmus to Spinoza*, Revised and expanded edition (Berkeley: University of California Press, 1979).

Popkin, Richard H., *Isaac La Peyrère, 1596-1676: His Life, Work and Influence* (Leiden: E. J. Brill, 1987).

> Includes many references to Spinoza.

Popkin, Richard H., *The Third Force in 17th Century Philosophy: Scepticism, Biblical Studies and Science* (Leiden: E. J. Brill, 1991).

> Includes the author's "Spinoza's Relations with the Quakers in Amsterdam," originally in *Quaker History*, Vol. 70 (1984), pp. 14-28, as well as other references to Spinoza.

Popkin, Richard H. (ed.), *The Philosophy of the Sixteenth and Seventeenth Centuries* (New York: The Free Press, 1966).

Popkin, Richard H., "Spinoza," in *Encyclopedia Judaica* (New York: Macmillan, 1971), Vol. 15, cols. 275-282.

Popkin, Richard H., "Spinoza and La Peyrère," in Shahan and Biro (1978), Chap. 9, pp. 177-195.

> Originally in the *Southwestern Journal of Philosophy*, Vol. 8, No. 3 (Fall 1977), pp. 177-195.

Popkin, Richard H., "Hume and Spinoza," *Hume Studies*, Vol. 5, No. 2 (November 1979), pp. 65-93.

Popkin, Richard H., "Spinoza's Skepticism and Anti-Skepticism," in Kogan (1979), pp. 5-35.

Popkin, Richard H., "Spinoza, the Quakers, and the Millenarians, 1656-1658," *Manuscrito* (Sao Paulo), Vol. 6 (1982), pp. 113-133.

Popkin, Richard H., "Spinoza and the Conversion of the Jews," in De Deugd (1984), pp. 171-183.

Popkin, Richard H., "Philosophy and the History of Philosophy," *The Journal of Philosophy*, Vol. 82 (November 1985), pp. 625-632.

> In *Humanities Index*, No. 860221.

Popkin, Richard H., "Spinoza and Samuel Fisher," *Philosophia* (Israel), Vol. 15, No. 3 (December 1985), pp. 219-236.

Popkin, Richard H., "Serendipity at the Clark: Spinoza and the Prince of Condé," *The Clark Newsletter*, No. 10 (University of California at Los Angeles, 1986), pp. 4-7.

Popkin, Richard H., "Could Spinoza Have Known Bodin's *Colloquium-Heptaplomares?*" *Philosophia* (Israel), Vol. 16, Nos. 3-4 (December 1986), pp. 307-314.

Popkin, Richard H., "Some New Light on the Roots of Spinoza's Science of Bible Study," in Grene and Nails (1986), pp. 171-188.

Popkin, Richard H., "The First Published Discussion of a Central Theme in Spinoza's *Tractatus Theologico-Politicus*," *Philosophia* (Israel), Vol. 17, No. 2 (March 1987), pp. 101-109.

Popkin, Richard H., "The Religious Background of Seventeenth-Century Philosophy," *Journal of the History of Philosophy*, Vol. 25 (1987), pp. 35-50.

> In Donagan (1989), p. 213.

Popkin, Richard H., "Some Seventeenth-Century Interpretations of Spinoza's Ideas," in Augustijn, Holtrop, Meyjer, and Van der Wall (1987), pp. 63-74.

Popkin, Richard H., "Spinoza's Earliest Philosophical Years, 1655-61," in *Studia Spinozana*, Vol. 4 (1988), pp. 37-55.

Popkin, Richard H., "The Dispersion of Bodin's Dialogues in England, Holland, and Germany," *Journal of the History of Ideas*, Vol. 49, No. 1 (1988), pp. 157-161.

> Discusses the possibility that Spinoza, among others, may have been familiar with Jean Bodin's *Colloque outre Sept Scavans*.

Popkin, Richard, H., "Spinoza and the *Three Imposters*," in Curley and Moreau (1990), pp. 347-358.

Popkin, Richard H., and Avrum Stroll, *Philosophy Made Simple* (Oxford: Heinemann Made Simple Books, 1969).

> Includes a section, "Philosophy of Spinoza," pp. 30-37, and other references.

Popkin, Richard H., and Michael A. Signer (eds.), *Spinoza's Earliest Publication? The Hebrew Translation of Margaret Fell's "A Loving Salutation to the Seed of Abraham Among the Jews, Wherever They Are Scattered Up and Down Upon the Face of the Earth,"* With an introduction by Richard H. Popkin and introductory observations on the Hebrew translation of *A Loving Salutation* by Michael A. Signer (Assen, The Netherlands: Van Gorcum, 1987).

Popper, Karl R., "How I See Philosophy," in Bontempo and Odell (1975), pp. 41-55.

Portnoy, E., "Spinoza: The Outcast Philosopher," *Holland Herald* (Amsterdam), Vol. 17, No. 10 (1982), pp. 13-18.

> In Van der Werf (1984), No. 1521, and Walther (1991), p. 88.

Powell, Elmer Ellsworth, *Spinoza and Religion: A Study of Spinoza's Metaphysics and of His Particular Utterances in Regard to Religion, With a View To Determining the Significance of His Thought for Religion and Incidentally His Personal Attitude Toward It* (Chicago: The Open Court Publishing Co., 1906).

> Reprinted under the same title in Boston by Chapman and Grimes, 1941.
> Also currently available from UMI Out-of-Print Books on Demand (Order No. OP52266 for the 1906 edition, 2017983 for the 1941 edition).

Prajnanamanda, Swami, *The God of Spinoza*, Prabuddha Bharata, Calcutta, June 1945.

> In Wetlesen (1968), p. 44.

Preus, Samuel J., "Spinoza, Vico, and the Imagination of Religion," *Journal of the History of Ideas*, Vol. 50, No. 1 (January/March 1989), pp. 71-93.

Pringle-Pattison, Andrew Seth, *The Idea of God in the Light of Recent Philosophy*, The Gifford Lectures delivered in the University of Aberdeen in the years 1912 and 1913 (New York: Oxford University Press, 1917).

Pringle-Pattison, Andrew Seth, *Idea of Immortality*, The Gifford Lectures delivered in the University of Edinburgh (Oxford: The Clarendon Press, 1922).

> Includes a section on Spinoza, pp. 148-152, and other references.

Pufendorf, Samuel, Of the law of nature and nations, Done into English by B. Kennett. 3rd Edition Added the notes of Barbeyrac. London, 1717.

> In Hertzberger (1950), No. 702. A translation of the 1672 Latin text, containing critical references to Spinoza.

Punjer, Bernhard, *History of the Christian Philosophy of Religion from the Reformation to Kant*, Translated by W. Hastie, with a preface by Robert Flint (Edinburgh: T. & T. Clark, 1887).

> Includes a chapter on Spinoza, pp. 407-454.

Pyun, Hae Soo, *Nature, Intelligibility and Metaphysics: Studies in the Philosophy of F. J. E. Woodbridge* (Amsterdam: Gruner, 1972).

> In *Philosopher's Index*, No. 073618, citing material on Spinoza and Woodbridge.

Quinn, Philip L., "Divine Conservation and Spinozistic Pantheism," *Religious Studies*, Vol. 15 (1979), pp. 289-302.

> *See* Oakes (1980) for a reply.

Rabenort, William Louis, *Spinoza as Educator* (New York: AMS Press, 1972).

> Facsimile reprint of Columbia University Contributions to Education, No. 38 (New York: Teachers College, Columbia University, 1911), which is the author's doctoral dissertation of the same title and year.

Rader, Melvin, *Wordsworth: A Philosophical Approach* (Oxford: The Clarendon Press, 1967).

> In *Philosopher's Index*, No. 076967.

Radhakrishnan, Sarvepalli, *et al.* (eds.), *History of Philosophy, Eastern and Western*, Sponsored by the Ministry of Education, Government of India (London: George Allen & Unwin, 1952-1953). 2 vols.

> Includes a chapter by Nikunja Vihari Banerjee, "Rationalism," Vol. 2, pp. 201-222, which contains a section on Spinoza, pp. 208-215. Also includes many other references to Spinoza.

Radner, Daisie, "Spinoza's Theory of Ideas," *The Philosophical Review*, Vol. 80, No. 3 (July 1971), pp. 338-359.

Radner, Daisie, "Malebranche's Refutation of Spinoza," in Shahan and Biro (1978), Chap. 5, pp. 113-128.

> Originally in the *Southwestern Journal of Philosophy*, Vol. 8, No. 3 (1977), pp. 113-128.

Raju, P. T., *Thought and Reality: Hegelianism and Advaita*, With foreword by J. H. Muirhead (London: George Allen & Unwin, 1937).

> Includes many references to Spinoza.

Rakhman, D., "Spinoza and Judaism," in Kline (1952), pp. 48-60.

[Ramsay, Andrew Michael] The philosophical principles of natural and re-vealed religion. Unfolded in a geometrical order by the Chevalier Ramsay ... Glasgow, Printed and sold by Robert [Foulls?], 1748-1749. 2 vols.

> In Oko (1964), p. 210. An appendix in Vol. 1 (pp. 497-541) includes "a refutation of the first book of Spinoza's Ethics; by which the whole structure is undermined."

Rand, Benjamin (ed.), *The Classical Moralists: Selections Illustrating Ethics from Socrates to Martineau* (Boston: Houghton Mifflin, 1909).

> Includes selections from Spinoza.

Rand, Benjamin (ed.), *The Classical Psychologists: Selections Illustrating Psychology from Anaxagoras to Wundt* (London, 1912).

> In Hertzberger (1950), No. 145, citing a selection from Spinoza's *Ethics*, pp. 191-207, in the Fullerton translation.

Randall, John Herman, Jr., *The Making of the Modern Mind: A Survey of the Intellectual Background of the Present Age* (Boston: Houghton Mifflin Co., 1926).

> Includes a section on Spinoza, pp. 244-248.

Randall, John Herman, Jr., *The Career of Philosophy from the Middle Ages to the Enlightenment* (New York: Columbia University Press, 1962).

> Includes a chapter, "Spinoza: Rational Naturalist," pp. 434-459.

Randall, John Herman, Jr., and Justus Buchler, *Philosophy: An Introduction*, Revised Edition (New York: Barnes & Noble, 1971).

> Includes a section, "Spinoza's Conception of Nature," pp. 239-241, and many other references.

Rapaport, David, *The History of the Concept of Association of Ideas* (New York: International Universities Press, 1974).

> Based on the author's 1938 doctoral dissertation. Traces the concept through the works of Bacon, Descartes, Spinoza, Locke, Leibniz, Hume, and Kant.

Raphael, D. D., chapter on Spinoza in Goldwater (1962).

Rappaport, S., "Spinoza's Spiritual Worth," *Jewish Affairs*, Vol. 37, No. 2 (1977), pp. 11-14.

> In Van der Werf (1984), No. 1556.

Rathbun, Constance, "On Certain Similarities Between Spinoza and Psychoanalysis," *Psychoanalytic Review*, Vol. 21 (1934), pp. 14ff.

> In Oko (1964), p. 308.

Ratner, Joseph, *Spinoza on God* (New York: Henry Holt and Co., 1930).

> From the author's doctoral dissertation, Columbia University, 1930. Currently available from UMI Out-of-Print Books on Demand (Order No. OP15708).

Ratner, Joseph. *See* Spinoza, *The Philosophy of Spinoza* ... (1927).

Ratner, Joseph, "In Defense of Spinoza," *The Journal of Philosophy*, Vol. 23, No. 5 (March 4, 1926), pp. 121-122.

> In Oko (1964), p. 116. *See* H. A. Wolfson, *Studies* ... (1977) for a reply.

Ratner, Joseph, "Spinoza on God," *The Philosophical Review*, Vol. 39 (January 1930), pp. 56-72; (March 1930), pp. 153-177.

Ravven, Heidi M., "Notes on Spinoza's Critique of Aristotle's Ethics: From Theology to Process Theory," *Philosophy and Theology*, Vol. 4 (Fall 1989), pp. 3-32.

Rawidowicz, Simon, *Studies in Jewish Thought* (Philadelphia: Jewish Publication Society of America, 1974).

> In Dienstag (1986), p. 400, citing an essay, "On Interpretation," pp. 45-80, discussing Spinoza's "rebellion against Maimonides"; originally in *Proceedings of the American Academy for Jewish Research*, Vol. 26 (1957), pp. 83-126.

Razumovski, I. P., "Spinoza and the State," in Kline (1952), pp. 149-161.

Reck, Andrew J., "Substance, Subject and Dialectic," *Tulane Studies in Philosophy*, Vol. 9 (1960), pp. 109-133.

> In *Philosopher's Index*, No. 010536, citing references to Hegel and Spinoza.

Redwood, John, *Reason, Ridicule and Religion: The Age of Enlightenment in England, 1660-1750* (Cambridge: Harvard University Press, 1976).

> Includes many references to Spinoza.

Ree, Jonathan, "History, Philosophy, and Interpretation: Some Reactions to Jonathan Bennett's *Study of Spinoza's Ethics*," in Hare (1988), pp. 44-61.

Reed, Edward Steven, *The Corporeal Ideas Hypothesis and the Origin of Scientific Psychology*, Unpublished doctoral dissertation, Boston University, 1980.

> Includes a discussion of the Cartesian origins of Spinoza's, Locke's, and Hume's account of the nature of the soul. Currently available from UMI (Order No. 80-24216).

Rees, Abraham. The cyclopaedia; or, Universal dictionary of arts, sciences, and literature. By Abraham Rees with the assistance of eminent professional gentlemen. London, Longman, Hurst, Rees, Orme & Brown, 1819. 39 vols.

> In Oko (1964), p. 127, citing an article, "Spinozism," in Vol. 33.

Reeves, Joan Wynn, *Body and Mind in Western Thought* (New York: Penguin Books, 1958).

> In *Philosopher's Index*, No. 020727.

Reeves, Joan Wynn, *Thinking about Thinking: Studies in the Background of Some Psychological Approaches* (New York: George Braziller; London: Secker & Warburg, 1965).

Includes a chapter, "Spinoza's Treatment of Thinking in Relation to Modern Approaches," pp. 36-53, and other references.

Renan, Ernest, *Studies in Religious History* (New York: Scribner and Welford, 1887).

Includes a chapter on Spinoza, pp. 453-481. Hertzberger (1950), No. 150, cites a 2-vol. London edition (n.d.).

Renan, Ernest, *Leaders of Christian and Anti-Christian Thought*, Translated by W. M. Thomson (London: Mathieson, 1891).

Includes a section on Spinoza, pp. 47-71.

Renan, Ernest, *The Poetry of the Celtic Races, and Other Studies*, Translated, with introduction and notes, by William G. Hutchison (London: W. Scott, Ltd., 1896).

Includes a chapter on Spinoza.

Renan, Ernest, "Spinoza: 1677, and 1877," Oration delivered at The Hague, February 21, 1877, translated by M. Stuart Phelps, *Contemporary Review*, Vol. 29 (1877), pp. 763-777.

Reprinted in *Popular Science Monthly*, Vol. 11 (1877), pp. 216-230; *The New Englander*, Vol. 37 (1878), pp. 763-781; and other publications, including Knight (1882), pp. 145-170.

Rensch, Bernard, "Spinoza's Identity Theory and Modern Biophilosophy," *The Philosophical Forum*, Vol. 3 (Winter 1972), pp. 193-206.

Rensma, Patricia Ann, *Eros and Wholeness in the Thought of Spinoza and Hegel*, Unpublished doctoral dissertation, Pennsylvania State University, 1970.

Currently available from UMI (Order No. 71-21793).

[Reynolds] The religion of Jesus delineated. London, 1726.

This citation is based on Hertzberger (1950), No. 913.

Reynolds, J. W., *The Mystery of Miracles*, 2nd Edition (London, 1881).

In Hertzberger (1950), No. 153, citing many references to Spinoza.

Rice, Lee C., *Moral Judgment in Benedict de Spinoza*, Unpublished doctoral dissertation, St. Louis University, 1967.

Currently available from UMI (Order No. 68-01288).

Rice, Lee C., "The Continuity of 'Mens' in Spinoza," *The New Scholasticism*, Vol. 43 (Winter 1969), pp. 75-103.

Rice, Lee C., "Methodology and Modality in the First Part of Spinoza's *Ethics*," in Van der Bend (1974), pp. 144-155.

Rice, Lee C., "Spinoza on Individuation," in Mandelbaum and Freeman (1975), pp. 195-214.

> Originally in *The Monist*, Vol. 55, No. 4 (October 1971), pp. 640-659.

Rice, Lee C., "Von Wright, Rationalism and Modality," *International Logic Review*, Vol. 8 (June 1977), pp. 53-56.

> In *Philosopher's Index*, No. 057551, noting the author's rejection of the axiomatized system of Von Wright, which he "claims to be a possible syntax underlying Spinoza's necessitarianism."

Rice, Lee C., "Emotion, Appetition, and Conatus in Spinoza," *Revue internationale de philosophie*, Vol. 31 (1977), pp. 101-116.

Rice, Lee C., "*Servitus* in Spinoza: A Programmatic Analysis," in Wetlesen (1978), pp. 179-191.

Rice, Lee C., "Piety and Philosophical Freedom in Spinoza," in De Deugd (1984), pp. 184-205.

Rice, Lee C., "Spinoza's Account of Sexuality," *Philosophy Research Archives*, Vol. 10 (1984), pp. 19-34.

Rice, Lee C., "Spinoza, Bennett, and Teleology," *The Southern Journal of Philosophy*, Vol. 23, No. 2 (Summer 1985), pp. 241-254.

Rice, Lee C., "Individual and Community in Spinoza's Social Psychology," in Curley and Moreau (1990), pp. 271-285.

[Rich, Elihu] *Appleton's Cyclopedia of Biography: Embracing a Series of Original Memoirs of the Most Distinguished Persons of All Times*, American Edition, ed. by Francis L. Hawkes (New York: D. Appleton and Co., 1856).

> In Oko (1964), p. 54, citing an entry on Spinoza, pp. 884-885.

Richter, John Blain, *New Light on Spinoza,* Unpublished doctoral dissertation, University of Missouri, Columbia, 1974.

    Currently available from UMI (Order No. 75-05789).

Richter, R., "Spinoza's Method," *Essays.*

    This incomplete citation is in Melamed (1933), p. 382.

Rickman, H. P., *Preface to Philosophy* (London: Routledge & Kegan Paul, 1964).

    Includes many references to Spinoza.

Rickman, H. P., *The Adventures of Reason: The Uses of Philosophy in Sociology* (Westport, CT: Greenwood Press, 1983).

    Includes a section on Spinoza, pp. 71-98, and other references.

Ricoeur, Paul, "Irrationality and the Plurality of Philosophical Systems," *Dialectica,* Vol. 39 (1985), pp. 297-319.

    In *Philosopher's Index,* No. 137774.

Riley, Woodbridge, *Men and Morals: The Story of Ethics* (New York: Frederick Ungar, 1960).

    Reprint of the 1929 edition published in Garden City, NY, by Doubleday, Doran & Company. Includes a section on Spinoza, pp. 219-229.

Ripley, George. Defence of "The latest form of infidelity" examined; a second letter to Andrews Norton, occasioned by his defence of a discourse on "The latest form of infidelity," by George Ripley. Boston, J. Munroe, 1840. 85 pp.

Ritchie, Eliza, "Notes on Spinoza's Conception of God," *The Philosophical Review,* Vol. 11, No. 1 (1902), pp. 1-15.

Ritchie, Eliza, "The Reality of the Finite in Spinoza's System," *The Philosophical Review,* Vol. 13, No. 1 (1904), pp. 16-29.

Robbins, William, *The Ethical Idealism of Matthew Arnold: A Study of the Nature and Sources of His Moral and Religious Ideas* (Toronto: University of Toronto Press, 1959).

    In *Philosopher's Index,* No. 072510.

Roberts, David, *The Nature of the Finite Mode in Spinoza's Metaphysics*, Unpublished doctoral dissertation, Emory University, 1973.

> Currently available from UMI (Order No. 74-00460).

Robertson, George Croom, *Elements of General Philosophy*, Edited from notes of lectures delivered at the University College, London, 1870-1892, by C. A. Foley Rhys Davids (London: Murray, 1905).

> Includes two sections on Spinoza, pp. 59-63 and pp. 274-295.

Robertson, George Croom, "Leibnitz and Spinoza," in Bain and Whittaker (1894), pp. 334-342.

Robertson, John M., *Pioneer Humanists* (London: Watts & Co., 1907).

> Includes a chapter on Spinoza, pp. 148-180.

Robertson, John M., *A Short History of Freethought, Ancient and Modern*, 2nd Edition (London: Watts & Co., 1906). 2 vols.

> Includes many references to Spinoza.

Robertson, John M., *A Short History of Morals* (London: Watts & Co., 1920).

> Includes a section on Spinoza, pp. 240-253.

Robertson, John M., "Spinoza," *The Reformer* (London), Vol. 4 (1900), pp. 7-20.

> In Oko (1964), p. 116.

Robinson, Henry W., and Walter Adams (eds.), *The Diary of Robert Hooke, 1672-1680*, Translated from the original in the possession of the Corporation of the City of London (Guildhall Library), with a foreword by Sir Frederick Gowland Hopkins (London: Taylor & Francis, 1935).

> Includes references to Spinoza, pp. 353-368.

Robinson, Lydia G. *See* Spinoza, *Short Treatise ...* (1909).

Robinson, Richard, *Definition* (Oxford: Clarendon Press, 1954).

> Includes many references to Spinoza.

Roe, Edward D., Jr., "The Probability of Freedom: A Critique of Spinoza's Demonstration of Necessity," *The Bibliotheca Sacra*, Vol. 51 (1894), pp. 641-659.

Rogers, Arthur Kenyon, *Morals in Review* (New York: The Macmillan Co., 1927).

> Includes a chapter on Spinoza's *Ethics*, pp. 159-190.

Rogers, Arthur Kenyon, *A Student's History of Philosophy*, 3rd Edition (New York: The Macmillan Co., 1932).

> Includes a section on Spinoza, pp. 254-272.

Rogers, Reginald A. P., *A Short History of Ethics, Greek and Modern* (London: Macmillan and Co., 1911).

> Includes a section, "Rationalistic Naturalism — Spinoza," pp. 143-146, and other references.

Rohatyn, Dennis A., "Internal Relations," *Philosophical Papers*, Vol. 4 (October 1975), pp. 116-120.

> In *Philosopher's Index*, No. 049340, citing references to Spinoza, Aristotle, and Hegel.

Rohatyn, Dennis A., "Spinoza's Emotivism," in Wilbur (1976), pp. 29-35.

Rome, Beatrice K., *The Philosophy of Malebranche: A Study of His Integration of Faith, Reason, and Experimental Observation* (Chicago: Henry Regnery Co., 1963).

> Includes many references to Spinoza.

Rorty, Amélie O., "The Two Faces of Spinoza," *The Review of Metaphysics*, Vol. 41, No. 2 (December 1987), pp. 299-316.

> Also in Curley and Moreau (1990), pp. 196-208.

Rorty, Richard, J. B. Schneewind, and Quentin Skinner (eds.), *Philosophy in History: Essays on the Historiography of Philosophy* (Cambridge: Cambridge University Press, 1984).

> Includes an essay by Bruce Kurlick, "Seven Thinkers and How They Grew: Descartes, Spinoza, Leibniz; Locke, Berkeley, Hume; Kant," pp. 125-139, and other references.

Rosen, Stanley, *Spinoza's Argument for Political Freedom*, Unpublished doctoral dissertation, University of Chicago, 1956.

Rosen, Stanley, *G. W. F. Hegel: An Introduction to the Science of Wisdom* (New Haven: Yale University Press, 1974).

> Includes a section, "Aristotelian and Spinozistic Elements in Hegel's Noetics," pp. 50-56, and other references.

Rosen, Stanley, "Spinoza's Argument for Political Freedom," *Giornale di metafisica*, Vol. 13, No. 4 (1958), pp. 487-499.

> In Rice (1967), p. 305, and Den Uyl (1983), p. 172.

Rosen, Stanley, "Benedict Spinoza," in Strauss and Cropsey (1972), pp. 431-450.

Rosen, Stanley, "Hegel, Descartes and Spinoza," in Wilbur (1976), pp. 115-132.

Rosenberg, A., *Tyssot de Patot and His Work, 1655-1738* (The Hague, 1972).

> In Van der Werf (1984), No. 1620, citing pp. 56-77.

Rosenthal, Henry M., *The Consolations of Philosophy: Hobbes's Secret, Spinoza's Way*, Edited with an introduction by Abigail L. Rosenthal (Philadelphia: Temple University Press, 1989).

Rosmarin, Trude Weiss, *Religion of Reason: Hermann Cohen's System of Religious Philosophy* (New York: Bloch Publishing Co., 1936).

> Includes a chapter on Spinoza.

Ross, Alexander. ΠΑΝΣΕΒΙΑ: or, A view of all religions in the World. Also, A discovery of all known heresies in all ages and places. 6th ed. Annexed, lives, actions and ends of notorius hereticks. With their effigies. London, 1683.

> In Hertzberger (1950), No. 707.

[Ross, Alexander] The philosophical touch-stone: or Observations upon Sir Kenelm Digbie's discourses of the nature of bodies and of the reasonable soul; and Spinoza's opinion of the mortality of the soul. London, 1645 [sic].

> In Oko (1964), p. 422; in Van der Linde, No. 406.

Ross, James F., *Philosophical Theology* (Indianapolis, IN: Bobbs-Merrill, 1969).

In *Philosopher's Index*, No. 019292, citing references to Aquinas, Duns Scotus, Anselm, Spinoza, and Hume.

Ross, James F., "Did God Create the Only Possible World?" *The Review of Metaphysics*, Vol. 16 (September 1962), pp. 14-25.

In *Philosopher's Index*, No. 006955, citing references to Aquinas, Spinoza, and Leibniz.

Ross, Stephen David, *Transition to an Ordinal Metaphysics* (Albany, NY: State University of New York Press, 1980).

Includes many references to Spinoza.

Ross, Stephen David, *Metaphysical Aporia and Philosophical Heresy* (Albany, NY: State University of New York Press, 1989).

Includes a chapter, "Spinoza: The Heresy of Heresy," pp. 117-150, and many other references.

Rotenstreich, Nathan, *From Substance to Subject: Studies in Hegel* (The Hague: Martinus Nijhoff, 1974).

Van der Werf (1984), No. 1624, cites a section contrasting Kant and Spinoza to Hegel, pp. 43-55.

Rotenstreich, Nathan, "On Shame," *The Review of Metaphysics*, Vol. 19 (September 1965), pp. 55-86.

In *Philosopher's Index*, No. 007069, citing references to Spinoza, Kant, Hegel, and other philosophers.

Rotenstreich, Nathan, "Freedom as a Cause and as a Situation," *Revue internationale de philosophie*, Vol. 24 (1970), pp. 53-71.

In *Philosopher's Index*, No. 039867.

Rotenstreich, Nathan, "Bergson and the Transformations of the Notion of Intuition," *Journal of the History of Philosophy*, Vol. 10 (July 1972), pp. 335-346.

In *Philosopher's Index*, No. 036334, citing references to Spinoza, Kant, and Bergson.

Rotenstreich, Nathan, "Freedom, Reflection, and Finitude," *Philosophy and Phenomenological Research*, Vol. 33 (December 1972), pp. 163-173.

In *Philosopher's Index*, No. 037946, noting the author's argument against
Spinoza's notion that freedom is an acknowledgment of necessity.

Rotenstreich, Nathan, "Conatus and Amor Dei: The Total and Partial Norm,"
Revue internationale de philosophie, Vol. 31 (1977), pp. 117-134.

Rotenstreich, Nathan, "Rationalism and Thinking," *Archives de philosophie*
(1978), pp. 312-325.

In Van der Werf (1984), No. 1627.

Rotenstreich, Nathan, and Norma Schneider (eds.), *Spinoza: His Thought and
Work* (Jerusalem: Israel Academy of Sciences and Humanities, 1983).

Papers presented at the International Institute of Philosophy's *Entretiens* in
Jerusalem, 6-9 September 1977, commemorating the tercentenary of
Spinoza's death. In addition to an essay by Rotenstreich — "The System and
Its Components," pp. 14-23 — includes papers in English by A. Bar-On, J.
Ben-Shlomo, G. Funke, S. Hampshire, W. Marx, R. McKeon, A. Naess, S.
Pines, P. Strawson, E. Urbach, G. von Wright, and Y. Yovel.

Roth, Leon, *Spinoza, Descartes, and Maimonides* (Oxford: The Clarendon
Press, 1924).

Reprinted (New York: Russell and Russell, 1963).

Roth, Leon, *Spinoza* (London: George Allen & Unwin, 1954).

Roth, Leon. *The Guide of the Perplexed: Moses Maimonides* (London:
Hutchinson's Universal Library, 1984).

In Dienstag (1986), p. 401, citing a section on Spinoza and Maimonides,
pp. 89-94, and other references.

Roth, Leon, "David Nieto and the Orthodoxy of Spinozism," in *Chronicon
Spinozanum*, Vol. I (1921), pp. 278-282.

Roth, Leon, "Spinoza and Cartesianism," *Mind*, Vol. 32, No. 125 (1923), pp.
12-37; No. 126, pp. 160-178.

Roth, Leon, "Spinoza in Recent English Thought," *Mind*, Vol. 36, No. 142
(April 1927), pp. 205-210.

Roth, Leon, "Jewish Thought in the Modern World," in Bevan (1927), discus-
sing Spinoza on pp. 449-457.

Royce, Josiah, *The Spirit of Modern Philosophy: An Essay in the Form of Lectures* (Boston and New York: Houghton, Mifflin and Co., 1892).

> Includes a section on Spinoza, pp. 41-67, and other references. A section on pp. 68-100, "The Rediscovery of the Inner Life: From Spinoza to Kant," is reprinted in John J. McDermott (ed.), *The Basic Writings of Josiah Royce* (Chicago: University of Chicago Press, 1969), Vol. 1, pp. 273-298.

Royce, Josiah, *Fugitive Essays*, With an introduction by J. Loewenberg (Cambridge: Harvard University Press, 1920).

> Includes an essay, "Natural Rights and Spinoza's Essay on Liberty," pp. 290-299.

Royce, Josiah, "Spinoza," in Warner (1897), Vol. XXXV, pp. 13785-13793.

Rubinoff, Lionel, *Collingwood and the Reform of Metaphysics: A Study in the Philosophy of Mind* (Toronto: University of Toronto Press, 1970).

> Includes a section on Spinoza, pp. 191-194, and other references.

Runes, Dagobert D. *See* Spinoza, under "Improvement of the Understanding," "Short Treatise," "Ethics," "Correspondence," and "Excerpts."

Runia, D. T., "History of Philosophy in the Grand Manner: The Achievement of H. A. Wolfson," *Philosophia Reformata* (Kampen), Vol. 49 (1984), pp. 112-133.

> In *Philosopher's Index*, No. 130662.

Russell, Bertrand, *A Critical Exposition of the Philosophy of Leibniz*, New edition (London: George Allen & Unwin, 1937).

> Includes many references to Spinoza.

Russell, Bertrand, *A History of Western Philosophy, and Its Connection with Political and Social Circumstances from the Earliest Times to the Present Day* (New York: Simon and Schuster, 1945).

> Includes a chapter on Spinoza, pp. 369-380.

Russell, John M., "Freedom and Determinism in Spinoza," *Auslegung*, Vol. 11, No. 1 (Fall 1984), pp. 378-389.

Rutherford, Mark. *See* William Hale White (1910).

Saccaro-Battisti, Guiseppa, "Democracy in Spinoza's Unfinished *Tractatus Politicus*," *Journal of the History of Ideas*, Vol. 38 (1977), pp. 623-634.

Saccaro-Battisti, Guiseppa, "Changing Metaphors of Political Structure," *Journal of the History of Ideas*, Vol. 44, No. 1 (1983), pp. 31-54.

> "Examines the metaphorical structures used by various thinkers from the 17th to the 20th century as cognitive and rhetorical devices [to conceptualize] the state and society." — *Historical Abstracts* database, No. 1085933.

Saccaro-Battisti, Guiseppa, "Herrera and Spinoza on Divine Attributes: The Evolving Concept of Perfection and Infinity," *Studi e richerche sulla cultura e sulla litteratura degli Elrei d'Italia*, Vol. 4 (1985), pp. 21-58.

> In Popkin (1988), p. 54.

Sachar, Abram Leon, *A History of the Jews* (New York: A. A. Knopf, 1930).

> Includes a section, "Acosta and Spinoza," pp. 245-248.

Sachs, Mendel, "Maimonides, Spinoza, and the Field Concept in Physics," *Journal of the History of Ideas*, Vol. 37, No. 1 (January-March 1976), pp. 125-131.

Sacksteder, William, "Spinoza on Democracy," in Mandelbaum and Freeman (1975), pp. 117-138.

Sacksteder, William, "Spinoza Today: Some Commentary on Commentaries," *Philosophia* (Israel), Vol. 7 (March 1977), pp. 135-161.

Sacksteder, William, "Spinoza on Part and Whole: The Worm's Eye View," in Shahan and Biro (1978), Chap. 7, pp. 139-159.

> Originally in the *Southwestern Journal of Philosophy*, Vol. 8, No. 3 (Fall 1977), pp. 139-159.

Sacksteder, William, "How Much of Hobbes Might Spinoza Have Read?" *Southwestern Journal of Philosophy*, Vol. 11, No. 2 (Summer 1980), pp. 25-40.

Sacksteder, William, "Communal Orders in Spinoza," in De Deugd (1984), pp. 206-213.

Sacksteder, William, "Simple Wholes and Complex Parts: Limiting Principles in Spinoza," *Philosophy and Phenomenological Research*, Vol. 45, No. 3 (March 1985), pp. 393-406.

Sacksteder, William, "Spinoza's Attributes, Again: An Hobbesian Source," in *Studia Spinozana*, Vol. 3 (1987), pp. 125-149.

Saint-Evremond. Works. Made English: With the life of the author by Des Maizeaux. Added the memoirs of the Dutchess of Mazarim, etc. 2nd Edition London, 1728. 3 vols.

> In Hertzberger (1950), No. 311, citing several references to Spinoza by his contemporaries.

Saisset, Emile, *Essay on Religious Philosophy*, Translated, with marginal analysis, notes, critical essay, and philosophical appendix (Edinburgh: T. & T. Clark, 1863). 2 vols.

> Includes a chapter, "Pantheism of Spinoza," Vol. 1, pp. 92-158, and other references.

Saito, Hiroshi, "Spinozism and Japan," in Hessing (1977), pp. 442-454.

Sajama, Seppo Eino, *Idea, Judgement and Will: Essays on the Theory of Judgement*, Unpublished doctoral dissertation, University of Turku (Finland), 1983.

> Includes material on Spinoza. Currently available from UMI (Order No. 84-00813).

Salas Ortueta, Jaime de, "Ethics and Politics in Spinoza and Leibniz," in *Studia Spinozana*, Vol. 6 (1990), pp. 201-217.

Salomon, H. P., "Baruch Spinoza, Ishac Orobio de Castro and Haham Mosseh Rephael d'Aguilar on the Noachites: A Chapter in the History of Thought," *Arquivos do Centro Cultural Portugues*, Vol. 14 (1979), pp. 253-286.

Saltus, Edgar, *The Anatomy of Negation* (London: Williams and Norgate, 1886).

> Includes a section on Spinoza, pp. 112-121.

Samuels, M. Memoirs of Moses Mendelssohn including the correspondence with J. C. Lavater. 2nd ed. London, 1827.

> In Hertzberger (1950), No. 886, citing many references to Spinoza and Spinozism.

Sanderson, Edgar, J. P. Lamberton, John McGovern, *et al., Six Thousand Years of History*, With introduction by Marshall S. Snow (New York: E. R. DuMont, Publisher, 1899). 10 vols.

Vol. IV, *Great Philosophers*, includes a chapter on Spinoza, pp. 263-272, and other references.

Sandys-Wunsch, J., "Spinoza: The First Biblical Theologian," *Zeitschrift für die Alttestamentliche Wissenschaft*, Vol. 93, No. 3 (1981), pp. 327-340.

Santayana, George, *Obiter Scripto: Lectures, Essays & Reviews*, Edited by Justus Buchler and Benjamin Schwartz (New York: Charles Scribner's Sons, 1936).

Includes an essay on Spinoza, "Ultimate Religion," pp. 280-297, first published in *Septimana Spinozana* (1933), pp. 105-115. Reprinted in Fisch (1951), pp. 317-326.

Santayana, George. *See* Spinoza, *Ethics* (1910).

Santayana, George, "The Ethical Doctrine of Spinoza," *The Harvard Monthly*, Vol. 2 (1886), pp. 144-152.

Sargent, Rose Mary C., *Robert Boyle and the Experimental Ideal*, Unpublished doctoral dissertation, University of Notre Dame, 1987.

Includes material on Spinoza. Currently available from UMI (Order No. 87-20775).

Sarton, George, "Spinoza: 1632-1677-1927," *Isis*, Vol. 10, No. 33 (March 1928), pp. 11-15, with plates.

Sass, Hans Martin, "Ideational Politics and the Word Tolerance," *Philosophy and Rhetoric*, Vol. 11 (Spring 1978), pp. 98-113.

In *Philosopher's Index*, No. 058952, citing references to Spinoza and Locke.

Satz, H., *Spinoza's Moral Philosophy and the Order of Odd Fellows* (Berlin, 1979).

In Van der Werf (1984), No. 1663.

Savan, David, "Spinoza and Language," in Kashap (1972), pp. 236-248, and in Grene (1979), pp. 60-72.

Originally in *The Philosophical Review*, Vol. 67, No. 2 (April 1958), pp. 212-225. A version of this paper was read at a meeting of the Eastern Division of the American Philosophical Association, December 1955.

Savan, David, "Spinoza on Death and the Emotions," in Wetlesen (1978), pp. 192-203.

Savan, David, "Spinoza on Man's Knowledge of God: Intuition, Reason, Revelation, and Love," in Kogan (1979), pp. 80-103.

Savan, David, "Spinoza: Scientist and Theorist of Scientific Method," in Grene and Nails (1986), pp. 95-123.

Savan, David, "Spinoza: Eternity, Duration and Time," in Hunter (1991).

Saw, Ruth Lydia, *The Vindication of Metaphysics: A Study in the Philosophy of Spinoza* (London: Macmillan and Co., 1951).

Saw, Ruth Lydia, "Spinoza," in Urmson (1960), pp. 367-371.

Saw, Ruth Lydia, "Personal Identity in Spinoza," in Kashap (1972), pp. 86-100.

> Originally in *Inquiry*, Vol. 12, No. 1 (1969), pp. 1-14.

Saw, Ruth Lydia, "The Task of Metaphysics for Spinoza," in Mandelbaum and Freeman (1975), pp. 235-244.

> Originally in *The Monist*, Vol. 55 (October 1971), pp. 660-667.

Schacht, Richard, *Hegel and After: Studies in Continental Philosophy Between Kant and Sartre* (Pittsburgh: University of Pittsburgh Press, 1975).

> Discusses the concept of freedom in Hegel and Spinoza, pp. 73-81.

Schacht, Richard, *Classical Modern Philosophers: Descartes to Kant* (London: Routledge & Kegan Paul, 1984).

> Includes a chapter on Spinoza, pp. 66-99, and many other references.

Scharfstein, Ben-Ami, *The Philosophers: Their Lives and the Nature of Their Thought* (Oxford: Basil Blackwood, 1980).

> Includes a section on Spinoza, pp. 149-156, and other references.

Scharfstein, Ben-Ami, *et al.* (eds.), *Philosophy East, Philosophy West: A Critical Comparison of Indian, Chinese, Islamic and European Philosophy* (New York: Oxford University Press, 1978).

> Includes an essay by Ilai Alon, "Between Fatalism and Causality: Al-Ash'ari and Spinoza," pp. 218-234, and other references.

Schaub, Edward L. (ed.), *Spinoza: The Man and His Thought: Addresses Delivered at the Spinoza Tercentenary* (Chicago: The Open Court Publishing Co., 1933).

> In addition to a paper by E. L. Schaub — "Spinoza: His Personality and His Doctrine of Perfection," which originally appeared in *The Monist*, Vol. 43 (January 1933), pp. 1-22 — includes essays by H. Chase, S. Freehof, C. Morris, and T. Smith.

Schelling, F. W. J., *Of Human Freedom*, Translated, with critical introduction and notes, by James Gutmann (Chicago: The Open Court Publishing Co., 1936).

> Includes a section on Spinoza, pp. 11-24.

Schelling, F. W. J., *Bruno, or On the Natural and the Divine Principle of Things* (1802), Edited and translated, with an introduction, by Michael G. Vater (Albany, NY: State University of New York Press, 1984.)

> Includes many references to Spinoza in the editor's introduction and the notes.

Schindler, Solomon, *Dissolving Views in the History of Judaism* (Boston: Lee and Shepard; New York: C. T. Dillingham, 1888).

> Includes a chapter, "Baruch Spinoza and His Time," pp. 215-227.

Schings, H. J., "Goethe's *Wilhelm Meister* and Spinoza," *Interdisciplinary Science Reviews*, Vol. 11, No. 2 (1986), pp. 118-121.

Schipper, Edith Watson, "Two Concepts of Human Freedom," *The Southern Journal of Philosophy*, Vol. 11 (Winter 1973), pp. 309-315.

[Schleiermacher, Friederich E. D.] *The Life of Schleiermacher as Unfolded in His Autobiography*, Translated by F. Rowan (London, 1860). 2 vols.

> In Hertzberger (1950), No. 165.

Schmidt-Biggemann, Wilhelm (ed.), *Baruch de Spinoza (1677-1977): His Work and Its Reception*, with an introduction (Baarn: M. Hertzberger, 1977).

> In Walther (1991), p. 45, who identifies this publication as Catalogue 19 of the August-Herzog Bibliothek.

Schmitz, Kenneth L., "Hegel's Assessment of Spinoza," in Kennington (1980), Chap. 13, pp. 229-246.

Schneider, Herbert W., "'Chevalier' Ramsay's Critique of Spinoza," *Journal of the History of Philosophy*, Vol. 3 (April 1965), pp. 91-96.

Schneider, Ivo, "Christian Huygen's Contribution to the Development of a Calculus of Probabilities," *Janus* (Netherlands), Vol. 67, No. 4 (1980), pp. 269-279.

> Discusses Huygen's work on probability and its impact on DeWitt, Spinoza, Sauveur, and Newton.

Schochet, Jacob Immanuel, *The Psychological System of Maimonides*, Unpublished thesis, University of Waterloo, 1973.

> In Dienstag (1986), No. 403, citing a section on Spinoza's critique of religion and of Maimonides, pp. 172-186.

Schoeman, Ferdinand D. (ed.), *Responsibility, Character, and the Emotions: New Essays in Moral Psychology* (New York: Cambridge University Press, 1988).

> Includes an essay by Lenn E. Goodman, "Determinism and Freedom," pp. 107-164, which discusses Aristotle, Maimonides, and Spinoza.

Schoen, Edward L., "The Role of Common Notions in Spinoza's *Ethics*," *The Southern Journal of Philosophy*, Vol. 15 (Winter 1977), pp. 537-550.

Schreiber, Emmanuel, "Baruch Spinoza," *The Platonist*, Vol. 3 (1887), pp. 423-434.

> In Oko (1964), p. 117.

Schultzer, Bent, *Transcendence and the Logical Difficulties of Transcendence: A Logical Analysis* (London: Oxford University Press; Copenhagen: Levin & Munks-gaard, 1935).

> Includes a section, "The Spinozistic Problem of Transcendence (Parallelism, Empedokles' Principle)," pp. 138-140, and many other references.

Schwartz, Joel, "Liberalism and the Jewish Connection: A Study of Spinoza and the Young Marx," *Political Theory*, Vol. 13, No. 1 (February 1985), pp. 58-84.

> A reply by Dennis Fischman was published in Vol. 13, No. 4, pp. 607-609.

Schwarzschild, Stephen S., "Do Noachites Have To Believe in Revelation? A Contribution to a Jewish View of Natural Law," *Jewish Quarterly Review*, Vol. 52 (1961-1962), pp. 297-308; Vol. 53 (1962-1963), pp. 30-65.

In Curley (1975), p. 311, noting that the focus here is on "a passage in dispute between Maimonides, Spinoza, Mendelssohn, and H. Cohen."

Schwegler, Albert, *A History of Philosophy in Epitome*, Translated from the 1st Edition by Julius H. Seelye, revised from the German 9th Edition, with an Appendix by Benjamin E. Smith (New York: D. Appleton and Co., 1881).

Includes a section on Spinoza, pp. 213-221. The original 1856 edition includes this chapter on pp. 184-191.

Schwegler, Albert, *Handbook of the History of Philosophy*, Translated and annotated by J. H. Stirling, 7th Edition (Edinburgh: Edmonston and Douglas, 1879).

In Oko (1964), p. 151, citing a chapter on Spinoza, pp. 168-176.

Schwegler, Albert, "Spinoza and His Metaphysics," in Robinson (1909).

Schweitzer, A., *Civilization and Ethics* (London: Unwin, 1961).

In *Philosopher's Index*, No. 075652.

Scruton, Roger, *From Descartes to Wittgenstein: A Short History of Modern Philosophy* (London: Routledge & Kegan Paul, 1981).

Includes a chapter, "Spinoza," pp. 50-56, and many other references.

Scruton, Roger, *Spinoza* (New York: Oxford University Press, 1986).

Sears, Edward I., "Spinoza and His Philosophy," *The National Quarterly Review*, Vol. 9 (1864), pp. 332-347.

Segal, Ora (ed.), *Further Studies in Philosophy* (Jerusalem: Magness Press, 1968).

Includes a chapter by Shlomo Pines, "Spinoza's *Tractatus Theologico-Politicus*, Maimonides and Kant," pp. 3-54.

Seligman, F., "Some Aspects of Spinozism," *Proceedings of the Aristotelian Society*, Vol. 61 (1960-1961), pp. 109-128.

Selsam, Howard, "Spinoza: Art and the Geometric Order," *Studies in the History of Ideas*, Vol. 3 (1935), pp. 253-269.

Sen, Sanat Kumar, *A Study of the Metaphysics of Spinoza* (Visva-Bharati, Santiniketan, India: Centre of Advanced Study in Philosophy, 1966).

Sen, Sanat Kumar, "The Method of Spinoza," *Philosophical Quarterly of India*, Vol. 31 (1958-1959), pp. 115-120.

Sen, Sanat Kumar, "Spinoza's Theory of Truth and Falsity," *Journal of the Indian Academy of Philosophy*, Vol. 1, pp. 75-88.

> In *Philosopher's Index*, No. 067968; date not given.

Sen, Sanat Kumar, "Spinoza on Philosophical Method," *Journal of the Indian Academy of Philosophy*, Vol. 3, pp. 80-90.

> In *Philosopher's Index*, No. 067983; date not given.

Sen, Sanat Kumar, "On the Ontological Argument," *Journal of the Philosophical Association*, Vol. 7, pp. 99-104.

> In *Philosopher's Index*, No. 068006, citing references to Spinoza and Kant; date not given. *See* Srinivasan (n.d.) for a reply.

Sen, Sanat Kumar, "Spinoza and Sankhya," *Journal of the Philosophical Association*, Vol. 8, pp. 41-44.

> In *Philosopher's Index*, No. 068021; date not given.

Sermoneta, Joseph B., "Biblical Anthropology in the *Guide of the Perplexed* by Maimonides and Its Reversal in the *Tractatus Theologico-Politicus* by Spinoza," *Topoi*, Vol. 7, No. 3 (December 1988), pp. 241-247.

Sessions, George, "Spinoza and Jeffers on Man in Nature," *Inquiry*, Vol. 20 (Winter 1977), pp. 481-528.

Sewall, Frank. *See* Spinoza, *Improvement of the Understanding, Ethics and Correspondence* (1901).

Shaffer, Jerome A., *Philosophy of Mind* (Englewood Cliffs, NJ: Prentice Hall, 1968).

> In *Philosopher's Index*, No. 019668, citing references to Descartes, Spinoza, Bretano, and Strawson.

Shaftesbury, Anthony Ashley Cooper, 3rd Earl of. Characteristics of men, manners, opinions, times. In three volumes ... London, Anno 1711.

> In Oko (1964), p. 310.

Shahan, Robert W., and J. I. Biro (eds.), *Spinoza: New Perspectives* (Norman: University of Oklahoma Press, 1978).

> Includes papers by E. Curley, C. Hardin, S. Kashap, D. Lachterman, D. Lewis, T. Mark, G. Parkinson, R. Popkin, D. Radner, W. Sacksteder, and E. Shmueli.

Shanks, Alexander, *An Introduction to Spinoza's Ethic* (London: Macmillan & Co., 1938).

> Currently available from UMI Out-of-Print Books on Demand (Order No. OP52310).

Sharif, M. M., "Muslim Philosophy and Western Thought," *Kant-Studien*, Vol. 54 (1963), pp. 188-197.

> In *Philosopher's Index*, No. 068164.

Shatsky, Jacob, "Spinoza and Modern Thought," in *Baruch Spinoza* (Spinoza Institute of America, 1933).

Sheldon, Mark, "Logic of the Self-Evident: Spinoza, Imagination and Metaphor," *Proceedings of the Heraclitian Society*, Vol. 2 (May-August 1974), pp. 62-90.

> In *Philosopher's Index*, No. 014965.

Sheldon, Mark, "Metaphor," *Philosophy Forum*, Vol. 7 (Fall 1975), pp. 56-70.

> In *Philosopher's Index*, No. 053677, noting discussion of the relationship of a theory of metaphor with Spinoza's theory of the imagination in the *Ethics*.

Sheldon, Mark, "Spinoza, Imagination and Chaos," *The Southern Journal of Philosophy*, Vol. 17 (1979), pp. 119-132.

Sheldon, Walter L., "Benedict Spinoza," *The Open Court*, Vol. 6 (1892), pp. 127-131, 135-137.

> In Oko (1964), p. 117.

[Shelley, Percy Bysshe] *Letters, 1812-1818*, Edited by Roger Ingpen (London: Published for the Julian Editions by E. Benn; New York: Scribner, 1926).

> In Oko (1964), p. 310, citing references to Spinoza, pp. 33-34, and pp. 39-40.

[Sheps, Elias] *The Strange Death of Barukh Spinoza*, by Eli A. Almi [pseud.] (Cambridge, MA: Sci-Art Publishers, 1952). 16 pp.

Sherlock, Thomas. A vindication of the corporation and test acts, in answer to the Bishop of Bangor's reasons for the repeal of them, to which is added a second part concerning the religion of oaths. London, Pemberton, 1718.

> In Oko (1964), p. 356.

Sherman, Ernest, "Spinoza and the Divine *Cogito*: God as 'Self-Performance,'" in Wilbur (1976), pp. 36-43.

Shestov, Lev, *In Job's Balances: On the Sources of the Eternal Truths*, Translated by Camilla Coventry and C. A. Macartney, with introduction by Bernard Martin (Athens, OH: Ohio University Press, 1975).

> Originally published in London by J. M. Dent, 1932. Includes as a Foreword on pp. xxx-l the essay, "Science and Free Inquiry," which focuses on Spinoza, as well as a chapter, "Children and Stepchildren of Time: Spinoza in History," pp. 247-273. Both of these essays were earlier published in *A Shestov Anthology*, Edited with an introduction by Bernard Martin (Athens, OH: Ohio University Press, 1970), pp. 193-214 and pp. 215-243, respectively.

Shestov, Lev, *Speculation and Revelation*, Translated by Bernard Martin (Athens, OH: Ohio University Press, 1982).

> Includes many references to Spinoza, as well as a discussion on pp. 74-86 of Vladimir Solovyov's article, "The Concept of God," which Solovyov intended as a "defense" of Spinoza.

Shimizu, Reiko, "Excommunication and the Philosophy of Spinoza," *Inquiry*, Vol. 23, No. 3 (September 1980), pp. 327-348.

Shirley, Samuel. *See* Spinoza, *Ethics* (1982) and *Tractatus Theologico-Politicus* (1989).

Shirmacher, Wolfgang, "Monism in Spinoza's and Husserl's Thought: The Ontological Background of the Body-Soul Problem," in Tymieniecka (1983), pp. 345-352.

> According to Van der Werf (1984), No. 2254, also in *Analecta Husserliana*, Vol. 16 (1983), pp. 345-352.

Shmueli, Efraim, *Crossroads of Modern Thought: Studies in Spinoza, Hegel, Marx, Husserl and Mannheim* (Tel-Aviv: Eked, 1984).

Includes four papers on Spinoza: (1) "The Geometrical Method, Personal Caution, and the Idea of Tolerance," pp. 7-25, published earlier in Shahan and Biro (1978), Chap. 10, pp. 197-215, and originally in the *Southwestern Journal of Philosophy*, Vol. 8, No. 3 (Fall 1977), pp. 197-215; (2) "Hegel's Interpretation of Spinoza's Concept of Substance," pp. 26-41, originally in *International Journal for Philosophy of Religion*, Vol. 1, No. 3 (1970), pp. 176-191; (3) "Some Similarities Between Spinoza and Hegel on Substance," pp. 42-54, originally in *The Thomist*, Vol. 36 (October 1972), pp. 645-657; and (4) "Thomas Aquinas' Influence on Spinoza's Concept of Attributes," pp. 55-66, originally in *Journal of Religious Studies*, Vol. 7 (1979), pp. 61-72.

Siebrand, Heine J., *Spinoza and the Netherlanders: An Inquiry into the Early Reception of His Philosophy of Religion* (Assen, The Netherlands: Van Gorcum, 1988).

From the author's dissertation in 1988 at Groningen.

Siebrand, Heine J., "On the Early Reception of Spinoza's *Tractatus Theologico-Politicus* in the Context of Cartesianism," in De Deugd (1984), pp. 214-225.

Siebrand, Heine J. "Is God an Open Place in Spinoza's Philosophy of Religion?" *Neue Zeitschrift für Systematische Theologie und Religionsphilosophie*, Vol. 28, No. 3 (1986), pp. 261-274.

See Naess (1986) for a reply.

Siebrand, Heine J., "Spinoza and the Rise of Modern Science in the Netherlands," in Grene and Nails (1986), pp. 61-91.

Silbermann, Isidor, "Some Reflections on Spinoza and Freud," *Psychoanalytic Quarterly*, Vol. 42, No. 4 (1973), pp. 601-624.

Singer, Brent A., "Spinoza on Returning Hatred with Love," *Journal of Moral Education*, Vol. 17, No. 1 (January 1988), pp. 3-10.

Singer, Brent A., "Spinoza, Heidegger, and the Ontological Argument," *Journal of the British Society for Phenomenology*, Vol. 21, No. 3 (1990), pp. 265-273.

Singer, Edgar A., *Modern Thinkers and Present Problems: An Approach to Modern Philosophy Through Its History* (New York: Henry Holt and Co., 1923).

Includes a chapter on Spinoza, pp. 37-61, followed by another entitled, "A Disciple of Spinoza (An Illustration)," pp. 65-93.

Singer, Irving, *The Nature of Love: Courtly and Romantic* (Chicago: University of Chicago Press, 1984).

In *Philosopher's Index*, No. 133634.

Singleton, Ira Custer, *The Rationality of Eighteenth Century Musical Classicism: A Study of the Relationships Between the Rationalistic Philosophies of Descartes, Spinoza and Leibniz and the Classicism of Haydn, Mozart and Beethoven*, Unpublished doctoral dissertation, New York University, 1954.

Currently available from UMI (Order No. 00-08012).

Siwek, Paul, *The Philosophy of Evil* (New York: Ronald Press, 1951).

In *Philosopher's Index*, No. 017665, citing references to Spinoza, Leibniz, Schopenhauer, and others.

Siwek, Paul, "Final Causes in the System of Spinoza," Translated by C. J. McNaspy, *The Modern Schoolman*, Vol. 13 (1936), pp. 37-39.

In Rice (1967), p. 305. According to Wetlesen (1968), p. 47, also in *Proceedings of the 10th International Congress of Philosophy* (Amsterdam, 1949), pp. 1136-1141.

Siwek, Paul, "How Pantheism Resolves the Enigma of Evil," *Laval théologique et philosophique* (Quebec), Vol. 2 (1955), pp. 213-221.

In *Philosophers's Index*, No. 071472.

Slote, Michael A., "Understanding Free Will," *The Journal of Philosophy*, Vol. 77 (March 1980), pp. 136-151.

In *Philosopher's Index*, No. 085741.

Slyomovics, Peter, "Spinoza: Liberal Democratic Religion," *Journal of the History of Philosophy*, Vol 23, No. 4 (October 1985), pp. 499-513.

Smith, Daniel Drake. *See* Spinoza, *Ethics* (1888).

Smith, Henry, *Spinoza and His Environment: A Critical Essay with a Translation of the Ethics* (Cincinnati: Robert Clarke & Co., 1886).

Smith, J. F., "Ethics of Spinoza," *Theological Review*, Vol. 7 (1870), pp. 550-571.

Smith, Joseph H. (ed.), *Thought, Consciousness, and Reality* (New Haven, CT: Yale University Press, 1977). 2 vols.

> In *Mental Health Abstracts*, No. 0314356, citing a chapter on "the concept of psychic freedom" in Spinoza, Freud, and Hampshire.

Smith, Kalmin D., "The Politics of Civil Religion," *American Benedictine Review*, Vol. 26, No. 1 (1975), pp. 89-106.

> Reviews the origins of civil religion in the thought of many philosophers, including Spinoza.

Smith, Maurice Hamlin, *Spinoza's Anticipation of Recent Psychological Developments* (Cambridge: Cambridge University Press, 1925).

> Reprinted from *The British Journal of Medical Psychology*, Vol. 5, No. 4 (1925), pp. 257-278.

Smith, Norman Kemp, *Studies in the Cartesian Philosophy* (New York: Garland Publishing, 1987).

> Facsimile reprint of the original 1902 edition published in London by Macmillan. Includes a section, "The Cartesian Principles in Spinoza and Leibniz," pp. 137-180, of which pp. 137-160 focus on Spinoza.

Smith, Norman Kemp, *The Philosophy of David Hume: A Critical Study of Its Origins and Central Doctrines* (London: Macmillan; New York: St. Martin's Press, 1966).

> A reprint of the first edition, 1941. Includes as an appendix to Chap. XXIII a section, "Bayle's Article on Spinoza, and the Use Which Hume Has Made of It," pp. 506-516.

Smith, T. V., *Creative Sceptics: In Defense of the Liberal Temper* (Chicago and New York: Willett, Clark & Co., 1934).

> Includes a chapter, "Doubting One's Way to Spiritual Peace, Being a Moral from Benedict Spinoza," pp. 67-105.

Smith, T. V., "Spinoza's Political and Moral Philosophy," in Schaub (1933).

> Originally in *The Monist*, Vol. 43 (January 1933), pp. 23-39.

Smith, T. V., and Marjorie Grene, *From Descartes to Kant: Readings in the Philosophy of the Renaissance and Enlightenment* (Chicago: University of Chicago Press, 1940).

Includes an essay on Spinoza, pp. 270-276, followed by selections from his works.

Snider, Denton J., *Modern European Philosophy: The History of Philosophy Psychologically Treated* (St. Louis: Sigma Publishing Co., 1904).

Includes a section on Spinoza, pp. 118ff.

Snow, Adolph J., "Spinoza's Use of the 'Euclidean Form' of Exposition," *The Monist*, Vol. 33, No. 3 (July 1923), pp. 473-480.

Snow, Dale Evarts, *Self and Absolute in the Early Schelling*, Unpublished doctoral dissertation, Emory University, 1984.

Includes material on Spinoza. Currently available from UMI (Order No. 84-20296).

Snow, Dale Evarts, "F. H. Jacobi and the Development of German Idealism," *Journal of the History of Philosophy*, Vol. 25 (July 1987), pp. 397-415.

Includes references to Spinoza.

Sokolow, Nahum, "Baruch Spinoza the Jew and His Time," *Avukah Annual* (1932), pp. 723-731.

In Oko (1964), p. 73.

Sokolow, Nahum, "Spinoza the Jew," *Jewish Review* (London), Vol. 1, No. 3 (1932-1933), pp. 35-44.

In Oko (1964), p. 118.

Sokolov, V. V., "On the Evolution of Spinoza's Political and Philosophical Ideas," *Soviet Studies in Philosophy*, Vol. 2 (Spring 1964), pp. 57-62.

Solomon, Hannah G., *A Sheaf of Leaves* (Chicago: Privately printed, 1911).

In Oko (1964), p. 504, citing a "review" of Spinoza's *Tractatus Theologico-Politicus*, pp. 9-15.

Sontag, Frederick, *Divine Perfection: Possible Ideas of God* (New York: Harper & Brothers, 1962).

Includes a chapter, "Spinoza and Leibniz," pp. 59-68, and other references.

Sontag, Frederick, *Problems of Metaphysics* (Scranton, PA: Chandler, 1970).

In *Philosopher's Index*, No. 019966.

Sontag, Frederick, *How Philosophy Shapes Theology: Problems in the Philosophy of Religion* (New York: Harper and Row, 1971).

Includes many references to Spinoza.

Sontag, Frederick, *Emotion: Its Role in Understanding and Decision* (New York: Peter Lang Publishing, 1989).

In *Philosopher's Index*, No. 165546.

Sontag, Frederick, "Being and Freedom: The Metaphysics of Freedom," *Process Studies*, Vol. 8 (Fall 1978), pp. 180-185.

In *Philosopher's Index*, No. 084516, citing the author's argument that freedom is an attribute of God, or substance, as defined in Spinoza's *Ethics*.

Sontag, Frederick, "Ethics of Spinoza," in Magill (1982), Vol. 2, pp. 886-893.

Sorley, William Ritchie, *Spinoza* (London: Published for the British Academy by E. Milford, Oxford University Press, 1918).

20pp. From *Proceedings of the British Academy*, Vol. VIII; Third Annual Lecture on a Master Mind.

Sorley, William Ritchie, *Moral Values and the Idea of God*, The Gifford Lectures delivered in the University of Aberdeen in 1914 and 1915, 3rd Edition (Cambridge: Cambridge University Press; New York: Putnam, 1935).

Includes a section on Spinoza, pp. 379ff., as well as other references.

Sorley, William Ritchie, "Spinoza and Jewish Medieval Philosophy," *Mind*, Vol. 5 (July 1880), pp. 362-384.

Spencer, Margaret E. N., *A Comparative Study of the Ethics of Spinoza and Nietzsche*, Unpublished doctoral dissertation, Yale University, 1924.

Spencer, Margaret E. N., "Spinoza and Nietzsche: A Comparison," *The Monist* (January 1931), pp. 67-90.

Spicker, Stuart F. (ed.), *The Philosophy of the Body* (Chicago: Quadrangle Books, 1970).

Includes a chapter by Hans Jonas, "Spinoza and the Theory of Organism." *See* Jonas (1974).

Spink, J. S., *French Free Thought from Gassendi to Voltaire* (London: The Athlone Press, University of London; New York: Oxford University Press, 1960).

> Includes two chapters on Spinoza: "Monopsychism and the Reaction to Spinoza," pp. 238-252, and "Le Grand Tout," pp. 253-279, as well as other references. Reprinted in New York by Greenwood Press, 1969.

Spinka, Matthew, *Christian Thought from Erasmus to Berdyaev* (Englewood Cliffs, NJ: Prentice Hall, 1962).

> Includes a section, "Baruch Spinoza's Deterministic Pantheism," pp. 34-39.

Sprague, Elmer, *Metaphysical Thinking* (New York: Oxford University Press, 1978).

> Includes a section, "God in Spinoza's Metaphysics," pp. 147-152.

Sprigge, T. L. S., *The Vindication of Absolute Idealism* (Edinburgh: Edinburgh University Press, 1983).

> Sprigge (1985), p. 180, describes this book as an attempt "to synthesize idealism and Spinozism."

Sprigge, T. L. S., *Theories of Existence: A Sequence of Essays on the Fundamental Positions in Philosophy* (Harmondsworth: Penguin Books, 1985).

> Includes a chapter, "Spinozistic Pantheism," pp. 153-176, and other references.

Sprigge, T. L. S., *The Rational Foundations of Ethics* (London: Routledge & Kegan Paul, 1988).

> Includes a section on Spinoza, pp. 82-90, and other references.

Sprigge, T. L. S., *The Significance of Spinoza's Determinism*, Mededelingen vanwege het Spinozahuis 58 (Leiden: E. J. Brill, 1989).

Sprigge, T. L. S., "Spinoza: His Identity Theory," in Honderich (1984).

> Originally published as "Spinoza's Identity Theory," *Inquiry*, Vol. 20 (Winter 1977), pp. 419-445.

Srinivasan, G., "Spinoza and Sankhya: Reply to Professor Sanat Kumar Sen," *Journal of the Philosophical Association*, Vol. 7, pp. 57-59.

> In *Philosopher's Index*, No. 068000; date not given.

Stace, W. T., *Mysticism and Philosophy* (London: The Macmillan Press, 1960).

Includes a section on Spinoza's pantheism, pp. 215-218, and other references.

Stackhouse, Thomas. A defence of the Christian religion from the several objections of modern antiscripturists; wherein the literal sense of the prophecies contained in the Old Testament, and of the miracles recorded in the New, is explained and vindicated, in which is included the whole state of the controversy between Mr. Woolston and his adversaries ... Second edition, corrected. London, Printed for Edward Symon, 1733.

In Oko (1964), p. 357.

Stafford, T. Polhill, *Neoplatonic Elements in the Philosophy of Spinoza: An Attempt To Show the Origin of Spinoza's Principal Thoughts*, Unpublished doctoral dissertation, Southern Baptist Theological Seminary, 1930.

Stallknecht, Newton P., and Robert S. Brumbaugh, *The Spirit of Western Philosophy* (New York: David McKay Co., 1950).

Includes a section, "The Parallelism of Spinoza," pp. 276-282, as well as quotations from the *Ethics*, in Chap. 9, "The Cartesian Problem of Interaction."

Stambaugh, Joan, *The Real Is Not the Rational*, SUNY Series in Buddhist Studies (Albany, NY: State University of New York Press, 1986).

Includes a section on Spinoza's discussion of the emotions, pp. 52-57, and many other references.

Staniland, H. S., "Psychological Hedonism," *Second Order* (Nigeria), Vol. 4 (1975), pp. 74-79.

In Van der Werf (1984), No. 1842.

Stebbing, L. Susan, *et al.*, "Symposium: The New Physics and Metaphysical Materialism," *Proceedings of the Aristotelian Society*, Vol. 43 (1943), pp. 167-214.

In *Philosopher's Index*, No. 066316, citing references to Spinoza, Jeans, Huxley, and others.

Stein, Siegfried, and Raphael Loewe (eds.), *Studies in Jewish Religious and Intellectual History*, Presented to Alexander Altmann on the Occasion of His Seventieth Birthday (Montgomery, AL: University of Alabama Press, 1979).

Includes an essay by Shlomo Pines, "The Jewish Religion after the Destruction of the Temple and the State: The Views of Bodin and Spinoza," pp. 215-234.

Steinberg, Diane, *Spinoza's Theory of the Mind*, Unpublished doctoral dissertation, University of Illinois, Urbana-Champaign, 1977.

Currently available from UMI (Order No. 77-26758).

Steinberg, Diane, "Spinoza's Theory of the Eternity of the Mind," *Canadian Journal of Philosophy*, Vol. 11, No. 1 (March 1981), pp. 35-68.

Steinberg, Diane, "Spinoza's Ethical Doctrine and the Unity of Human Nature," *Journal of the History of Philosophy*, Vol. 22, No. 3 (July 1984), pp. 303-324.

Steinberg, Diane, "A Note on Bennett's 'Transattribute Differentiae' and Spinoza's Substance-Monism," *The Southern Journal of Philosophy*, Vol. 24, No. 3 (Fall 1986), pp. 431-435.

Steinberg, Diane, "Necessity and Essence in Spinoza," *The Modern Schoolman*, Vol. 64, No. 3 (March 1987), pp. 187-195.

Stepelevich, Lawrence S., "Hegel and Stirner: Thesis and Antithesis," *Idealistic Studies*, Vol. 6 (Spring 1976), pp. 263-278.

In *Philosopher's Index*, No. 051889.

Stephen, Leslie, *A History of English Thought in the Eighteenth Century* (London: Smith, Elder, 1876). 2 vols.

Includes a section on Spinoza, Vol. 1, pp. 30-33. The 1881 edition is currently available from UMI Out-of-Print Books on Demand (Order No. BH16568). The third edition (1902) was reprinted in Bristol by Thoemmes in 1991.

Stephen, Leslie, "Spinoza," *Fortnightly Review*, Vol. 23 (1880), pp. 752-772.

In Oko (1964), p. 497, identifying this essay as a review of Pollock's *Spinoza: His Life and Philosophy* (1880).

Sterling, Ada, *The Jews and Civilization* (New York: Aetco Publishing Co., 1924).

Includes a section on Spinoza, pp. 291-295.

Sternfeld, Robert, "Reason and Necessity in Classical Rationalism," *The Review of Metaphysics*, Vol. 12 (September 1958), pp. 48-56.

In *Philosopher's Index*, No. 006804, citing references to Spinoza, Descartes, and Leibniz.

Sternheim, Emmanuel, "Spinoza: An Essay," *Monthly Review*, Vol. 27, No. 3 (June 1907), pp. 36-50.

In Oko (1964), p. 119.

[Stewart, Dugald] *The Works of Dugald Stewart* (Cambridge, MA: Hilliard and Brown, 1829). 7 vols.

Includes a section on Spinoza, Vol. 6, pp. 273-280. The *Collected Works*, edited by Sir William Hamilton and published in 11 vols. by T. & T. Clark in 1877 in Edinburgh, presents the same material in Vol. I, pp. 298-306.

Stillingfleet, Edward. Origines sacrae or a rational account of the grounds of natural and reveal'd religion. 7th Edition. Added part of another book on the same subject. Cambridge, 1702.

In Hertzberger (1950), No. 922, citing a discussion of Spinoza and his works in Part II, pp. 100 ff.

[Stillingfleet, Edward] The works of that eminent and most learned prelate, Dr. Edw. Stillingfleet, late lord bishop of Worcester. Together with his life and character. London, Printed by J. Heptinstall, for Henry and George Mortlock, 1709-1710. 6 vols.

In Oko (1964), p. 357, citing references to Spinoza.

Stirling, Amelia Hutchison. *See* Spinoza, *Ethics* (1910) and *Tractatus de Intellectus Emendatione* (1969).

Stirling, J. H., *Philosophy and Theology* (Edinburgh, 1890).

In Hertzberger (1950), No. 172, citing many references to Spinoza.

Stitskin, Leon D., *Jewish Philosophy: A Study in Personalism* (New York: Yeshiva University Press, 1976).

Includes a section on Spinoza, pp. 61-69, and other references.

Stock, Irwin, *William Hale White (Mark Rutherford): A Critical Study*, With foreword by Lionel Trilling (London: George Allen & Unwin, 1956).

Includes a section on Spinoza, pp. 70-74.

Stokes, G. J., "Gnosticism and Modern Pantheism," *Mind*, Vol. 4 (1895), pp. 320-333.

> In Oko (1964), p. 446.

[Stouppe, Jean Baptiste] The Religion of the Dutch. Represented in several Letters from A Protestant Officer in The French Army to A Pastor and Professor of Divinity at Berne in Swisserland. Out of the French. London, Printed for Samuel Heyrick at Grayes-Inn Gate in Holbourn. 1680.

> 66pp. Citation follows Van der Linde, No. 65. Oko (1964), p. 73, is alone in giving the author's name as Giovanni Battista Stoppa.

Strauss, Joseph, *Essays*, 2nd Edition (London and New York: Walter Scott Publishing Co., 1911).

> Includes an essay, "Benedictus Spinoza," pp. 25-72, originally in *Gentleman's Magazine*, Vol. 50 (1892), pp. 379 ff.

Strauss, Leo, *Persecution and the Art of Writing* (Glencoe, IL: The Free Press, 1952).

> Includes a chapter, "How To Study Spinoza's *Theologico-Political Treatise*," pp. 142-201; originally in *Proceedings of the American Academy for Jewish Research*, Vol. 17 (1948), pp. 69-131.

Strauss, Leo, *Spinoza's Critique of Religion*, Translated by E. M. Sinclair (New York: Schocken Books, 1965).

> The preface in this volume was reprinted in Goldin (1974) and Strauss (1968).

Strauss, Leo, *Liberalism Ancient and Modern* (New York: Basic Books, 1968).

> Includes on pp. 224-259 the author's "Preface" to his *Spinoza's Critique of Religion* (1965).

Strauss, Leo, and Joseph Cropsey (eds.), *History of Political Philosophy* (Chicago: Rand McNally, 1972).

> Includes an essay by Stanley Rosen, "Benedict Spinoza," pp. 431-450.

Strawson, P. F. (ed.), *Studies in the Philosophy of Thought and Action* (London: Oxford University Press, 1968).

> Includes an essay by Stuart Hampshire, "Spinoza and the Idea of Freedom," pp. 48-70.

Strawson, P. F., "Liberty and Necessity," in Rotenstreich and Schneider (1983), pp. 120-129.

Strickler, Nina, *The Problem of the Absolute: A Study in Spinoza, Hegel and Wittgenstein*, Unpublished doctoral dissertation, De Paul University, 1973.

>   Currently available from UMI (Order No. 73-28663).

Stroll, Avrum, and Richard H. Popkin, *Introduction to Philosophy* (New York: Holt, Rinehart and Winston, 1961).

>   Includes a section, "Spinoza's Metaphysical Theory," pp. 159-165, and another, "The Ethics of Spinoza," pp. 279-288, and many other references.

Strycovski, Z. H., *The Jewish Background of Spinozism*, Unpublished doctoral dissertation, St. Louis, MO, 1926.

>   In Van der Werf (1984), No. 2232.

Stumpf, Samuel Enoch, *Socrates to Sartre: A History of Philosophy*, 3rd Edition (New York: McGraw-Hill Book Co., 1982).

>   Includes a section on Spinoza, pp. 239-245, and many other references.

Sullivan, Celestine J., Jr., *Critical and Historical Reflections on Spinoza's "Ethics,"* University of California Publications in Philosophy, Vol. 32 (Berkeley: University of California Press, 1958). 45 pp.

>   Currently available from UMI Out-of-Print Books on Demand (Order No. 2021178).

Sullivan, Constantine J., Jr., "Spinoza and Hume on Causation," *Proceedings of the 12th International Congress of Philosophy*, Vol. 12, *History of Modern and Contemporary Philosophy* (Firenze: Sansomi, 1961), pp. 431-467.

>   Citation based on details in Wetlesen (1968), p. 47, and Curley (1975), p. 312.

Sullivan, R. E., *John Toland and the Deist Controversy: A Study in Adaptations* (Cambridge, 1982).

>   In Van der Werf (1984), No. 1872.

Swabey, William Curtis, *Ethical Theory from Hobbes to Kant* (New York: Philosophical Library, 1961).

>   Includes a chapter on Spinoza, pp. 15-25. Currently available from UMI Out-of-Print Books on Demand (Order No. OP40948).

Tagliacozzo, Giorgio, and Donald Phillip Verene (eds.), *Giambattista Vico's Science of Humanity* (Baltimore: Johns Hopkins University Press, 1976).

> Includes an essay by Amos Funkenstein, "Natural Science and Social Theory: Hobbes, Spinoza, and Vico," pp. 187-212.

Tanner, A. E., "Spinoza and Modern Psychology," *American Journal of Psychology*, Vol. 18 (October 1907), pp. 514-518.

Tawney, G. A., "In Memoriam: George Stuart Fullerton and Spinoza," in *Chronicon Spinozanum*, Vol. IV (1926), pp. 246-252.

Taylor, A. E., *The Faith of a Moralist*, The Gifford Lectures delivered in the University of St. Andrews, 1926-1928 (London: Macmillan and Co., 1930). 2 vols.

> Includes many references to Spinoza.

Taylor, A. E., "The Conception of Immortality in Spinoza's *Ethics*," *Mind*, Vol. 5 (1896), pp. 145-166.

Taylor, A. E., "A Further Word on Spinoza," *Mind*, Vol. 55, No. 218 (April 1946), pp. 97-112.

Taylor, A. E., "Some Incoherencies in Spinoza," in Kashap (1972), Part I, pp. 189-211; Part II, pp. 289-309.

> Originally in *Mind*, Vol. 46 (April 1937), pp. 137-158; and Vol. 46 (July 1937), pp. 281-301.

Taylor, Henry Osborn, *Human Values and Verities* (New York: Macmillan and Co., 1928).

> Includes a section on Spinoza, pp. 163-178.

Teichler, Jacob L., "Why Was Spinoza Banned?" *The Menorah Journal*, Vol. 45 (1957), pp. 41-60.

Tennemann, Wilhelm Gottlieb, *A Manual of the History of Philosophy*, Translated by the Rev. Arthur Johnson (Oxford: D. A. Talboys, 1832).

> Includes a section on Spinoza, pp. 322-329. Later editions — 1852 and 1875 in Bohn's Philosophical Library, with revisions and additions by J. B. Morell — appear to retain these pages.

Teo, Wesley K. H., "The Relation of Substance to Attributes in Spinoza," *Kinesis*, Vol. 1 (Fall 1968), pp. 15-21.

Terrenal, Quentin C., *Causa Sui and the Object of Intuition in Spinoza* (Cebu City, The Philippines: University of San Carlos, 1976).

> From the author's doctoral dissertation, Catholic University of America, 1975. The latter is currently available from UMI (Order No. 75-13039).

Thayer, Vivian T., *A Comparison of the Ethical Philosophies of Spinoza and Hobbes*, Unpublished doctoral dissertation, University of Wisconsin, Madison, 1922.

Thayer, Vivian T., "Comparison of Bergson and Spinoza," *The Monist*, Vol. 29 (January 1919), pp. 96-105.

Thayer, Vivian T., "Comparison of the Ethical Philosophies of Spinoza and Hobbes," *The Monist*, Vol. 32 (October 1922), pp. 553-568.

Thilly, Frank, *A History of Philosophy*, Revised by Ledger Wood (New York: Henry Holt and Co., 1951).

> Includes a chapter on Spinoza, pp. 319-332, and other references.

Thilly, Frank, "Spinoza's Doctrine of the Freedom of Speech," in *Chronicon Spinozanum*, Vol. III (1923), pp. 88-107.

Thomas, Calvin, *Goethe and the Conduct of Life*, University of Michigan Philosophical Papers, First Series, No. 2 (Ann Arbor: Andrews & Witherby, 1886).

> 28 pp. Includes a discussion of the *Ethics*.

Thomas, George Finger, *Religious Philosophies of the West* (New York: Scribner's, 1965).

> In Curley (1975), p. 289.

Thomas, Henry, *Understanding the Great Philosophers* (Garden City, NY: Doubleday & Company, 1962).

> Includes a chapter on Spinoza, pp. 207-217.

Thomas, Henry, and Dana Lee Thomas, *Living Biographies of Great Philosophers: Plato to Santayana* (Garden City, NY: Halcyon House, 1947).

Includes a chapter on Spinoza, pp. 115-132.

Thomas, Wendell Marshall, *On the Resolution of Science and Faith* (New York: Island Press, 1947).

In *Philosopher's Index*, No. 017395.

Thomson, James, *Essays and Phantasies* (London: Reeves and Turner, 1881).

Includes an essay, "A Few Words on the System of Spinoza," pp. 303-312.

Tice, Terrence, and Thomas P. Slavens, *Research Guide to Philosophy*, Sources of Information on the Humanities, No. 3 (Chicago: American Library Association, 1983).

Includes an article on Spinoza, pp. 85-88.

Tiebout, Harry M., "Deus, sive Natura...," *Philosophy and Phenomenological Research*, Vol. 16 (June 1956), pp. 512-521.

Tigner, Joyce A., "An Analysis of Spinoza on Pride and Self-Abasement," *American Journal of Psychoanalysis*, Vol. 45, No. 3 (1985), pp. 208-220.

Tilley, Terrance W., *Talking of God: An Introduction to Philosophical Analysis of Religious Language* (New York: Paulist Press, 1978).

In *Philosopher's Index*, No. 089328, citing the author's discussion of Spinoza as a representative of one group of analysts of religious language.

[Tindal, Matthew] Christianity as old as the creation: or, The gospel, a republication of the religion of nature. The 2d ed. in octavo ... London, Printed in the year 1732.

In Oko (1964), p. 402. Hertzberger (1950), No. 923, cites the first edition (1730).

[Toland, John] Christianity not mysterious or a treatise showing, that there is nothing in the Gospel contrary to reason, nor above it, and that no Christian doctrine can be properly call'd a mystery. London, 1696.

In Hertzberger (1950), No. 924. A facsimile edition was published in New York by Garland Publishing, as Vol. 15 in the Garland Series on the Philosophy of John Locke.

Toland, John, *Letters to Serena*, British Philosophers and Theologians of the 17th and 18th Centuries, No. 58 (New York: Garland Publishing, 1976).

> A facsimile of the original 1704 edition, printed in London for Bernard Lintot at the Middle-Temple Gate in Fleetstreet. Discusses Spinoza in Part IV, pp. 131-162 ("A Letter to a Gentleman in Holland, showing Spinoza's System of Philosophy to be without any Principle or Foundation"), and in Part V, pp. 163-239 ("Motion essential to Matter, in Answer to some Remarks by a Noble Friend on the Confutation of Spinoza"). The 1704 edition is cited in Van der Linde, No. 330; in Oko (1964), p. 228; and in Hertzberger (1950), No. 927.

[Toland, John] Nazerenus or Jewish, Gentile and Mahometan Christianity .... Also, the original plan of Christianity occasionally explain'd in the history of the Nazarens ... With the relation of an Irish manuscript of the four Gospels ... and the reality of the Keldees. London, 1718.

> In Oko (1964), p. 228; in Hertzberger (1950), No. 931. *See* Mangey (1718) and Paterson (1718).

Toland, John. Tetradymus. Containing I. Hodegus; or, The pillar of cloud and fire, that guided the Israelites in the wilderness, not miraculous .... II. Clidophorous; or, Of the exoteric and esoteric philosophy, that is, of the external and internal doctrines of the ancients: the one open and public, accommodated to popular prejudices and the establish'd religions; the other private and secret, wherin, to the few capable and discrete, the real truth stript of all disguises. III. Hypatia; or, The history of a most beautiful, most virtuous, most learned, and every way accomplish'd lady; who was torn to pieces by the clergy of Alexandria, to gratify the pride, emulation, and cruelty of their Archbishop Cyril ... IV. Mangoneutes: being a defense of Nazarenus, address'd to the Right Reverend John, lord bishop of London; against his lordship's chaplain Dr. Mangey, his dedicator, Mr. Patterson, and ... the Reverend Dr. Brett ... London, Printed: and sold by J. Brotherton and W. Meadows ... 1720.

> In Oko (1964), p. 229. *See* Mangey (1718) and Paterson (1718).

[Toland, John] Pantheisticon: or, the form of celebrating the Socratic-Society ... subjoined a short dissertation upon a two-fold philosophy of the pantheists. Rendered into English. London, 1751.

> In Hertzberger (1950), No. 926. First English edition of the 1720 Latin original. A facsimile edition was published in New York by Garland Publishing.

[Toland, John] A collection of several pieces of Mr. John Toland, now first publish'd from his original manuscripts: with some memoirs of his life and writings ... London, J. Peele, 1726. 2 vols.

In Oko (1964), p. 228.

Tomm, Winnifred A., "Autonomy and Interrelatedness: Spinoza, Hume, and Vasubandhu," *Zygon*, Vol. 22, No. 4 (December 1987), pp. 459-478.

Toole, Robert, "Shaftesbury on God and His Relationship to the World," *International Studies in Philosophy*, Vol. 8 (Fall 1976), pp. 81-100.

Tovey, Barbara, and George Tovey, "Women's Philosophical Friends and Enemies," *Social Sciences Quarterly*, Vol. 55, No. 3 (1974), pp. 586-604.

In *Historical Abstracts* database, No. 776245.

Tripathi, Rama Kanta, *Spinoza in Light of the Vedanta* (Banaras, India: Banaras Hindu University, 1957).

Trompetter, Linda A., *Substance and Attributes in Spinoza's Philosophy*, Unpublished doctoral dissertation, University of Massachusetts, 1977.

Currently available from UMI (Order No. 77-21517).

Trompetter, Linda A., "Spinoza: A Response to De Vries," *Canadian Journal of Philosophy*, Vol. 11, No. 3 (September 1981), pp. 525-538.

Tsanoff, Radoslav A., *Ethics of Spinoza*, Rice Institute Pamphlets, No. 20 (April 1933), pp. 216-237.

Tsanoff, Radoslav A., *The Great Philosophers* (New York: Harper & Brothers, 1953).

Includes a chapter, "Spinoza: Monistic Determinism and Moral Values," pp. 309-327.

Tsanoff, Radoslav A., *Science and Human Perspectives* (London: Routledge & Kegan Paul, 1962).

Also published in the U.S. as *Worlds To Know* (New York: Humanities Press, 1962). Includes a section that focuses on Spinoza, "Psychophysical Parallelism," pp. 16-19, and other references.

Tulloch, J., *Rational Theology and Christian Philosophy in England in the 17th Century*, 2nd Edition (Edinburgh, 1874). 2 vols.

> In Wetlesen (1968), p. 12.

Turck, Hermann, *The Man of Genius* (London: Black, 1923).

> Includes a section on Spinoza, pp. 208-214. According to Oko (1964), p. 282, the first English edition — apparently published in Germany in 1914 (and translated from the German 6th Edition by George J. Tamson) — includes a chapter, "Genius and Freedom of Mind in Schopenhauer's and Spinoza's Teachings," pp. 199-214.

Turner, William, *History of Philosophy* (Boston: Ginn & Co., 1903).

> Includes a chapter on Spinoza, pp. 289-309.

Tymieniecka, Anna-Teresa (ed.), *Soul and Body in Phenomenology* (Dordrecht: D. Reidel Publishing Co., 1983).

> Includes an essay by Wolfgang Schirmacher, "Monism in Spinoza's and Husserl's Thought: The Ontological Background of the Body-Soul Problem," pp. 345-352.

Ueberweg, Friedrich, *History of Modern Philosophy from Thales to the Present Time*, Translated by George S. Morris (London: Hodder and Stoughton, 1874). 2 vols.

> Includes a section on Spinoza, Vol. 2, pp. 55-78.

Umphrey, Stewart, "Spinoza's Defense of Human Freedom," in Wilbur (1976), pp. 44-65.

Umphrey, Stewart, "*De Natura*," in Kennington (1980), Chap. 15, pp. 273-292.

Upton, Charles Barnes, "Dr. Martineau's and Mr. Pollock's Spinoza," *Modern Review* (London), Vol. 3 (1882), pp. 757-797, and Vol. 4 (1883), pp. 137-176.

> In Oko (1964), p. 498. Review of Martineau's *A Study of Spinoza* (1882) and Pollock's *Spinoza: His Life and Philosophy* (1880).

Urbach, E. E., "Greetings from the Israel Academy of Sciences and Humanities," in Rotenstreich and Schneider (1983), pp. 9-10.

Urmson, J. O. (ed.), *The Concise Encyclopedia of Western Philosophy and Philosophers* (New York: Hawthorn Books, 1960).

> Includes an article by Ruth Lydia Saw on Spinoza, pp. 367-371.

Ursery, Danney, "Spinoza's Primary Emotions," *Dialogue: Journal of Phi Sigma Tau*, Vol. 22, Nos. 2-3 (April 1980), pp. 57-62.

Usmani, M. A., "Spinoza: A First-Rate Scientific Rationalist," *Pakistan Philosophical Congress*, Vol. 11 (1964), pp. 258-262.

> In *Philosopher's Index*, No. 067769.

Valentiner, W. R., *Rembrandt and Spinoza: A Study of the Spiritual Conflicts in Seventeenth-Century Holland* (London: Phaidon Press, 1957).

Valleé, Gerard (ed.), *The Spinoza Conversations Between Lessing and Jacobi: Text with Excerpts from the Ensuing Controversy*, Translated by G. Valleé, J. B. Lawson, and C. G. Chapple, with introduction by G. Valleé (Lanham, MD: University Press of America, 1988).

> Includes translations of relevant sections from Mendelssohn's *Morgenstunden* (1785), pp. 65-77; Jacobi's *Über die Lehre des Spinoza* (1819), pp. 79-125; Mendelssohn's *An die Freunde Lessings* (1786), pp. 127-149; and Jacobi's *Wider Mendelssohns Beschuldigungen* (1819), pp. 151-160.

Van Bunge, Wiep, "A Tragic Idealist: Jacob Ostens (1630-1678)," in *Studia Spinozana*, Vol. 4 (1988), pp. 263-279.

Van Bunge, Wiep, "Johannes Bredenburg and the *Korte Verhandeling*," in *Studia Spinozana*, Vol. 4 (1988), pp. 321-328.

Van Bunge, Wiep, "On the Early Dutch Receptions of the *Tractatus Theologico-Politicus*," in *Studia Spinozana*, Vol. 5 (1989), pp. 225-251.

Van der Bend, J. G. (ed.), *Spinoza on Knowing, Being and Freedom*, Proceedings of the Spinoza Symposium at the International School of Philosophy in The Netherlands, September 1973 (Assen, The Netherlands: Van Gorcum, 1974).

> In addition to an essay by Van der Bend — "Some Idealistic Tendencies in Spinoza," pp. 1-5 — includes papers by H. De Dijn, G. Floistad, A. Furlan, J. Groen, K. Hammacher, O. Hansen, E. Harris, H. Hubbeling, A. Naess, G. Parkinson, L. Rice, P. van der Hoeven, A. Wernham, J. Wetlesen, and T. Zweerman.

Van der Hoeven, P., "The Significance of Cartesian Physics for Spinoza's Theory of Knowledge," in Van der Bend (1974), pp. 114-125.

Vanderhoof, Frank M. *See* Spinoza, *Theologico-Political Treatise* (1952).

Van der Merwe, E. (ed.), *Old and New Questions in Physics, Cosmology, Philosophy and Theoretical Biology* (New York, 1983).

> In Van der Werf (1984), No. 1397, citing an essay by Arne Naess, "Einstein, Spinoza and God," pp. 683-687.

Van der Tak, W. G. *See* Vaz Dias (1982, 1989).

Van der Wal, G. A., "Spinoza and the Idea of *Reason of State*," in *Studia Spinozana*, Vol. 1 (1985), pp. 275-304.

Van der Werf, Theo, Heine Siebrand, and Coen Westerveen, *Spinoza Bibliography 1971-1983*, Mededelingen XLVI vanwege het Spinozahuis (Leiden: E. J. Brill, 1984).

> Cited in the present bibliography as "Van der Werf (1984)," followed by the item number.

Van Loon, Hendrik Willem, *Tolerance* (Garden City, NY: Garden City Publishing Co., 1927).

> Includes a chapter on Spinoza, pp. 277-289. Also published under the title, *The Liberation of Mankind: The Story of Man's Struggle for the Right To Think* (London: George G. Harrap & Co., 1926), with the chapter on Spinoza on pp. 225-235.

Van Mildert, William. An historical view of the rise and progress of infidelity, with a refutation of its principles and reasoning; in a series of sermons preached for the lecture founded by the Hon. Robert Boyle, in the parish church of St. Mary Le Bow, London, from the year 1802 to 1805. 5th ed. Oxford, Printed by T. Combe for J. H. Parker, 1839. 3 vols.

> In Oko (1964), p. 392, citing references to Spinoza in Vol. 1, pp. 280-285 and 454-457, and in Vol. 2, p. 401.

Van Straaten, Zak (ed.), *Philosophical Subjects: Essays Presented to P. F. Strawson* (Oxford: Oxford University Press, 1980).

> Includes an essay by J. Bennett, "Accountability," pp. 14-47, containing a section, "Why the Spinozist Attack Is Persuasive," pp. 25-28.

Van Suchtelen, Guido, "The Spinoza Houses at Rijnsburg and The Hague," in Hessing (1977), pp. 475-478.

Van Suchtelen, Guido. See *Studia Spinozana*, Vol. 4 (1988).

Van Vloten, J., "Spinoza: An Oration," Translated by Allan Menzies, in Knight (1882), pp. 129-143.

> The full title is "Spinoza: The (Glad) Herald to Mankind of the Good News of the Majority."

Van Zandt, Joe D., "*Res Extensa* and the Space-Time Continuum," in Grene and Nails (1986), pp. 249-266.

Vater, M. G., "The Human Mind as *Idea* in the Platonic Tradition and in Spinoza," *Diotima* (Athens), Vol. 8 (1980), pp. 134-143.

Vaughan, Charles Edwyn, *Studies in the History of Political Philosophy Before and After Rousseau*, Edited by A. G. Little (Manchester: Manchester University Press; London and New York: Longmans, Green, 1925). 2 vols.

> Reprinted (New York: Russell and Russell, 1960). Includes a chapter, "The Social Contract: Spinoza," Vol. 1, pp. 62-129.

Vaughan, Frederick, *The Political Philosophy of Giambattista Vico: An Introduction to "La scienza nuova"* (The Hague: Martinus Nijhoff, 1972).

> In Van der Werf (1984), No. 2005, citing pp. 44-50.

Vaz Dias, A. M., *Spinoza and Simon Joosten de Vries*, Mededelingen vanwege het Spinozahuis 59 (Delft: Eburon, 1989).

> This issue also includes two papers by W. G. van der Tak, "Jarich Jellesz' Origins" and "Jellesz' Life and Business." The entire issue, including an introduction by Theo van der Werf, was translated into English by S. Bijvoet-Hart.

Vaz Dias, A. M., and W. G. Van der Tak, *Spinoza: Merchant & Autodidact*, Translated by S. Bijvoet-Hart, with preface by G. van Suchtelen (The Hague: Martinus Nijhoff, 1982).

This translation of the 1932 original edition in Dutch was first published in *Studia Rosenthaliana*, Vol. 16, No. 2 (1982), with the title essay on pp. 113-171. This edition also includes, in translation, A. M. Vaz Dias, "Did Spinoza Live in ''t Opregte Tappeythuys'?" pp. 172-175; W. G. van der Tak, "Van den Enden and Kerckrinck," pp. 176-177; A. M. Vaz Dias and W. G. van der Tak, "The Firm of Bento y Gabriel de Spinoza," pp. 178-189; and W. G. van der Tak, "Spinoza's Payments to the Portuguese-Israelitic Community, and the Language in Which He Was Raised," pp. 190-195.

Vazquez, Amaral Pedro Jorge, *Descartes and Suarez: An Introduction to the Theory of Ideas*, Unpublished doctoral dissertation, University of Pittsburgh, 1984.

Presents Descartes' theory of mind as a transition from Suarezian scholasticism to Spinozism. Currently available from UMI (Order No. 84-21310).

Veil, Charles Marie de. A letter to the honourable Robert Boyle, esq., defending the divine authority of the Holy Scripture, and that it alone is the rule of faith. In answer to Father Simon's Critical history of the Old Testament ... London, Printed for Thomas Malthus, 1683.

18pp. In Oko (1964), p. 398.

Veitch, John. *See* Descartes (n.d.).

Versfeld, Martin, *The Mirror of Philosophers* (London and New York: Sheed and Ward, 1960).

Includes a section on Spinoza, pp. 240-244, and many other references.

Vesey, G. N. A. (ed.), *Reason and Reality*, Royal Institute of Philosophy Lectures, Vol. 5 (London: The Macmillan Press, 1972).

Includes essays by P. T. Geach, "Spinoza and the Divine Attributes," pp. 15-27, and J. J. MacIntosh, "Spinoza's Epistemological Views," pp. 28-48.

Viereck, George Sylvester, and Paul Eldridge, *My First Two Thousand Years: The Autobiography of the Wandering Jew* (London: Duckworth, 1929).

Includes a chapter, "I Discuss God with Spinoza," pp. 393-400. The U.S. edition, published in New York by Macaulay in 1928, presents this chapter on pp. 420-428.

Vincent, Andrew (ed.), *The Philosophy of T. H. Green* (Gower).

This citation is based on details in *Philosopher's Index*, No. 152700. Includes an essay by Rex Martin, "Green on Natural Rights in Hobbes, Spinoza and Locke," pp. 104-126.

Volfson, S. Ya., "Spinoza's Ethical World-View," in Kline (1952), pp. 131-148.

Voltaire, F.-M. A. de. Letters addressed to his Highness the prince of *****, containing comments on the writings of eminent authors, accused of attacking Christian religion. London, 1768.

In Hertzberger (1950), No. 936, citing a section on Spinoza, pp. 103-111.

Voltaire, F.-M. A. de. The ignorant philosopher. Translated from the French. Glasgow, 1767.

In Hertzberger (1950), No. 937, citing a section on Spinoza, pp. 49-59. Hertzberger, No. 938, cites another volume incorporating *The Ignorant Philosopher* and other essays, London, 1779, with a section on Spinoza, pp. 25-31.

Voltaire, F.-M. A. de, *A Philosophical Dictionary*, Ten volumes in two (New York: Coventry House, 1932). 2 vols.

Reprint of the 1901 edition by E. R. Dumont. Spinoza is incidentally mentioned (e.g., in the articles, "Atheism," "Atheists," and "Dictionary"), and is sometimes discussed at greater length (e.g., in the articles, "God" and "Liberty of the Press").

Voltaire, F.-M. A. de, *Essays and Criticisms* (Chicago: The de Laurence Company, n. d.).

Combines books with sections on Spinoza: *Voltaire's Letters on the Eminent Writers Who Have Been Accused of Attacking the Christian Religion* (New York: Peter Eckler Publishing Co., n.d.), Letter X, "Of Spinoza," pp. 83-88. Also *The Ignorant Philosopher, With an Address to the Public upon the Parricides Imputed to the Families of Calas and Sirven* (New York: Peter Eckler Publishing Co., n.d.), Section XXIV, "Spinoza," pp. 24-29.

Von Leyden, W., *Seventeenth-Century Metaphysics: An Examination of Some Main Concepts and Theories* (London: Gerald Duckworth & Co., 1968).

Includes major sections on Spinoza.

Von Wright, G. H., "Greetings from the International Institute of Philosophy," in Rotenstreich and Schneider (1983), pp. 11-13.

Voss, Stephen H., "How Spinoza Enumerated the Affects," *Archiv für Geschichte der Philosophie*, Vol. 63, No. 2 (1981), pp. 167-179.

Vygotski, L. S., "Spinoza's Theory of Emotions in Light of Contemporary Psychoneurology," Translated by E. E. Berg, *Soviet Studies in Philosophy*, Vol. 10, No. 4 (Spring 1972), pp. 362-382.

Wade, Ira O., *The Intellectual Development of Voltaire* (Princeton: Princeton University Press, 1969).

> Includes a section on Spinoza, pp. 693-711, and many other references.

Wade, Ira O., *The Intellectual Origins of the French Enlightenment* (Princeton: Princeton University Press, 1971).

> Includes a section, "Spinoza and the Ethical Problem of *Deus sive Natura*," pp. 322-346; a discussion of Spinoza and Leibniz, pp. 455-462; a discussion of Bayle's treatment of Spinoza, pp. 606-614; and many other references.

Wade, Ira O., *The Structure and Form of the French Enlightenment* (Princeton: Princeton University Press, 1977). 2 vols.

> Includes a discussion of the influence of Spinoza's *Tractatus Theologico-Politicus*, Vol. I, pp. 180 ff., and many other references.

Wade, Robert H. B., *The Influence of Spinoza's "Tractatus Theologico-Politicus" in France, 1670-1750*, Unpublished doctoral dissertation, Yale University, 1942.

> Currently available from UMI (Order No. 82-05191).

Wahl, Jean, *The Philosopher's Way* (New York: Oxford University Press, 1948).

> Includes many references to Spinoza.

Waite, A. E., *The Brotherhood of the Rosy Cross: Being Records of the House of the Holy Spirit in Its Inward and Outward History* (London, 1924).

> In Hertzberger (1950), No. 270.

Walker, Jeremy, "Philosophy in the Present Age," *Dialogue* (Ottawa), Vol. 13 (September 1974), pp. 561-576.

> In *Philosopher's Index*, No. 045353, citing references to Aristotle, Descartes, and Spinoza.

Walker, Ralph C. S., *The Coherence Theory of Truth: Realism, Anti-Realism, Idealism* (London: Routledge, 1989).

> Draws upon the author's earlier article, "Spinoza and the Coherence Theory of Truth," *Mind*, Vol. 94, No. 373 (January 1985), pp. 1-18.

Wallace, Robert. Antitrinitarian biography; or, Sketches of the lives and writings of distinguished antitrinitarians; exhibiting a view of the state of Unitarian doctrine and worship in the principal nations of Europe, from the Reformation to the close of the seventeenth century ... London, E. T. Whitfield, 1850. 5 vols.

> In Oko (1964), p. 358.

Walsh, Francis, "The God of Spinoza," *The New Scholasticism*, Vol. 3 (1929), pp. 309-321.

Walsh, Martin J., *A History of Philosophy* (London: Geoffrey Chapman, 1985).

> Includes a section on Spinoza, pp. 237-244, and other references.

Walther, Manfred. See *Studia Spinozana*, Vol. 1 (1985), Vol. 3 (1987), and Vol. 6 (1990).

Walther, Manfred, "Bibliographie," in his *Baruch de Spinoza: Briefwechsel*, 3rd Edition (Hamburg: Meiner, 1976).

Walther, Manfred, "Spinoza and Literature: A Supplementary Bibliography," in *Studia Spinozana*, Vol. 5 (1989), pp. 377-386.

Walther, Manfred, "Negri on Spinoza's Political and Legal Philosophy," in Curley and Moreau (1990), pp. 286-297.

Walther, Manfred, "Bibliography on Spinoza's Life," in Carl Gebhardt, *Spinoza: Lebensbeschriebungen und Dokumente*, Revised edition (Hamburg: Felix Meiner, 1991).

Walther, Manfred, "Spinoza's Critique of Miracles: A Miracle of Criticism?" in Hunter (1991).

Warburton, William. A critical and philosophical commentary on Mr. Pope's Essay on man, in which is contain'd a vindication from the misrepresentations of Mr. De Resnel and Mr. De Creusas. London, J. and P. Knapton, 1742.

> In Oko (1964), p. 313.

Ward, James, *Naturalism and Agnosticism,* The Gifford Lectures delivered before the University of Aberdeen in the Years 1896-1898, 4th Edition (London: Adam and Charles Black, 1915).

> Iverach (1904), pp. vii-viii, notes 'useful references' to Spinoza and Descartes.

Ward, James, *Essays in Philosophy,* With a memoir of the author by Olwen Ward Campbell (Cambridge: Cambridge University Press, 1927).

> Includes many references to Spinoza.

Ward, Richard. The life of the learned and pious Dr. Henry More, late fellow of Christ's college in Cambridge. To which are annex'd divers of his useful and excellent letters. By Richard Ward ... London, Printed and sold by Joseph Downing, 1710.

> In Oko (1964), p. 212.

Ward, S., *Ethics: An Historical Introduction* (London, 1924).

> In Hertzberger (1950), No. 188, citing a section on Spinoza, pp. 47-51.

Warner, Charles Dudley (ed.), *A Library of the World's Best Literature, Ancient and Modern* (New York: The International Society, 1897). 45 vols.

> Includes an essay by Josiah Royce on Spinoza, Vol. XXXV, pp. 13785-13793, along with a selection from Spinoza's writings.

Wartofsky, Marx W., *Feuerbach* (Cambridge: Cambridge University Press, 1977).

> Includes a section on Spinoza, pp. 85-88, and many other references.

Wartofsky, Marx W., *Models: Representation and the Scientific Understanding,* Boston Studies in the Philosophy of Science, Vol. 48 (Dordrecht: D. Reidel Publishing Co., 1979).

> Includes the chapters, "Action and Passion: Spinoza's Construction of a Scientific Psychology," pp. 231-254, first published in Grene (1979), pp. 329-353; "Nature, Number and Individuals: Motive and Method in Spinoza's Philosophy," pp. 255-276, originally in *Inquiry,* Vol. 20 (Winter 1977), pp. 457-479; and "Diderot and the Development of Materialistic Monism," pp. 297-337.

Watkins, J. W. N., "The Posthumous Career of Thomas Hobbes," *Review of Politics,* Vol. 19, No. 3 (1957), pp. 351-360.

> Discusses the impact of Hobbes' political philosophy on those of Spinoza, Leibniz, Locke, Kant, Marx, and others.

Watkins, J. W. N., "Three Views Concerning Human Freeman," in Peters (1975), pp. 200-228.

Watkins, J. W. N., "Minimal Presuppositions and Maximal Metaphysics," *Mind*, Vol. 87 (April 1978), pp. 195-209.

> In *Philosopher's Index*, No. 058348, and Van der Werf, No. 2057.

Waton, Henry, *The Kabbalah and Spinoza's Philosophy as a Basis for an Idea of Universal History* (New York: Spinoza Institute of America, 1931-32). 2 vols.

Waton, Henry, *A True Monistic Philosophy, Comprehending the Absolute, God, Existence, Man, Society, and History* (New York: J. J. Little & Ives, 1947).

> In Trompetter (1977), p. 153. Oko (1964), p. 438, and the *Philosopher's Index*, No. 018478, give the publisher as the Spinoza Institute of America.

Waton, Henry, "The Historic Significance of Spinoza's Philosophy," in *Baruch Spinoza* (Spinoza Institute of America, 1933).

Waton, Henry, "The Jewish Question and Spinoza's Philosophy," in *Baruch Spinoza* (Spinoza Institute of America, 1933).

Waton, Henry, "Why a Spinoza Institute?" in *Baruch Spinoza* (Spinoza Institute of America, 1933).

Watt, A. J., "Spinoza's Use of Religious Language," *The New Scholasticism*, Vol. 46 (Summer 1972), pp. 286-307.

Watt, A. J., "The Causality of God in Spinoza's Philosophy," *Canadian Journal of Philosophy*, Vol. 2, No. 2 (December 1972), pp. 171-189.

> *See* Harris (1972) for a reply.

Watt, A. J., "Reply to Harris," *Canadian Journal of Philosophy*, Vol. 2, No. 4 (June 1973), pp. 541-544.

Watt, A. J., "Transcendental Arguments and Moral Principles," *The Philosophical Quarterly*, Vol. 25 (January 1975), pp. 40-57.

> In *Philosopher's Index*, No. 046338, citing references to Spinoza, Kant, and Collingwood.

Watts, Isaac. Discourses of the love of God, and the use and abuse of the passions in religion, with a devout meditation suited to each discourse ... London, Printed for J. Clark and R. Hett, 1729.

> In Oko (1964), p. 458.

Watts, Isaac. An essay on the freedom of will in God and in creatures ... London, J. Roberts, 1732.

> In Oko (1964), p. 412.

[Watts, Isaac] Philosophical Essays on Various Subjects, viz. Space, Substance, Body, Spirit, the Operations of the Soul in Union with the Body, innate Ideas, perpetual Consciousness, [etc.]: With some Remarks on Mr. Locke's Essay on the Human Understanding. To which is subjoined A brief Scheme of Ontology, or The Science of Being in general, with its Affections. By I. W. London: Printed for Richard Ford at the Angel, and Richard Hett at the Bible and Crown, 1733.

> In Oko (1964), p. 441. Currently available from UMI Out-of-Print Books on Demand (Order No. OP35217). The third edition, printed in London for James Brackstone (1742) was reprinted with a new introduction by John Yolton (Bristol: Thoemmes, 1990). Spinoza is mentioned explicitly on pp. 62-63 of the 1742 edition.

Watts, Isaac. Logick: Or, The Right Use of Reason in the Enquiry after Truth. With A Variety of Rules to guard against Error, in the Affairs of Religion and Human Life, as well as in the Sciences. The Third Edition, Corrected. London: Printed for John Clark and Richard Hett ... 1729.

> A facsimile reprint of the second edition (1726) was issued by Garland Publishing in New York as Vol. 16 in the Garland Series on the Philosophy of John Locke. Oko (1964), p. 429, cites a 7th Edition printed in London for Richard Hett and James Brackstone in 1740.

Wawrytko, Sandra A., *The Undercurrent of Feminine Philosophy in Eastern and Western Thought* (Lanham, MD: University Press of America, 1981).

> From the author's doctoral dissertation, *The Philosophical Systematization of a "Feminine" Perspective in Terms of Taoism's "Tao te Ching" and the Works of Spinoza*, Washington University, 1976. The latter is currently available from UMI (Order No. 76-23103).

Waxman, Meyer, *The Philosophy of Don Hasdai Crescas* (New York: Columbia University Press, 1920).

Includes a section on Spinoza's relation to Crescas. Originally in *Jewish Quarterly Review*, Vol. 9 (1918-1919), pp. 209-210, 212; and Vol. 10 (1919-1920), p. 299.

Waxman, Meyer, "Baruch Spinoza's Relation to Jewish Philosophical Thought and to Judaism," *Jewish Quarterly Review*, Vol. 19, No. 4 (April 1929), pp. 411-430.

Webb, Clement C. J., *God and Personality*, Being the Gifford Lectures, 1918-1919 (London: George Allen & Unwin; New York: The Macmillan Co., 1918).

Includes a section on Spinoza, pp. 68 ff., and other references.

Webb, Clement C. J., *A History of Philosophy*, Home University Library, No. 96 (New York: Henry Holt and Co.; London: Williams and Norgate [1922?]).

Includes a section on Spinoza, pp. 157-164, and other references.

Webb, M. O., "Natural Theology and the Concept of Perfection in Descartes, Spinoza, and Leibniz," *Religious Studies*, Vol. 25, No. 4 (1989), pp. 459-475.

Weber, Alfred, *History of Philosophy*, Authorized translated by Frank Thilly, with *Philosophy Since 1860*, by Ralph Barton Perry (New York: C. Scribner's Sons, 1925).

Includes a section on Spinoza, pp. 258-275, and many other references.

Wedberg, Anders, *A History of Philosophy* (Oxford: The Clarendon Press, 1982). 3 vols.

Includes two sections, "The Motives of Spinoza and Leibniz," Vol. 2, pp. 57-58, and "Spinoza's System," Vol. 2, pp. 59-63, and other references.

Wedeck, H. E.. *See* Spinoza, *Principles of Cartesian Philosophy* (1961).

Weine, Max, "Three Rationalists: Some Parallels," *Reconstructionist*, Vol. 45, No. 6 (1979), pp. 22-28.

In Dienstag (1986), p. 409, identifying the three as Maimonides, Spinoza, and Mordecai Kaplan.

Weiss, Paul, "Some Pivotal Issues in Spinoza," in Kennington (1980), Chap. 1, pp. 3-16.

Weitz, Morris, *Theories of Concepts: A History of the Major Philosophical Tradition* (London: Routledge, 1988).

> Includes a section on Spinoza, pp. 79-83, and other references.

Wells, Donald A., *God, Man and the Thinker: Philosophies of Religion* (New York: Random House, 1962).

> In *Philosopher's Index*, No. 015556.

Weltoch, F., "The Perennial Spinoza," *Commentary*, Vol. 21 (1956), pp. 448-453.

> In Wetlesen (1968), p. 58.

Wernham, A. G. *See* Spinoza, *The Political Works* (1958).

Wernham, A. G., "A Survey of Work on 17th Century Rationalism, 1945-1952: Part II: Spinoza," *Philosophical Quarterly*, Vol. 3 (January 1953), pp. 76-79.

> In *Philosopher's Index*, No. 065320.

Wernham, A. G., "Spinoza's Account of Cognition in *Ethics*, Part II, Prop. 9-13," in Van der Bend (1974), pp. 156-161.

Westcott, Malcolm R., *Toward a Contemporary Psychology of Intuition* (New York: Holt, Reinhart and Winston, 1968).

> Discusses the views of Spinoza, Bertson, Croce, Ewing, Stocks, Bahm, and Bunge on intuition in the chapter, "Philosophical Intuitionism and Its Critics," pp. 5-23.

Wetlesen, Jon, *A Spinoza Bibliography* (Oslo: The Institute of Philosophy, University of Oslo, 1968).

> A second edition was published in 1971.

Wetlesen, Jon, *Internal Guide to the Ethics of Spinoza: Index to Spinoza's Cross References in the Ethics, Rearranged So As To Refer from Earlier to Later Statements* (Oslo: *Inquiry* and The Institute of Philosophy, University of Oslo, 1974).

Wetlesen, Jon, *The Sage and the Way: Spinoza's Ethics of Freedom* (Assen, The Netherlands: Van Gorcum, 1979).

> From the author's doctoral dissertation of the same title, Oslo, 1976.

Wetlesen, Jon (ed.), *Spinoza's Philosophy of Man: Proceedings of the Scandinavian Spinoza Symposium, 1977* (Oslo: Universitetsforlaget, 1978).

> In addition to Wetlesen's paper—"Freedom as Contemplation or Action? A Reply to Arne Naess," pp. 204-210—includes papers by E. Curley, H. De Dijn, G. Floistad, J. Friedman, E. Giancotti Boscherini, J. Groen, E. Harris, H. Hubbeling, A. Naess, H. Parsons, L. Rice, D. Savan, and P. Wienpahl.

Wetlesen, Jon, "A Reconstruction of Basic Concepts in Spinoza's Social Psychology," *Inquiry*, Vol. 12, No. 1 (Spring 1969), pp. 105-132.

Wetlesen, Jon, "Normative Reasoning in Spinoza: Two Interpretations," in Van der Bend (1974), pp. 162-171.

Wetlesen, Jon, "Body Awareness as a Gateway to Eternity: A Note on the Mysticism of Spinoza and Its Affinity to Buddhist Meditation," in Hessing (1977), pp. 479-494.

Wettersten, John, "Free from Sin: On Living with Ad Hoc Hypotheses," *Conceptus*, Vol. 18 (1984), pp. 86-100.

> In *Philosopher's Index*, No. 128587.

[Whitby, Daniel] A dissuasive from enquiring into the doctrine of the Trinity: or, The difficulties and discouragements which attend the study of that doctrine. In a letter to a friend. London, Printed for John Baker, 1714.

> In Oko (1964), p. 212.

White, Alan, *Schelling: An Introduction to the System of Freedom* (New Haven: Yale University Press, 1983).

> Includes many references to Spinoza. From the author's doctoral dissertation, *The End of Philosophy: A Study of Hegel and Schelling*, Pennsylvania State University, 1980. The latter is currently available from UMI (Order No. 80-24506).

White, William Hale, *Pages from a Journal, With Other Papers*, 2nd Edition (London: Oxford University Press, 1910).

> Includes a chapter on Spinoza, pp. 32-58. Also in the first edition (London: T. F. Unwin, 1901).

White, William Hale. *See* Spinoza, *Ethic* (1910) and *Tractatus de Intellectus Emendatione* (1969).

White, William Hale, "Spinoza's Doctrine of the Relationship Between Mind and Body," *International Journal of Ethics*, Vol. 6 (October 1895-July 1896), pp. 515-518.

White, William Hale, "Coleridge on Spinoza," *Athenaeum*, Vol. 1 (1897), pp. 680 ff.

Whittaker, Thomas, *Reason, A Philosophical Essay with Historical Illustrations* (New York: Greenwood Press, 1968).

> Reprint of the 1934 edition published by Cambridge University Press. Includes a section on Spinoza.

Whittaker, Thomas, "Transcendence in Spinoza," *Mind*, Vol. 38, No. 151 (July 1929), pp. 293-311.

Whittemore, Robert C., "Hegel as Pantheist," *Tulane Studies in Philosophy*, Vol. 9 (1960), pp. 134-164.

> In *Philosopher's Index*, No. 010537.

Whyte, Lancelot Law, *The Next Development in Man* (New York: Henry Holt, 1948).

> In *Philosopher's Index*, No. 017314.

Wiener, Max, "John Toland and Judaism," *Hebrew Union College Annual*, Vol. 16 (1941), pp. 215-242.

> In Oko (1964), p. 229.

Wiener, Max, "Spinoza's Contribution to Anti-Semitism," *Reconstructionist*, Vol. 8, No. 11 (October 1942), pp. 9-11.

> In Oko (1964), p. 378.

Wiener, Philip P. (ed.), *Dictionary of the History of Ideas: Studies of Selected Pivotal Ideas* (New York: Charles Scribner's Sons, 1973). 5 vols.

> Includes many references to Spinoza.

Wienpahl, Paul, *The Radical Spinoza* (New York: New York University Press, 1979).

> Concludes on pp. 171-257 with the author's translation of the definitions, axioms, postulates, and propositions of the *Ethics*, with Latin text opposite, and notes.

Wienpahl, Paul, "Spinoza and Wang Yang-Ming," *Religious Studies*, Vol. 5, No. 1 (1969), pp. 19-27.

Wienpahl, Paul, "Ch'an Buddhism, Western Thought, and the Concept of Substance," *Inquiry*, Vol. 14 (Summer 1971), pp. 84-101.

Wienpahl, Paul, "Spinoza and Mental Health," *Inquiry*, Vol. 15, Nos. 1-2 (Summer 1972), pp. 64-94.

Wienpahl, Paul, "Wang Yang-Ming and Meditation," *Journal of Chinese Philosophy*, Vol. 1 (March 1974), pp. 199-227.

> In *Philosopher's Index*, No. 043393. Van der Werf (1984), No. 2091, identifies this paper as a "sequel" to Wienpahl (1969).

Wienpahl, Paul, "On Translating Spinoza," in Hessing (1977), pp. 495-524.

Wienpahl, Paul, "Spinoza and Mysticism," in Wetlesen (1978), pp. 211-224.

Wieseltier, Leon, "Philosophy, Religion, and Harry Wolfson," *Commentary*, Vol. 61, No. 4 (1976), pp. 57-64.

> Discusses the influence of Spinoza on Wolfson's philosophy.

Wightman, W. P. D., *Science and Monism* (London: George Allen & Unwin, 1934).

> Includes a section, "The Failure of Spinozism," pp. 65-114.

Wilbur, James B. (ed.), *Spinoza's Metaphysics: Essays in Critical Appreciation* (Assen, The Netherlands: Van Gorcum, 1976).

> In addition to an essay by Wilbur — "Is Spinoza's God Self-Conscious?" pp. 66-85 — includes papers by H. Allen, R. Beck. W. Edgar, E. Harris, R. Pasotti, D. Rohatyn, S. Rosen, E. Sherman, and S. Umphrey.

Wild, John. *See* Spinoza, *Spinoza Selections* (1930).

Williams, Forrest, "Some Reflections on Spinoza's 'Ethics' as Edifying Ontology," in Casey (1986), pp. 95-110.

Williamson, R. K., "On Curley's Interpretation of Spinoza," *Australasian Journal of Philosophy*, Vol. 51 (August 1973), pp. 157-161.

> *See* Curley (1973).

Willis, R., *Benedict de Spinoza: His Life, Correspondence, and Ethics* (London: Trübner & Co., 1870).

> Includes the author's translation of the correspondence, pp. 216-413, and the *Ethics*, pp. 414-647. Also includes a translation of the Jacobi-Lessing conversations, pp. 149-162. Walther (1991), p. 121, cites an edition published in London by Trübner in 1870 entitled, *Spinoza, His Ethics, Life, Letters, and Influence on Modern Religious Thought*; he also indicates that this was reprinted in New York by Gordon in 1977.

Willis, R. *See* Spinoza, *Tractatus Theologico-Politicus* ... (1862).

Wilson, Catherine, *Leibniz's Metaphysics: A Historical and Comparative Study* (Princeton: Princeton University Press, 1989).

> Includes many references to Spinoza.

Wilson, Colin, "Spinoza: The Outsider," in Hessing (1977), pp. 525-542.

Wilson, Margaret D., "Objects, Ideas, and 'Minds': Comments on Spinoza's Theory of Mind," in Kennington (1980), Chap. 7, pp. 103-120.

Wilson, Margaret D., "Notes on Modes and Attributes," *The Journal of Philosophy*, Vol. 78 (1981), pp. 584-586.

> In Van der Werf (1984), No. 2103.

Wilson, Margaret D., "Infinite Understanding, *Scientia Intuitiva*, and *Ethics* I.16," *Midwest Studies in Philosophy*, Vol. 8 (1983), pp. 181-192.

Wilson, Margaret D., "Comments on J. M. Beyssade: 'De l'émotion intérieure chez Descartes à d'affect actif spinoziste," in Curley and Moreau (1990), pp. 191-195.

> Beyssade's paper is in Curley and Moreau, pp. 176-190.

Windelband, Wilhelm, *A History of Philosophy*, Translated by James H. Tufts, Revised edition (New York: Harper Torchbooks, Harper & Brothers, 1958). 2 vols.

> Reprint of the revised translation published by Macmillan in 1901. The German original was published in 1892. Includes many references to Spinoza.

Windelband, Wilhelm, *An Introduction to Philosophy*, Translated by J. McCabe (London, 1923).

> In Hertzberger (1950), No. 200.

Winston, David, "Barukh Spinoza," in Eliade (1987), Vol. 14, pp. 7-11.

Wise, R. B. A., "The Parallelism of Attributes," *Philosophical Papers*, Vol. 11 (October 1982), pp. 23-37.

> In *Philosopher's Index*, No. 117383.

Wolf, A., *The Oldest Biography of Spinoza* (London: George Allen & Unwin, 1927).

> Presents the first English translation of the *Life of the Late Mr. de Spinoza*, the French original of which was completed in 1678 or 1688 (though not published until 1719) and is usually attributed to Jean Maximilien Lucas. Also includes a translation of additions in the printed texts of 1719 and 1735, the French text of both the *Life* and the additions, and translations of additional biographical materials selected from the record of Spinoza's excommunication, Meyer's preface to Spinoza's *Principles*, Jelles' preface to the *Opera Posthuma*, Bayle's *Dictionary*, and S. Kortholt's preface to his father's *On Three Great Imposters*. This volume is currently available from UMI Out-of-Print Books on Demand (Order No. OP56284).

Wolf, A., *A History of Science, Technology, and Philosophy in the 16th and 17th Centuries*, With the cooperation of F. Dannemann and A. Armitage, new edition prepared by Douglas McKie (London: George Allen & Unwin, 1950).

> Includes sections on Spinoza's psychology, pp. 571-575, and his philosophy, pp. 650-656, and many other references.

[Wolf, A.] *Spinoza (1632-1677): The Library of the Late Prof. Dr. A. Wolf, Head of the Department of the History and Philosophy of Science, University of London*, Catalogue No. 150 (Amsterdam: International Antiquariaat, Menno Hertzberger, 1950).

> Citations from this catalogue in the present bibliography are given as "Hertzberger (1950)," followed by the item number.

Wolf, A. *See* Spinoza, *Short Treatise* (1910) and *Correspondence* (1966).

Wolf, A., "Spinoza the Conciliator," in *Chronicon Spinozanum*, Vol. II (1922), pp. 3-13.

Cited in Oko (1964), p. 104, as a separate 13 pp. publication (Hagae
Comitis, 1922).

Wolf, A., "Huxley and Spinoza," in *Chronicon Spinozanum*, Vol. IV (1926),
pp. 261-263.

Wolf, A., "Spinoza," *Journal of Philosophical Studies*, Vol. 2, No. 5 (January
1927), pp. 3-19.

Wolf, A., "Spinoza's Synoptic Vision," *Philosophy*, Vol. 8, No. 20 (1933), pp.
3-13.

Wolf, A., "An Addition to the Correspondence of Spinoza," *Philosophy*, Vol.
10 (1935), pp. 200-204.

Wolf, A., "Spinoza's Conception of the Attributes of Substance," in Kashap
(1972), pp. 16-27.

Originally in *Proceedings of the Aristotelian Society*, Vol. 27 (1927). pp.
177-192.

Wolfenden, J. F., *The Approach to Philosophy* (London: Edward Arnold & Co.,
1932).

Includes sections on Spinoza, pp. 69-72, and pp. 90-93, and other references.

Wolfson, Abraham, *Spinoza: A Life of Reason*, 2nd enlarged edition (New York:
Philosophical Library, 1969).

Wolfson, Harry Austryn, *The Philosophy of Spinoza: Unfolding the Latent
Processes of His Reasoning* (Cambridge: Harvard University Press, 1934). 2
vols.

Published in a one-volume edition by Harvard in 1948. Reprinted in
Cleveland by World Publishing Co., 1958, and in New York by Schocken
Books, 1969. Also published in New York in a one-volume paperback
edition by Meridian Books, 1978.

Wolfson, Harry Austryn, *Spinoza and Religion* (New York: New School for
Social Research, 1950).

Originally read as the Horace M. Kallen Lecture, New York, November 16,
1949; also published under the same title in *The Menorah Journal* (Autumn
1950), pp. 146-167.

Wolfson, Harry Austryn, *Religious Philosophy: A Group of Essays* (Cambridge: Harvard University Press, 1961).

> Includes two essays, "The Veracity of Scripture in Philo, Halevi, Maimonides and Spinoza," pp. 217-245, and "Spinoza and the Religion of the Past," pp. 246-249. The former first appeared in *Alexander Marx Jubilee Volume* (New York: Jewish Theological Seminary of America, 1950), pp. 603-630. The second is included in the following work.

Wolfson, Harry Austryn, *From Philo to Spinoza: Two Studies in Religious Philosophy*, Edited by Isadore Twersky (New York: Behrman House, 1977).

> 64 pp. Includes the essay, "Spinoza and the Religion of the Past."

Wolfson, Harry Austryn, *Studies in the History of Philosophy and Religion*, Edited by Isadore Twersky and George H. Williams (Cambridge: Harvard University Press, 1977). 2 vols.

> Vol. 2 includes three essays on Spinoza: "Some Guiding Principles in Determining Spinoza's Medieval Sources," pp. 577-592 (originally in *The Jewish Quarterly Review*, Vol. 27, No. 4 [1937], pp. 333-348); "Spinoza's Mechanism, Attributes, and Panpsychism," pp. 593-600 (originally in *The Philosophical Review*, Vol. 46, No. 3 [May 1937], pp. 307-314); and "Towards an Accurate Understanding of Spinoza," pp. 601-605 (originally in *The Journal of Philosophy*, Vol. 23, No. 10 [May 13, 1926], pp. 268-273). The latter is a reply to criticisms by Ratner (1926) of the author's first three articles in *Chronicon Spinozanum*, cited below.

[Wolfson, Harry Austryn] *Harry Austryn Wolfson: Jubilee Volume on the Occasion of His Seventy-Fifth Birthday* (Jerusalem: American Academy for Jewish Research, Saul Lieberman, 1965). 2 vols.

> Includes an essay by Richard McKeon, "Spinoza on the Rainbow and on Probability," Vol. II, pp. 533-559.

Wolfson, Harry Austryn, "Spinoza's Definition of Substance and Mode," in *Chronicon Spinozanum*, Vol. I (1921), pp. 101-112.

Wolfson, Harry Austryn, "Spinoza on the Unity of Substance," in *Chronicon Spinozanum*, Vol. II (1922), pp. 92-117.

Wolfson, Harry Austryn, "Spinoza on the Simplicity of Substance," in *Chronicon Spinozanum*, Vol. III (1923), pp. 142-178.

Wolfson, Harry Austryn, "Spinoza on the Infinity of the Corporeal Substance," in *Chronicon Spinozanum*, Vol. IV (1926), pp. 79-103.

Wolfson, Harry Austryn, "A Case Study in Philosophic Research and Spinoza," *The New Scholasticism*, Vol. 14, No. 3 (July 1940), pp. 268-294.

> In Oko (1964), p. 501. A critique of Bidney's *The Psychology and Ethics of Spinoza* (1940).

Wolfson, Harry Austryn, "The Philonic God of Revelation and His Latter Day Deniers," *Harvard Theological Review*, Vol. 53 (1960), pp. 101-124.

> In Curley (1975), p. 315.

Wolfson, Harry Austryn, "Behind the Geometrical Method," in Grene (1979), pp. 3-24.

> A reprint of H. A. Wolfson (1934), Vol. I, pp. 3-31.

[Wollaston, W.] The religion of nature delineated. 6th ed. London, 1738.

> In Hertzberger (1950), No. 945.

Wolstein, Benjamin, "The Romantic Spinoza in America," *Journal of the History of Ideas*, Vol. 14 (June 1953), pp. 439-450.

Wood, Ledger, *Theories of Space and Time in Spinoza*, Unpublished doctoral dissertation, Cornell University, 1926.

Wood, Wallace, *The Hundred Greatest Men: Portraits of the One Hundred Greatest Men of History Reproduced from Fine and Rare Steel Engravings*, With general introduction by Ralph Waldo Emerson (New York: D. Appleton and Co., 1885).

> Includes a Spinoza portrait and biography, pp. 232-235.

Woodbridge, Frederick J. E., *Spinoza*, Lecture delivered at Columbia University, January 26, 1933 (New York: Columbia University Press, 1933).

> Reprinted in Gutmann's edition of the *Ethics*, pp. xxiii-xxxiv. *See* Spinoza, *Ethics* (1949).

Woodbridge, J. D., "Richard Simon's Reaction to Spinoza's *Tractatus Theologico-Politicus*," in Grunder and Schmidt-Biggemann (1984), pp. 201-226.

Woolhouse, R. S., "Leibniz's Reaction to Cartesian Interaction," *Proceedings of the Aristotelian Society*, Vol. 86 (1985-1986), pp. 69-82.

> In *Philosopher's Index*, No. 143281.

Wotton, William. A letter to Eusebia; occasioned by Mr. Toland's Letters to Serena. London, Printed for Tim. Godwin, 1704. 75 pp.

In Oko (1964), p. 229; in Hertzberger (1950), No. 933. *See* Toland (1704).

Wren, Thomas E., "Is Hope a Necessary Evil? Some Misgivings about Spinoza's Metaphysical Psychology," *Journal of Thought*, Vol. 7, No. 2 (April 1972), pp. 67-76.

Wright, Charles James, *Miracle in History and in Modern Thought; or, Miracle and Christian Apologetic* (New York: Holt [1930?]).

Includes a section on Spinoza, pp. 192-200.

Wright, William Kelley, *A History of Modern Philosophy* (New York: The Macmillan Company, 1941).

Includes a chapter on Spinoza, pp. 90-113, and other references.

Wundt, Wilhelm, *Ethical Systems*, Translated by Margaret Floy Washburn (London: Swan Sonnenschein; New York: Macmillan, 1897).

Includes a section on Spinoza, pp. 92-97.

Wundt, Wilhelm, *Ethics: An Investigation of the Facts and Laws of the Moral Life*, Translated by E. B. Titchener, J. H. Gulliver, and M. F. Washburn (London, 1897-1922 [sic]). 3 vols.

In Hertzberger (1950), No. 203.

Wurzer, William S., "'Mens et corpus' in Spinoza and Nietzsche: A Propaedeutic Comparison," *Dialogos* (Puerto Rico), Vol. 16 (November 1981), pp. 81-92.

Wurzer, William S., "Spinoza's Monism," *The Philosophical Review*, Vol. 90 (1981), pp. 503-530.

Wuttke, Adolf, *Christian Ethics*, Translated by John P. Lacroix, with a special preface by Dr. Riehm (New York: Nelson & Phillips, 1876). 2 vols.

Includes a section on Spinoza, Vol. 1, pp. 281-290.

Yakira, Elhanan, "What Is A Mathematical Truth?" in *Studia Spinozana*, Vol. 6 (1990), pp. 73-101.

Yarros, Victor S., "Ethics and the Spinoza Revival," *The Open Court*, Vol. 36, No. 12 (December 1922), pp. 714-720.

Yerushalmi, Y. H., *From Spanish Court to Italian Ghetto* (New York: Columbia University Press, 1971).

In Scharfstein (1980), p. 423, citing biographical information on Spinoza.

Yoshizawa, D., "Natural Science and Moral Science: Studies of the Theories of Spinoza and Leibniz," Tetsugaku Zasshi, Japan, 1952, pp. 90-109.

This citation is based on Wetlesen (1968), p. 81.

Young, J. Michael, "The Ontological Argument and the Concept of Substance," *American Philosophical Quarterly*, Vol. 11 (July 1974), pp. 181-191.

In *Philosopher's Index*, No. 044441.

Yovel, Yirmiyahu, *Nietzsche as Affirmative Thinker* (Dordrecht: Martinus Nijhoff, 1986).

Includes the essay, "Nietzsche and Spinoza: 'Amor Fati' and 'Amor Dei,'" pp. 183-203.

Yovel, Yirmiyahu, *Spinoza and Other Heretics* (Princeton: Princeton University Press, 1989). 2 vols.

Vol. 1 is entitled *Marrano of Reason*; Vol. 2, *The Adventures of Immanence*.

Yovel, Yirmiyahu (ed.), *Spinoza by 2000* (Philosophia Verlag, 1990), Vol. 1.

Cited by Garrett in *Studia Spinozana* (1990), p. 42.

Yovel, Yirmiyahu, "Bible Interpretation as Philosophical Praxis: A Study of Spinoza and Kant," *Journal of the History of Philosophy*, Vol. 11, No. 2 (April 1973), pp. 189-212.

Yovel, Yirmiyahu, "Why Spinoza Was Excommunicated," *Commentary*, Vol. 64, No. 5 (1977), pp. 46-52.

Yovel, Yirmiyahu, "Substance Without Spirit — On Hegel's Critique of Spinoza," in Rotenstreich and Schneider (1983), pp. 71-84.

See Marx (1983) for a reply.

Yovel, Yirmiyahu, "Reply to Professor Marx," in Rotenstreich and Schneider (1983), pp. 99-100.

Yovel, Yirmiyahu, "Spinoza and His People: The First Secular Jew?" *Jerusalem Quarterly* (Israel), Vol. 33 (1984), pp. 50-63.

Yovel, Yirmiyahu, "Marrano Patterns in Spinoza," in Giancotti Boscherini (1985), pp. 461-485.

Originally in *La rassegna mensile di Israel*, Vol. 49 (1983), pp. 543-564.

Yovel, Yirmiyahu, "Spinoza: The Psychology of the Multitude and the Uses of Language," in *Studia Spinozana*, Vol. 1 (1985), pp. 305-333.

Yovel, Yirmiyahu, "God's Transcendence and Its Schematization: Maimonides in Light of the Spinoza-Hegel Dispute," in Pines and Yovel (1986), pp. 269-282.

Yovel, Yirmiyahu, "Spinoza: The First Secular Jew?" *Tikkun*, Vol. 5, No. 1 (January-February 1990), pp. 40-46.

Yovel, Yirmiyahu, "The Third Kind of Knowledge as Alternative Salvation," in Curley and Moreau (1990), pp. 157-175.

Zac, Sylvain, "Life in the Philosophy of Spinoza," *Philosophy and Theology*, Vol. 1 (Spring 1987), pp. 255-266.

Zangwill, I., *Dreamers of the Ghetto* (New York: Bloch Publishing Co., 1923).

In Walther (1989), p. 384, citing a section on Spinoza, "The Maker of Lenses," pp. 186-220. Walther (1991), p. 114, also identifies an edition published in two volumes in Philadelphia by the Jewish Publication Society of America, 1898, with the Spinoza section in Vol. 2, pp. 211-248. Hertzberger (1950), No. 1241, cites an edition published in London in 1906 with the section on Spinoza on pp. 169-201.

Zellner, Harold, "Spinoza's Causal Likeness Principle," *Philosophy Research Archives*, Vol. 11 (1985), pp. 453-462.

Zellner, Harold, "Spinoza's Puzzle," *History of Philosophy Quarterly*, Vol. 5, No. 3 (July 1988), pp. 233-243.

Zellner, Harold, "Spinoza's Temporal Argument for Actualism," *Philosophy Research Archives*, Vol. 14 (1988-1989), pp. 303-309.

Zerffi, George Gustavus, "The Historical Development of Idealism and Realism: IV. Modern Period: Descartes — Spinoza — John Locke," *Transactions of the Royal Historical Society* (London), Vol. 8 (1880), pp. 331-355.

In Oko (1964), p. 157.

Zilsel, Edgar, "The Genesis of the Concept of Physical Law," *The Philosophical Review*, Vol. 51 (May 1952), pp. 245-279.

> In *Philosopher's Index*, No. 005714, citing references to Aquinas, Galileo, Kepler, Descartes, Spinoza, and Newton.

Zimmern, H., *Lessing: His Life and His Works* (London, 1878).

> In Hertzberger (1950), No. 853.

Zinberg, Israel, *The History of the Jewish Literature* (Vilno: "Tomor," 1929-1933). 4 vols.

> In Oko (1964), p. 379, citing a section on Spinoza, Vol. 4, pp. 407-415.

Zurcher, J. R., *The Nature and Destiny of Man: Essay on the Problem of the Union of the Soul and the Body in Relation to the Christian Views of Man*, Translated by Mabel R. Bartlett (New York: Philosophical Library, 1969).

> Includes a section, "The Monistic Parallelism of Spinoza," pp. 64-68.

Zweerman, Theo, "The Method in Spinoza's *Tractatus de Intellectus Emendatione*: Some Remarks on This Problem Inspired by the *Tractatus Theologico-Politicus* and by *Epistola* 37," in Van der Bend (1974), pp. 172-183.

Zweig, Arnold. *See* Spinoza, under "Excerpts."

Zycinski, Joseph M., "The Doctrine of Substance and Whitehead's Metaphysics," *Review of Metaphysics*, Vol. 42 (June 1989), pp. 765-781.

> In *Philosopher's Index*, No. 165013.

BRILL'S STUDIES
IN
INTELLECTUAL HISTORY

1. POPKIN, R.H. *Isaac la Peyrère (1596-1676)*. His Life, Work and Influence. 1987. ISBN 90 04 08157 7
2. THOMSON, A. *Barbary and Enlightenment*. European Attitudes towards the Maghreb in the 18th Century. 1987. ISBN 90 04 08273 5
3. DUHEM, P. *Prémices Philosophiques*. With an Introduction in English by S.L. Jaki. 1987. ISBN 90 04 08117 8
4. OUDEMANS, TH.C.W. & LARDINOIS, A.P.M.H. *Tragic ambiguity*. Anthropology, Philosophy and Sophocles' *Antigone*. 1987. ISBN 90 04 08417 7
5. FRIEDMAN, J.B. (ed.). *John de Foxton's Liber Cosmographiae* (1408). An Edition and Codicological Study. 1988. ISBN 90 04 08528 9
6. AKKERMAN, F. & VANDERJAGT A.J. (eds.). *Rodolphus Agricola Phrisius, 1444-1485*. Proceedings of the International Conference at the University of Groningen, 28-30 October 1985. 1988. ISBN 90 04 08599 8
7. CRAIG, W.L. *The Problem of Divine Foreknowledge and Future Contingents from Aristotle to Suarez*. 1988. ISBN 90 04 08516 5
8. STROLL, M. *The Jewish Pope*. Ideology and Politics in the Papal Schism of 1130. 1987. ISBN 90 04 08590 4
9. STANESCO, M. *Jeux d'errance du chevalier médiéval*. Aspects ludiques de la fonction guerrière dans la littérature du Moyen Age flamboyant. 1988. ISBN 90 04 08684 6
10. KATZ, D. *Sabbath and Sectarianism in Seventeenth-Century England*. 1988. ISBN 90 04 08754 0
11. LERMOND, L. *The Form of Man*. Human Essence in Spinoza's *Ethic*. 1988. ISBN 90 04 08829 6
12. JONG, M. DE. *In Samuel's Image*. Early Medieval Child Oblation. (in preparation)
13. PYENSON, L. *Empire of Reason*. Exact Sciences in Indonesia, 1840-1940. 1989. ISBN 90 04 08984 5
14. CURLEY, E & MOREAU P.-F. *Spinoza. Issues and Directions*. The Proceedings of the Chicago Spinoza Conference. 1990. ISBN 90 04 09334 6
15. KAPLAN, Y., MÉCHOULAN H. & POPKIN R.H. (eds.). *Menasseh Ben Israel and His World*. 1989. ISBN 90 04 09114 9
16. BOS, A.P. *Cosmic and Meta-Cosmic Theology in Aristotle's Lost Dialogues*. 1989. ISBN 90 04 09155 6
17. KATZ, D.S. & ISRAEL J.I. (eds.) *Sceptics, Millenarians and Jews*. 1989. ISBN 90 04 09160 2
18. DALES, R.C. *Medieval Discussions of the Eternity of the World*. 1990. ISBN 90 04 09215 3
19. CRAIG, W.L. *Divine Foreknowledge and Human Freedom*. The Coherence of Theism: Omniscience. 1991. ISBN 90 04 09250 1
20. OTTEN, W. *The Anthropology of Johannes Scottus Eriugena*. 1991. ISBN 90 04 09302 8
21. ÅKERMAN, S. *Queen Christina of Sweden*. The Transformation of a Seventeenth Century Philosophical Libertine. 1991. ISBN 90 04 09310 9
22. POPKIN, R.H. *The Third Force in Seventeenth Century Thought*. 1990. ISBN 90 04 09324 9

23. DALES, R.C. & ARGERAMI, O. (eds.). *Medieval Latin Texts on the Eternity of the World*. 1990. ISBN 90 04 09376 1
24. STROLL, M. *Symbols as Power*. The Papacy Following the Investiture Contest. 1991. ISBN 90 04 09374 5
25. FARAGO, C.J. *Leonardo da Vinci's 'Paragone'*. 1991. ISBN 90 04 09415 6
26. JONES, R. *Learning Arabic in Renaissance Europe*. (in preparation)
27. DRIJVERS, J.W. *HELENA AUGUSTA*. The Mother of Constantine the Great and the Legend of her Finding of the True Cross. 1991. ISBN 90 04 09435 0
28. BOUCHER, W.I., *Spinoza in English*. A Bibliography from the Seventeenth Century to the Present. 1991. ISBN 90 04 09499 7